VITH

D1387131

global policing

SAGE has been part of the global academic community since 1965, supporting high quality research and learning that transforms society and our understanding of individuals, groups, and cultures. SAGE is the independent, innovative, natural home for authors, editors and societies who share our commitment and passion for the social sciences.

Find out more at: **www.sagepublications.com**

global policing

Ben Bowling & James Sheptycki

Los Angeles | London | New Delhi
Singapore | Washington DC

© Ben Bowling and James Sheptycki 2012

First published 2012

Apart from any fair dealing for the purposes of research
or private study, or criticism or review, as permitted
under the Copyright, Designs and Patents Act, 1988, this
publication may be reproduced, stored or transmitted in
any form, or by any means, only with the prior permission
in writing of the publishers, or in the case of reprographic
reproduction, in accordance with the terms of licences
issued by the Copyright Licensing Agency. Enquiries
concerning reproduction outside those terms should be
sent to the publishers.

SAGE Publications Ltd
1 Oliver's Yard
55 City Road
London EC1Y 1SP

SAGE Publications Inc.
2455 Teller Road
Thousand Oaks, California 91320

SAGE Publications India Pvt Ltd
B 1/I 1 Mohan Cooperative Industrial Area
Mathura Road
New Delhi 110 044

SAGE Publications Asia-Pacific Pte Ltd
3 Church Street
#10-04 Samsung Hub
Singapore 049483

Library of Congress Control Number: 2011929077

British Library Cataloguing in Publication data

A catalogue record for this book is available from the British Library

ISBN 978-1-84920-081-3
ISBN 978-1-84920-082-0 (pbk)

Typeset by C&M Digitals (P) Ltd, Chennai, India
Printed and bound by CPI Group (UK) Ltd, Croydon, CR04YY
Printed on paper from sustainable resources

For Samson, Liam, Johannes, Frederik and Nadia

CONTENTS

ABBREVIATIONS

4-Cs	Communication, co-operation, coordination and collaboration
ACCP	Association of Caribbean Commissioners of Police
AFP	Australian Federal Police
ASEAN	Association of South East Asian Nations
ASEANAPOL	ASEAN Chiefs of Police
ATF	Bureau of Alcohol, Tobacco, Firearms and Explosives, US
BKA	Bundeskriminalamt, Germany
BKP	Bundeskriminalpolizei, Germany
CIA	Central Intelligence Agency, US
CDO	Collateralized Debt Obligation
CID	Criminal Investigation Department
CITES	Convention on International Trade in Endangered Species
CIVPOL	Civilian Police Programme, UN
DEA	Drug Enforcement Administration, US
DHS	Department of Homeland Security, US
EAW	European Arrest Warrant
EC	European Community
EDE	European Convention on Extradition
EIS	European Information System
EU	European Union
EUROPOL	European Police Office
FATF	Financial Action Task Force
FBI	Federal Bureau of Investigation, US
FBN	Federal Bureau of Narcotics, US
FCO	Foreign and Commonwealth Office, UK
FDA	Food and Drug Administration, US
FinCEN	Financial Crimes Enforcement Network, US
FIU	Financial Intelligence Unit
G7/8/20	Group of 7/8/20 countries
GATT	General Agreement on Tariffs and Trade
GDR	German Democratic Republic
HIV	Human immunodeficiency virus
HQ	Headquarters
ICC	International Criminal Court

ICHCDC	International Convention on Harmonized Commodity Description and Coding
ICSHCP	International Convention on the Simplification and Harmonization of Customs Procedures
ICT	Information and communications technologies
IGO	Intergovernmental Organisation
ILO	International Liaison Officer
ILOAT	International Labour Organisation Administrative Tribunal
IMF	International Monetary Fund
INS	Immigration and Naturalization Service, US
JCF	Jamaica Constabulary Force
JHA	EU Justice and Home Affairs Council
JSB	Joint Supervisory Body
LED	Law Enforcement Detachment
MINUSTAH	Mission des Nations Unies pour la Stabilisation en Haïti
MLAT	Mutual Legal Assistance Treaty
MOU	Memorandum of Understanding
MSF	Médecins Sans Frontières
NATO	North Atlantic Treaty Organization
NCB	National Central Bureau, Interpol
NCIS	National Criminal Intelligence Service, UK
NCS	National Crime Squad, UK
NGO	Non-governmental organisation
NPOIU	National Public Order Intelligence Unit, UK
NSA	National Security Agency, US
NYC	New York City
NYPD	New York City Police Department
OECD	Organisation for Economic Co-operation and Development
PR	Public Relations
R2P	Responsibility to Protect
RIC	Royal Irish Constabulary
RCMP	Royal Canadian Mounted Police
SAFE	Standards to Secure and Facilitate Global Trade
SARPOL	Southern African Regional Police
SOCA	Serious Organised Crime Agency, UK
STR	Suspicious Transaction Reports
SWAT	Special Weapons and Tactics
TNCs	Transnational corporations
TSA	Transportation Security Administration, US
UN	United Nations
UNCLOS	United Nations Convention of the Law of the Sea
UNODC	United Nations Office on Drug Control and Crime
UNDP	United Nations Development Programme

UNPOL	United Nations Police
UK	United Kingdom of Great Britain and Northern Ireland
US	United States
USCG	United States Coast Guard
WCO	World Customs Organisation
WTO	World Trade Organisation
ZfV	Zentralstelle für Verdachtsanzeigen, Germany

PREFACE AND ACKNOWLEDGEMENTS

Many of the ideas in this book were stimulated by Stan Cohen, David Downes, Michael Mann, Paul Rock, Robert Reiner and Leslie Sklair, whose work we encountered as postgraduate research students at the London School of Economics in the mid-1980s. This scholarship provided us with an understanding of the sources of social power and how these related to the problems of order and governance. Individually we have been able to work through these ideas through empirical research on policing from the very local (including domestic violence and racist violence in London) to the transnational (such as the English Channel region and the Caribbean islands).[1]

Encountering policing in various forms in different parts of the world led to lengthy discussions about what we saw and the issues that were raised from what we learned from our fieldwork. At the heart of the matter is the observation that the use of coercion and the power of surveillance which lie at the heart of policework are globalising. This raises obvious questions about accountability and control. After many years of verbal fencing about these issues, it is gratifying finally to have written a general theory of global policing.

We would like to thank a number of people who have read parts of the book and discussed it with us – Katja Franko Aas, Malcolm Anderson, Margaret Beare, Kevin Haggerty, Valsamis Mitselegas, Maurice Punch, Bill Saulsbury, Leanne Weber and the anonymous peer-reviewers. Philip Stenning in particular offered very forthright comments, which put the spurs to our thought. Conversations with Mike Larsen were very helpful in shaping the analysis of policing mega events. Derek Bond deserves a special mention for taking the time to discuss with us his first-hand experience of global policing and we are also grateful to Richard Bond for sharing his thoughts with us. Jasmine Chadha and Cian Murphy provided excellent research assistance and Lea Schönfeld was an oustanding editor. At Sage, thanks are due to Caroline Porter and Sarah-Jayne Boyd for commissioning this book and guiding us gently but firmly to the finish line. We are reponsible for all the remaining theoretical and factual errors.

We wish also to say some words of appreciation for Richard Ericson and Jean-Paul Brodeur for their kindness and generosity. Their contributions to theory and research defy categorisation and have been an inspiration. Both will be enormously missed.

This book is dedicated to our grown up children.

INTRODUCTION

Around the world, police officers are travelling abroad to work. This might be a plane, train or automobile journey to collect evidence on an unsolved murder. It might be a year's commitment to a United Nations Police (UNPOL) operation in a war-torn state, such as Afghanistan, or a three-year posting to serve as an international liaison officer in a 'drugs transit country', such as Jamaica. It might involve extensive overseas travel while seconded to Interpol or investigating war crimes for the International Criminal Court. Many more officers in domestic police forces, especially those working in fields such as organised crime, terrorism and cybercrime, spend their working lives communicating with their counterparts in other countries by email, fax and phone, or consulting international databases of criminal records, names, faces, fingerprints and DNA.

The usual justification for policing beyond borders is the globalisation of crime and insecurity: complex crimes and conspiracies spanning numerous countries are said to require extensive international police collaboration. We question this straightforward functional logic, but note nonetheless that, as crime and insecurity have become defined as global issues, police are frequently deployed to travel to other countries to interview witnesses, apprehend suspects and render them abroad for interrogation, trial or detention. International police organisations are growing in power and ambition, and at the same time, national police agencies are broadening their global reach.

Discussions of this profoundly important shift towards the global governance of crime have happened behind the closed doors of international bureaucracies. Most of the policy and planning and a great deal of the operational practice of global policing takes place backstage, secretly and as far as possible without attracting media attention. There has been almost no public discussion of the globalisation of policing – its priorities, policies, practices or accountability. With this lacuna in mind, the main aim of this book is to examine contemporary global policing and to explain its rapid development in the context of an emerging transnational-state-system. We set out to explore some of the challenging legal, political and social issues that arise in this field. Our goal is an empirically grounded theory of global policing.

The lack of public understanding of global policing is partly because it only recently became the subject of systematic research. The first books in this area – Malcolm Anderson's *Policing the World* and *Policing the European Union* and Ethan Nadelmann's *Cops Across Borders* – were published only within the last couple of decades.[2] These ground-breaking studies described the political background, organisational structures, harmonisation of criminal law and criminal procedure and emerging law enforcement strategies. Anderson et al.'s astonishing finding based on research in Europe during the 1990s was that the control of internal and external security was being transferred gradually from the nation-state to international institutions. Transnational policing, they wrote, opened a Pandora's Box of issues and problems.[3]

Examining the field from an American perspective, Nadelmann reached quite a different conclusion about the increasing international capacity of police forces. Rather than observing the emergence of international institutions, he concluded that the US was aggressively promoting its own criminal justice norms in the transnational realm. The process of transnationalisation, in Nadelmann's analysis, has been mostly about *Americanisation*.[4] According to him, through a three-fold process of *regularisation, accommodation* and *homogenisation*, foreign governments accommodated themselves to a US federal model of international law enforcement. This involved expanding the scope of criminal law and the use of enforcement methods such as electronic surveillance, informers, undercover policing and 'controlled deliveries'. It also meant using legal innovations developed in the US such as asset forfeiture and counter-money laundering.

By the early 1990s, the US was leading the development of transnational policing. Formulations of international agreements such as the 1988 United Nations Convention on Narcotic and Psychotropic Drugs illustrated the predominance of distinctly American preoccupations and techniques. For Nadelmann, the field comprised a complex array of international police organisations, co-operative mechanisms, regional police conferences and dozens of multi-lateral law enforcement arrangements all of which were 'intended to help law enforcement agencies reduce, transcend or circumvent frictions generated by conflicting sovereignties, political tensions and differences among law enforcement systems'.[5]

Following these early pioneers, researchers have gradually documented the co-operation required in policing border zones and island regions, the work of international liaison officers and the roles of supranational bodies such as the United Nations and European Union in transnational policing. This descriptive and explanatory empirical work has been complemented by valuable historical and theoretical accounts.[6] As the field has matured, several collections of articles exploring various aspects of transnational policing have opened up new directions of study.[7] Now that there is a solid body of empirical evidence published in various disciplines and from a wide variety of perspectives there is a need for an integrative inter-disciplinary theory of global policing. The pace of change has been so rapid that global policing practice is running ahead of policy and the thinking that might guide it. This book examines the theoretical dimensions of transnational policing and outlines an agenda of empirical research in this rapidly developing field.

Our broad working definition of transnational policing includes any form of order maintenance, law enforcement, peacekeeping, crime investigation, intelligence sharing, or other form of policework that transcends or traverses national boundaries. In Chapter 1, we explain the broad range of different *types of policing* that this involves and in Chapter 2 we set out the context of the emerging transnational-state-system. In Chapter 3 we describe the *architecture* of the worldwide policing system and in Chapter 4 the *subculture* of the global cops. In Chapter 5 we describe some examples of *transnational policing in practice* on the ground. In some instances, co-operation is based on bilateral relationships between two police forces, or multi-agency policing in three or four neighbouring countries, such as in the Benelux region or across the Caribbean islands. A distinction can be made between *transnational policing* and the related ideas of *international* and *global* policing. Political sociologists use the (intentionally hyphenated) term 'inter-national' to describe interactions among nation-states, while 'transnational' denotes phenomena that transgress national boundaries. In recent times, co-operation and collaboration have become increasingly ambitious to the extent that some forms of policing now claim a global reach. As will become clear, the idea of a *global police force* is a chimera, but *global policing* is a reality.

Collaboration among police officers from different countries is almost as old as modern policing itself. Policing archipelagos such as those in the Caribbean or Indonesia required police officers to travel by boat between neighbouring islands from time-to-time. Policing oceans, seas and other waterways is geographically transgressive. Since their inception, European police have had to cross national frontiers regularly as they went about their work – especially those policing border towns. Nadelmann notes that one of the early tasks of the US Marshals Service was to pursue runaway slaves escaping to Canada or Mexico. Not long after the Metropolitan Police formed an investigative branch in 1842, Scotland Yard detectives were asked by European police agencies to conduct surveillance on émigrés resident in Britain and when the first CID was formed in 1878, its duties included carrying out investigations for foreign governments.[8]

At the close of the 19th century, collaboration among police officers concerned with 'international anarchist terrorism' increased significantly. As well as formalising extradition processes, the 1898 Rome Conference agreed protocols for sharing information about suspected 'anarchists' and standardised the use of the Bertillon criminal identification system.[9] At the beginning of the 20th century public anxiety about the 'white slave' trade, what would now be called human trafficking, also stimulated the development of an organisation for international police co-operation that eventually became Interpol.[10] From then on, as global mobility became easier, faster and cheaper, police agents often travelled overseas to pursue fleeing suspects, collect evidence or interview witnesses. Increasingly, global police power has been used to arrest suspects on foreign soil and then to extradite, deport or render them abroad to face trial or prison. Over time, as transport and information communication technologies have developed, the shape and nature of criminal investigation shifted into the transnational realm.

By the end of the 20th century a number of entirely new policing mechanisms had been created. Interpol grew from a small club of police chiefs in 1923 into a 188 member organisation with a global communication and intelligence sharing capacity, 'wanted persons' databases and the ability to offer training and operational support for member police forces. The Interpol logo – encompassing a globe, scales and sword – may invoke the idea of global policing, but at the 'sharp end' Interpol has, in fact, little operational capacity and functions principally to facilitate communication, co-operation and coordination among police officers around the world. This said, Interpol's leadership has far-reaching ambitions for the organisation and its work has grown in scope and complexity. According to its website, the organisation provides investigative resources, intelligence analysis, liaison facilities and other similar activities to support domestic police in difficult cases. Interpol remains mainly a mechanism for sharing information, but is increasingly involved in operational policework on the ground. In recent years it has provided operational assistance to a murder investigation in Jamaica, credit card fraud investigations in Trinidad and Tobago, identifying plane-crash victims in Cameroon and fugitive tracking in Austria.[11] It has become embedded within domestic police forces, with officers based in the National Central Bureaux identifying with Interpol's global policing mission and playing a key role in transnational activity in local police divisions.[12]

The United Nations (UN) first put police on the ground to support its peacekeeping operation in Congo in 1960. A few years later, UN Secretary-General U. Thant declared that, 'I have no doubt that the world should eventually have an international police force which will be accepted as an integral and essential part of life in the same way as national police forces are accepted'.[13] Since then, UN policing capacity has grown dramatically. What started out as a few hundred police officers on the ground fifty years earlier had swelled by 2010 to more than 17,500 police officers from 98 countries deployed in peace operations around the world.[14] Still mainly concerned with peacekeeping, the UN policing mandate has been extended to other things like targeting gangs in Haiti, drugs in Afghanistan and Guinea-Bissau, and arms trafficking in the Democratic Republic of Congo. In 2009 Interpol and the UN signed a co-operation agreement linking UN Security-Council backed enforcement powers with Interpol databases of wanted persons, fingerprints, DNA and criminal intelligence. Speaking about these developments to the 77th Interpol General

Assembly, UN Police Adviser Andrew Hughes observed that practical collaboration between UNPOL and Interpol 'brings the combined weight of a majority of the world's States to bear on organised crime networks'.[15]

When the International Criminal Court (ICC) was established at the end of the millennium, it created a seedling police force with the power to collect and examine evidence and to interview suspects and witnesses in cases of war crimes, crimes against humanity and genocide. In 2008, under the direction of a former Belgian Gendarme, the ICC investigative division employed 165 people and had a budget of €21 million.[16] The ICC may issue arrest warrants but cannot, itself, enforce them.[17] The lack of a power of arrest led to calls for the ICC to have a 'strongly empowered policing arm which is able to work transnationally to take suspects into custody regardless of the desires or ability of the home nation'.[18] This has not yet come to pass. Although the ICC remit is narrowly restricted to a strict set of 'international crimes' and it has strictly limited enforcement powers, it nevertheless partially embodies the idea of an international *Police Judiciare*. This has profound implications for how global policing might develop in the future.

Alongside the emergence of these global policing entities and their rapid growth in size, power and ambition, regional organisations have been created in many places. The Association of South East Asian Nations Chiefs of Police (ASEANAPOL), Southern African Regional Police (SARPOL), Association of Caribbean Commissioners of Police (ACCP) and the European Police Office (EUROPOL) are umbrella organisations seeking, in various ways and under different legal or political auspices, to facilitate inter-agency collaboration and the exchange of information and personnel. While regional policing bodies tend, like Interpol, to be largely concerned with information sharing, they also play a key role in agenda setting and policymaking. They too sometimes provide operational functions.

Echoing these developments, domestic police forces have also become far more closely linked transnationally. Around the turn of the 21st century, many countries created 'national policing hubs', or centralised criminal intelligence services, to provide points of contact for international collaboration. Most countries now have national police in one form or another. Transnational liaison officers are the 'practical glue' that binds global policing together. They give advice and build capacity, train and mentor other police personnel and coordinate joint operations, often spanning continents. Led by the US, which has posted FBI liaison officers overseas since 1940, many countries now have an international policing capacity. In 2008, the FBI had around 340 people assigned permanently overseas and aimed to have an agent in every country.[19] The US DEA had 78 offices in 58 countries and the US Treasury Department, State Department Diplomatic Security Service, Bureau of Alcohol Tobacco and Firearms (ATF) and the Federal Marshals Service also had overseas posts. Police agencies in other countries, especially from what we call 'seigneurial states', started catching up. The UK and France have had liaison officers since the period of decolonisation. In 2010, the UK Serious Organised Crime Agency (SOCA) had 140 overseas liaison officers and there were 130 officers drawn from the French *Police Nationale*, *Police Judiciare* and *Gendarmerie* posted overseas. Having observed that 80 per cent of Canadian federal investigations extend beyond national borders, The Royal Canadian Mounted Police (RCMP) posted 35 Mounties in 25 locations around the world while the Australian Federal Police (AFP) had 80 liaison officers in 27 countries in 2009.

This list reveals a 'Western bias' and the fact that our analysis focuses primarily on an evolutionary process led by police from the over-developed world. Empirical research in this area has generally been limited to the work of these regions rather than the newly emerging economic powerhouses such as China, India, Brazil, Russia and Turkey. Our thesis rests on a conceptualisation of the world system as dominated by ideas that impose a transnational-state-system and our interest lies in understanding the effects of policing actors upholding those ideas through their operations at the middle and lower bureaucratic tiers of the global system more generally. Our focus is below that of sovereign states' representatives working bilaterally and through the auspices of supranational organisations.[20] Police agents from seigneurial states have a technological edge that gives them the upper hand in influencing the nature and extent of the global policing mission. Future research will no doubt open up the study of transnational policing subculture in other countries. Over time, as police actors from newly ascendant states gain influence we would expect them to have more impact on global policing. The effect of this evolution is an empirical question that depends on the living relationships between the transnational subculture of policing and the evolving global system more generally.

In the police research tradition, 'blue uniformed' public police officers are placed at the centre of analysis. Building on insights from the sociology of policing, we focus primarily on 'ordinary law policing' authorised and delivered by state agents. For this reason, private security providers, port and airport security officers, secret intelligence agencies, the military and other members of the wider policing family get less attention than they perhaps deserve. The place of private transnational police and secret agents in the background of our analysis reflects the fact that, unsurprisingly, there is less empirical research about their activities. Anecdotally, our encounters with private transnational policing agents and advisers suggests to us that the majority are in their second career (after working in one or another public policing agency) and that their ability to call upon networks of collegial contacts from their prior engagements facilitates their effectiveness in the system. It seems that state-based policing agents dominate the culture of global policing frequently operating at a distance. Transnational cops, private eyes and private spies are kith and kin and where scholarly literature exists, we show how private transnational policing contributes to the shape of the global system.

This book shows how globalisation impacts upon concepts of crime, security, justice and the law. It examines the origins of transnational policing, the forms it takes in contemporary society and speculates on the trajectory of its future development. It describes the evolution of a 'new security agenda' – focusing on serious organised crime and terrorism – and how this is driving a transformation in all spheres of policing. It explores the restructuring of local policing so that it is 'globally aware'; the creation of national policing agencies with a transnational reach; regional entities, such as Europol, and global organisations, such as Interpol, the World Customs Organisation and the policing roles of the UN and the ICC.

We set out a theory of policing practice in a variety of contexts linking the local with the global. Through an analysis of emerging political, legal and managerial regimes in the transnational realm, the book considers the effects, legitimacy and accountability of policing as it stretches beyond national borders. We offer a sceptical appraisal of both the 'dream' of global policing as the key to a safe world society and its opposite: the 'dystopian nightmare' of unaccountable and uncontrolled global law enforcers that threaten democratic values, human rights and civil liberties. We think that policing, broadly understood, is an essential component of any society and the gradual emergence of a 'world society' is no exception. Policing practices with a global reach and power are already an existing empirical reality and they seem likely to expand rather than contract in the decades ahead. Numerous questions arise about the form and function of global policing, how priorities, policies and practices are established and implemented and how normative issues are settled.

The most important question is: to what extent does global policing provide safety, protect liberty and reduce the sum total of human misery? If our assessment is often negative, it is because we have found that both the norms of police subculture and the outcomes of law enforcement practice too often run contrary to solemn oaths to 'protect and serve' society and to maintain its general well-being. The evidence from many places is that the goal of a peaceful and prosperous world society remains elusive. Our hope is that by making global policing theoretically visible it can be made more responsive to the desire of people everywhere to live in a world commonwealth fit for all.

1

THEORISING GLOBAL POLICING

Our first task is to contextualise our subject with regard to theories of policing, globalisation, social order and governance. We examine the role of the police within the classic nation-state system and how this has become problematic. We explore the idea of the 'social contract' and how this has been re-shaped by an emerging transnational-state-system. The chapter also sets out two typologies of policing that mark the conceptual boundaries of the field. The first explores the distinctions between policing that aims to *secure territory* and that which aims to maintain *surveillance over suspect populations*. It distinguishes between *high policing* (seeking to maintain particular interests of state and social elites) and *low policing* (seeking to maintain the interests of the social order more generally) and between *public* and *private* forms. A second typology suggests four geographical spheres of policing – *glocal, national, regional* and *global*. These typologies create the conceptual space within which the various forms of transnational policing explored in later chapters are theorised and understood. The groundwork covered here provides the basis for making global policing visible as a theoretical object.

──────────── **The problem of global policing** ────────────

There is no such thing as a global police force but there is global policing. *Global policing* refers to the capacity to use coercive and surveillant powers around the world in ways that pass right through national boundaries unaffected by them.[21] The many examples that we provide in this book include police officers who live permanently overseas or regularly use phones and computers to collect and share intelligence, investigate criminal conspiracies, to authorise arrest, or provide emergency services across a wide number of jurisdictions. A *global police force* would be different in subtle but important ways. If it existed, it would be an institution with universal jurisdiction, global mobility and the formal powers to arrest and detain suspects anywhere in the world. It would also have to have solid foundations in public international law and have some kind of system of control and accountability linking it to the peoples who inhabit the globe. Such a thing exists only in fiction and in the imagination of a small number of scholars and policymakers.[22]

The idea of a global police force occasionally appears in books and films, most hilariously in the 2004 action-comedy film *Team America: World Police*. Declaring that 'world crime is at an all time high', a US paramilitary force of marionettes is given a global mandate to eliminate criminals, terrorists and their backers, and to 'put the F back in freedom'. A more dramatic and edgy portrayal is the 2005 thriller *Lord of War*. The villain, a gunrunner played by actor Nick Cage, is pursued internationally by actor Ethan Hawke, a 'global cop', complete with Interpol badge, gun, body-armour and power to arrest his quarry anywhere in the world. These movies provide distorted images of something that is really happening: policework is globalising and many thousands of police officers work transnationally. At any given moment somewhere such agents are in the air travelling to provide consultancy services, training, investigative assistance, conference presentations and much else. Some will be local beat cops, others intelligence officers or private investigators. They might be identified with big city police forces, national agencies or supranational institutions such as the UNPOL or Interpol.

Stories about policing transnational organised crime, terrorism, people trafficking and cybercrime are now part of the standard daily commercial news diet, often garnished with snippets about Interpol or FBI involvement. Sensationalised global crime stories are hot topics that convey anxiety, fear and insecurity. However, global cops seem distant from everyday life. Global crime stories always seem to happen to other people: 'wanted criminals' or 'terrorist suspects' arrested in murky circumstances in far away places. The tone of the reportage signals that the forces of law and order are protecting good people from the 'dangerous classes' of the world – the global 'folk devils'.

The perception that global cops are a problem only for suspect populations consigned to the margins of the world system is one reason that we were interested in the story of Mr Derek Bond, a 72-year-old British citizen, retired engineer, unassuming mild-mannered grandfather of six who was arrested and held in custody while on a South African wine tasting holiday in January 2003.[23]

Mr Bond was first questioned by immigration authorities at Cape Town airport. Later he was arrested on the basis of an Interpol Red Notice and locked up in the cells of Durban central police station. Red Notices, naming a suspect wanted by police for an alleged crime, are circulated through the Interpol communications network of National Central Bureaux (NCBs) to police forces around the world. They are not 'international arrest warrants', because there is no international authority with the power to issue such things, but in most jurisdictions they are interpreted as authorising, or even compelling, local police to arrest.

Mr Bond was detained by the South African police as a suspected fugitive because the details of his passport, stated on the Interpol Red Notice, matched that of another Englishman, one Derek Lloyd Sykes. Accused of a US$4.8 million telemarketing fraud in the United States, Sykes was on the FBI's 'most wanted list' and was known to use Derek Bond as a false name. On the basis of an arrest warrant for Mr Sykes (alias Mr Bond) issued by the FBI in Houston, Texas in 1999, a Red Notice was circulated through the Interpol network. Unfortunately, this resulted in the detention of the real Mr Bond four years later at the insistence of the FBI legal attaché in Pretoria. The repercussions of this case of mistaken identity eventually prompted into action officials at the UK Foreign Office and the FBI Headquarters in Washington DC. The diplomatic spat between the USA and UK embassies in South Africa seems to have led to some activity on the ground and the real Mr Sykes was arrested in a Las Vegas hotel on 26 September, three weeks after the unfortunate Derek Bond had been arrested in South Africa.[24] On release and return to the UK on 28 September, Mr Bond described in vivid detail the dire conditions of his three weeks sleeping on the filthy concrete floor of a Durban police cell.

Like a character from a Franz Kafka novel, Bond found himself accused of a crime of which he had no knowledge, imprisoned by an impenetrable transnational policing system with no helpful means to protest his innocence or provide redress. Afterwards Mr Bond considered the merits of a civil case seeking compensation from US authorities but abandoned it on the advice of his solicitor and in the interests of a quiet life.[25] The case of Mr Bond raises questions about the relations between the individual and the complex web of institutions that makes up the global policing enterprise. Derek Bond was powerless to resist while his family, desperately trying to help, were trapped in a bureaucratic hall of mirrors.

The Red Notice issued by the FBI and circulated by Interpol in the Bond case contained inaccurate and incomplete information. It lacked a clear photograph or fingerprints. This case raises many questions. Who is responsible for checking the facts on a document that can result in depriving someone of their liberty? When police power is deployed intercontinentally, which laws are enforced? Where? By which authority? In whose name? What system of external accountability regulates policing beyond borders? Who is in charge when things go wrong and from whom can redress be sought? Who pays for the globe-trotting police? How are global cops recruited and trained? How are the problems known to afflict domestic policing – legal and procedural errors, corruption, racism and the abuse of force – remedied in the transnational realm? In the following pages we aim to provide the theoretical basis on which to answer these questions.

The case of Mr Bond is far from typical, not least because as a white, middle-class English retiree, he does not fit the stereotypical image of the 'usual suspect'. Across the world uncounted numbers of people are held in custody as a result of some aspect of global policing, the vast majority of whom are economically marginal people often with black or brown skin. The atypical case of Mr Bond piques curiosity about how the world is policed. In trying to make global policing theoretically visible we draw from an inter-disciplinary mix of sociological, legal and political theory, and extend our thinking to include insights from cultural anthropology, international relations, critical geography and history. Our aim is to make the idea of 'global policing' theoretically comprehensible to students of the social sciences and humanities generally.

Policing and social theory

One way to begin to think about contemporary policing would be to provide an overview of globalisation theory for criminologists.[26] We certainly think that understanding the evolution of policing offers a uniquely useful window through which to view globalisation. Many books on similar subjects begin by assuming that the meaning of 'police' is self-evident, a position that has an underlying functional logic: there are criminals so we need police to go after them.[27] Most accounts of transnational policing simply extend this logic: there are international criminals so we obviously need international police to go after them.[28] Instead of taking this 'common sense' approach, we have chosen to build a theory about global policing from first principles. We begin this by asking 'who are the police?' and 'what is policing?' and seek answers by turning to some basic sociological theories of social ordering.

The police idea is a modern one. It came into political parlance during the period known as the European Enlightenment and should be understood as much more than mere criminal law enforcement. The 'science of police' refers to a broad set of social practices intended to order and control, organise and regulate. As Pasquale Pasquino put it: 'What police regulations regulate, or try to regulate, or purport to regulate, is everything which in the life of this society [...] goes unregulated'.[29] Similarly, for Marcus Dubber, 'among the powers of government none is greater than the power to police and none less circumscribed'.[30] The order ensured by a 'science of policing' is underpinned and facilitated by statistical information on populations, the conditions of prosperity, health and public happiness. Statistics (a concept derived from 'Staat', ie. 'the State') becomes the *science of the state*; political arithmetic in which a calculative rationality is used to govern citizens and the life of a society.

This broad definition of policing is both forward and backward looking. It is *forward looking* because it seeks to prevent future ills, and *backward looking* because it also concerns itself with past misdeeds and seeking out those who break the law. It follows from this definition that our concern with policing must take in the complex mode of functioning of an entire network of institutions encompassing the administrative apparatus of the modern state.[31] Adam Smith, founder of classical economics, and Cesare Beccaria, founder of classical criminology, both agreed that policing in this broad sense is central to a healthy and happy economic order.[32] Beccaria declared, in 1769, that 'the sciences of education, good order, security and public tranquillity, objects all comprehended under the name of police [...] constitute the last object of public economy'.[33]

The modern sociology of policing defines its object somewhat differently. According to Egon Bittner, the functions of police in modern society centre on the Weberian sociological dictum that 'the State' claims the monopoly of coercive power in the maintenance of social order.[34] Bittner referred to coercive force as *the core of the police function*.[35] The police, he argued, are 'nothing else than a mechanism for the distribution of situationally justified force in society'.[36] This view of the police focuses on a central problem of society, which is how to contain (for the good of all) violence, dishonesty, conflict and other contingent harms that are detrimental to social life. This branch of the sociology of policing focused almost entirely on urban police conceptualised, in William Muir's words, as 'streetcorner politicians'.[37] The police are the keystone in the system of modern governance and an essential political interface between the state and society. Police are to government 'as the edge is to the knife'.[38] Of course, it makes a difference whether the knife is a scalpel or a bayonet.[39]

The pathways from the Enlightenment idea of 'police science' to today's manifestations of policing are many and varied.[40] The policing idea has been broken up into a hotchpotch of institutions, each with their own specific functional logic, sometimes working at cross-purposes, rarely rationally harmonised and without a reasoned separation of powers. For example, in the United States drugs are policed by two major federal agencies, the DEA and the FDA. There are points of tension between the rationality of these two agencies: illegal drugs have medical uses and medicines can be used unlawfully. There is, as yet, no overarching theoretical rationality of policing governance that reconciles the potential of this conflicting irrationality. The practical Balkanisation of the policing idea into a myriad of enforcement, regulatory and security agencies – policing everything from street crime and tax evasion, to water and food quality – provides the institutional surface of emergence for policing subcultures that we explore in further detail later in this book. Some social theorists have argued that these policing institutions are united by a common governmentality or risk discourse.[41] Our view is that the complexity of the field of transnational policing activities also gives rise to institutional friction. Consequently, policing may, contrary to its professed ideals to 'protect and serve society', actually contribute to harm.[42]

Policing and the social contract

The modern idea of police sprang from the same intellectual ground as the idea of the social contract, which itself is integral to thinking about the modern state. The social contract is the key to police legitimacy and forms the basis of the liberal idea of policing by consent. The language of the social contract is one for justifying political authority and describing the structure and content of just political authority. That is why the notion of 'policing by consent' is a key constituent of the language game of social contract theory and, by extension, liberal political philosophy and the practice of liberal democratic government.[43]

Simplifying for the sake of clarity and brevity, we outline four positions relevant to social contract theory.[44] On the left, we have the vision of Jean Jacques Rousseau who foregrounded the 'general will' whereby the sovereign resides in the entire people who are all equally free. On the right, we have the vision of Thomas Hobbes, according to whom society consists of a people beneath the sovereign authority. The difference between the two lies in their conception of human beings 'in a state of nature'. For Hobbes the natural state of humanity is 'poor, nasty, brutish and short' and in a perpetual 'war of all against all', which requires that the social contract ultimately be ensured through the might of the sovereign. For Rousseau, human beings in a state of nature hate to witness suffering and are naturally empathetic and compassionate. That is why, according to Rousseau, the sovereignty that ensures the social contract can lie with the people. Put simply, a Hobbesian version of the social contract gives overriding authority to the sovereign who is ultimately responsible for peace, order and good government; whereas the Rousseauian social contract grants all 'power to the people'. Hobbes risks autocratic tyranny; Rousseau a tyranny of the majority.

Social contract theory requires both points of view and gives rise to the third position that we identify with John Locke.[45] The edifice of Lockean social contract theory is built upon a principled insistence on the separation of political powers, which can be viewed as an attempt to occupy the 'golden mean' between the extremes of Hobbes and Rousseau. The strategy of separation of powers is also associated with Montesquieu, whose tripartite distinction between the power of the executive, the legislature and the judiciary was inspired by his observations of the British system (which, at the time, separated the powers of the Crown, parliament and the judiciary). These ideas were woven into the Constitution of the United States. Such a practical set up can be aptly associated with Lord Acton's historical maxim: 'all power tends to corrupt, absolute power corrupts absolutely'. These words of warning remain relevant to would be citizens of a liberal and democratic world society, especially in relation to policing power.

By separating political powers, the Lockean social contract legitimises liberal state governance by providing it with internal mechanisms with which to 'guard the guards'. In the tug-of-war between the two poles of liberal constitutional theory, Rousseau on the left Hobbes on the right, sometimes the centre fails to hold and the edifice of government comes under stress. This can give rise to the 'Machiavellian moment' when the politics of criticism by words and persuasion give way to the politics of brute force. Niccolo Machiavelli lived during the Italian Renaissance – a period that saw: city-states vying against each other for hegemony; France, Spain, Switzerland and the Holy Roman Empire battling for regional influence and control; and the armies of the Papacy fighting for the continuing dominance of the Throne of St Peter. The Italian Renaissance, despite the glory of its name, was a time of troubles. Machiavelli's discussion of the fall of Rome offered a coded pretext for discussing the virtues of republican government. He had good personal reasons to espouse one of the earliest conceptions of 'checks and balances' in the governance of governance. Such were the political dangers of his time that he personally suffered imprisonment and torture, and was eventually charged with conspiracy and exiled. Looking at the present policing of the new world order, one might conclude that a global Machiavellian moment has arrived.

Liberal theories of policing come out of this broad conversation about the nature of the social contract, the state and the practice of government. The idea of policing by consent plays a central and paradoxical role in the tenuous social ordering that results. Where matters concern policing there is always the possibility of a dangerous Machiavellian moment. This is a hazard for any state regardless of the specifics of its Constitution. In that moment lies the potential for power to corrupt or to turn its violence back on the people that it is intended to protect. A practical shortcoming of classical social contract theory that adds stress to the world system is that it is very limited regarding International relations. In Hobbes this is especially evident. There is not a word in *Leviathan* to suggest any relation between states except war and conquest interrupted by interludes of peace, which are merely a preparation for the next war. Kant's 1795 essay *Perpetual Peace* is the first work of western philosophy to broach the possibility that peace could be anything other than an interlude between wars.[46] In the absence of some principle of global governance, the modern nation-state system could, and indeed did, lead to a war of all against all.

This problem helps to explain how, under the pressure of globalisation, the separation of powers envisaged in the Constitution of the United Sates has slowly become imbalanced. Arthur M. Schlesinger argued that the growth in the power of the executive branch happened as the United States became a world power and then a superpower. His analysis shows how the power of the executive branch of government, the Office of the President, accumulated during wartime. The exercise of military force abroad facilitated the accretion of domestic policing powers. Schlesinger explained how the reasoned separation of powers between President, Congress, Senate and the Courts gradually became unbalanced.[47]

In our view, the Office of the President of the United States is one site of power in a polycentric global system. The palpable disaggregation of 'the State' left behind what some critics have described as a media-televisual 'simulation' of democracy wherein the public relations expert (using the techniques of mass psychology, spin and media manipulation) became a crucial player in the legitimation games of governance.[48] Classical social contract theories have no concept of media manipulation. The institutional drift occurred slowly over centuries but shifted radically in the recent past. What appears normal today differs greatly from what was originally intended more than two centuries ago in legal and political documents based on ideas about the social contract and policing with the consent. The state *qua* 'State' now appears as disaggregated and can no longer be understood as the basic building block of the world system.

In the context of the contemporary world system, traditional liberal democratic notions, such as the 'social contract' and 'policing by consent', are challenged in new ways. The power of globalised private property, embodied in transnational corporations, has grown far beyond anything that classic social contract theorists could have envisaged. As Bertrand Russell remarked in his conclusions on John Locke, a global social contract is an ultimate necessity, but it will look different from that which is depicted in classical theories. That is because 'the single separate citizen has no longer the power and independence that he had in Locke's speculations'. Our age, Russell said, is 'one of organization, and its conflicts are between organizations, not between separate individuals'.[49] He merely gestured at the problems that classic social contract theory has in grappling with the implications of global corporate power in a neo-liberal social order. We shall have more to say about this in later chapters, but for now we conclude that the transgressive nature of power in the transnational-state-system makes it very different from the nation-state-system that preceded it. This has profound consequences for policing.

Policing and political theory

The original notion of policing encompassed the whole art of government designed to control populations and secure territories. Policing, in its modern sense, was aimed at the internal order of states while the military staked out their perimeters, sometimes leading to warfare. Observing this, the American political scientist Charles Tilly likened state-making and war-making to protection rackets.[50] From very early on, policing was about the deployment of the state's monopoly claim to the use of force in the maintenance of social order, and maintaining a knowledge system capable of future planning so as to optimise the social life of the burgeoning capitals of Europe. As the modern state system developed and spread around the world, the practical implementation of the police idea was uneven and manifested differently in societies with different ideas about governance.

Understanding policing as integral to the national-state-system requires a distinction between 'high' and 'low' policing.[51] In early modern thinking, police functions for the maintenance of safe populations, such as emergency fire response, crime prevention or securing the food supply, were considered *basse police*, that is 'low policing'. This is distinct from *haute police*, 'high policing', which aims to secure the interests of 'the state' and political elites. Low policing is for the 'general interest' in contrast to high policing for the 'particular interest' defined by the powerful. Historically, elites were motivated to provide the services of low policing in order to maintain a population capable of engaging in military competition between states. The resulting insecurity of the international-state-system is partly what gave rise to the need for high policing functions. In different countries the policing idea was shaped in different ways. In continental Europe, the 'well-ordered police-state' stressed legality and centralised police authority.[52] In the United States 'the police' were representatives of a self-governing capitalist democracy affected by a mixture of cultures. Consequently, the occupational police subculture that emerged in the US had a lot more room for freewheeling individual aggression.[53]

The nation-state-system has evolved into a transnational-state-system and this has implications for policing and military roles. The specifics of high policing have also changed as a result of this transformation. Because of the impact of global neo-liberal market rationality, the idea of the central state as a 'monopoly security provider' is not as pervasive as it was in Max Weber's time. This problematic has been recognised by a range of thinkers who are interested in the way this new global system can or should be governed. Our contribution to this literature is to foreground police institutions and their occupational subcultures in shaping these transformations.

The evolution towards some kind of 'world system' challenges basic concepts of political rationality and legitimacy, with policing at the sharp end. There are different ways of coming at this. Antonio Negri and Michael Hardt propose that 'sovereignty has taken a new form, comprised of a series of national and supranational organisms united under single logic of rule'.[54] This they call *Empire*. There are affinities between Hardt and Negri and our own mode of theorising. By drawing attention to the power of institutions based in seigneurial states we signal an agreement that the post-national world system tends to function as a construct among ruling powers. We also agree with Hardt and Negri that the recent transformation created a new kind of political enemy – the criminal, a threat not to the political system but to law. Under the 'civilisation' they call Empire, the 'enemy' is simultaneously 'banalised' (i.e. reduced to a routine set of police repression procedures), 'absolutised' (i.e. represented as an absolute threat to the social order) and globalised.[55] Critical criminologists refer to these variously as 'suitable enemies', 'folk devils' and 'the usual suspects'.

Alternatively, there is the view of Anne Marie Slaughter who looks at the world system 'through the lens of disaggregated rather than unitary states'.[56] Using a very broad notion of 'networks', she captures a sense of vertical and horizontal connections between governmental actors in a global system of 'disaggregated sovereignty'. Her aim has been to show that networks of government actors have the capacity to enter into international regulatory regimes of various types and can thereby be bound to a body of international law. Our approach to socio-legal theory is rather different, as we outline in the next section, but we agree with Slaughter that states are not unitary billiard-ball-like entities that articulate and pursue a single national interest. We are similarly interested in horizontal and vertical governmental networks, but our specific interest is with policing because, not unlike Hardt and Negri, we see that the projection of suitable enemies is an ideological construct that provides a justificatory rhetoric useful in shoring up the idea of the transnational-state-system as an appropriate container of insecurity. For symbolic and practical reasons, policing provides the critical infrastructure to project the transnational-state conceptual scheme onto the world system map.

We aspire to something better for the politics of the global system. George Monbiot advocates a one-person-one-vote world government, a utopian vision of a global democratic order that transcends the obsolete nation-state. Monbiot would revitalise the United Nations General Assembly and replace the Security Council with a directly elected World Parliament.[57] David Held and others propose cosmopolitan democracy, a complex multi-level polity with administrative capacity and independent political resources at regional and global levels to complement local and national polities.[58] We would rather the institutional processes Held outlines led to the global social-democratic outcome Monbiot postulates, but the policing-insecurities of the present stand in the way of these hoped-for developments. Our inter-disciplinary theory seeks to add to discussions about how global policing influences the politics of the world system and constitutes a major modality of global governance. As we show in later chapters, currently existing global policing promulgates taken for granted assumptions regarding the transnational-state-system as a container for insecurity. By acting to shore up those assumptions, the transnational practices of policing act as a brake on the development of a new democratic global social contract.

Policing and law

Socio-legal theorists and legal scholars are apt to place policing under the rubric of the Rule of Law. Slaughter is not alone in her hope that legal rules can somehow be deployed in the effort to engineer a safe and just new world order. We detect many difficulties with the assumption that transnational policing practices can be easily tamed by law. Nation-state jurisdiction once seemed to determine the framework of the Law – the 'command of the sovereign', in the words of the American legal theorist John Austin. It was possible then to look to the sovereign state as the basis for the *Grundnorm* – the 'grounding norm' in Hans Kelsen's 'pure theory of law' – as providing a basis for the Rule of Law's apparent solidity.[59] In a transnationalising world in which all jurisdictions are increasingly multicultural and the state is no longer the uncontested basis of social order, the concept of Rule of Law is squeezed between the requirements of legal pluralism,[60] on the one hand, and the politics of law, on the other.[61] There is an intrinsic ambiguity in the relationship between law and policing that frequently belies the democratic expectation that police are somehow beholden to law. The practical policing task is the reproduction of the already constituted social order using 'whatever works' in the circumstances.

The paradox that police are required to use coercion to protect interests endorsed by the constitutional order of which they are a part is what makes them more liable than any other agency to corrupt that order.[62] A primary source of police power and legitimacy are the enabling legal provisions – sometimes referred to as the Ways and Means Act to 'get the job done'.[63] It is sometimes argued (not without evidence) that, as long as there is the perception of procedural fairness, legitimation of the whole enterprise can usually be achieved, even under conditions of significant legal and material inequality.[64] The law provides an enabling device for the police to accomplish the work of ordering. As Doreen McBarnet observes, there are many ways in which police use the law as an all-purpose control device.[65] Therefore, when it comes to law, 'whether the hand is wearing an "iron fist" or a "velvet glove", the police will hold the upper hand'.[66] Socio-legal research has shown that the law is a tool which policing agents use in a discretionary way, frequently in conditions of low visibility.[67]

To make matters more complex, law is also a double-edged sword. That is to say, while *enabling* policing, law may also be invoked as a brake on police power. Legal proceedings in civil courts symbolically shape and influence policing practice in some jurisdictions.[68] For example, the pressures on big city police departments in North America to change their response to reports of domestic and sexual violence came from civil proceedings and class action suits.[69] The significant increase in officer time spent on cases of domestic violence that took place during the latter half of the 20th century resulted from widening the ambit of criminal law enforcement to include violence against women in the home.[70]

In public law the legal instruments that may serve to constrain policing power are those that confer 'civil' or 'human rights'. Ambivalence arises in policing when the double-edged nature of law gives rise to 'counter-law' – using law against the law – and policing is fundamental to this. When police action becomes problematic, law creates rules to constrain and shape action, ideas that are themselves subject to interpretation. Using 'law against law' has paradoxical effects that confound simple Rule of Law expectations. The relation between policing and law is ambiguous for other reasons. There are lacunae in law that leave room for improvisation by police agents who often respond to situational exigencies that are unforeseeable. As Bittner put it, the role of the police is to find 'an unknown solution to an unknown problem'.[71]

Furthermore, the opportunities for the police to use discretion are growing. The widening scope of legal discourse now encompasses not only those who actually cause harm, but also those merely *suspected of being harmful*, as well as authorities who are deemed responsible for security failures. Each instance invites discretion and choice, not rule-governed behaviours. As civil and administrative law become more salient in processes of exerting power, the police use of law has also moved beyond the traditional principles, standards and procedures of criminal law.[72] This is particularly evident in criminal asset forfeiture, where civil law (with the lower standard of proof: the 'balance of probabilities') can be used to confiscate the 'proceeds of crime' without the necessity of a successful criminal prosecution (which has the higher standard of proof: 'beyond reasonable doubt').

From a global point of view, it is possible to see a 'transnational space between' where both legal and non-legal actors can 'jurisdiction shop'. The transnational space between jurisdictions has created opportunities for 'process laundering'. The Belgian courts, for example, naturally require criminal convictions to be based on evidence lawfully obtained under Belgian law. But during the 1990s when telephone wiretap interception was not allowed in that jurisdiction, Belgian police requested Dutch, French and Swedish colleagues to conduct telephone interceptions on their territories. The intercept evidence was relied upon in Belgian prosecutions and in each instance the court upheld prosecutions on the grounds that it was legally obtained in the jurisdictions concerned, even though it was unlawfully obtained according to the letter of Belgian law. It may be comforting that the relevant Dutch, French and Swedish laws complied with the European Convention on Human Rights, but the transnational-state-system is not limited to European countries, it is global. As we demonstrate later in this book, the policing activities, agencies and authorities that co-mingle in the transnational space between are diffuse and defy simple and traditional systems of accountability. Informalism and discretion are seen as practical solutions to the organisational difficulties the policing occupation presents.[73]

The commonly held notion that the 'Rule of Law' idea has teeth – that it somehow directs, or could in principle direct, policing action – is wide of the mark.[74] Police use law as a tool, just as other actors sometimes use law as a tool. Paradoxically, law in practice is always counter-law since it is by means of human discretion, choice and contestation that law is enacted. As it passes outside of itself to become real living law, it emerges as an instrument in the hands of knowing actors. Thus, the policing mission, both locally and globally, amounts to 'Rule *with* Law'. This nuanced perspective concerning policing and law has implications for understanding the attempt to make policing subject to democratic controls and accountable to law in any given instance. It is also why we pass up the opportunity to parse forensically the details of legal instruments such as the US Patriot Act. From our point of view, laws such as this politically assert the 'right of the sovereign' in a powerfully symbolic way and, although worthy of detailed examination by socio-legalists and others, it must be glossed over in a work of theoretical synthesis such as we are attempting here. Ultimately, we conclude that cultural change is more important than the changing letter of the law because it is from the meanings inherent in the occupational subculture of policing that meanings about the application of law derive (see Chapter 4).

Colonial policing

The modern police idea, and the system of government of which it was a part, emerged *sui generis* in the developed countries of the West during the Enlightenment period and took shape gradually over more than two centuries. The many particular state forms that emerged as the nation-state-system was built up over time manifest their own domestic systems of policing. Each had domestic legitimation requirements and appealed to a national social contract and thereby an exclusionary social good. For example, the former East Germany was formally the German *Democratic* Republic (GDR). Even in what was one of the most efficient (and oppressive) police states in modern Western history, a gesture was made to an implied social contract that excluded the capitalist Germans of 'the West'. Marx's sententious notion of the 'dictatorship of the proletariat', echoing a Rousseauian tyranny of the majority, was justified on the grounds that the communist system that it would supposedly evolve towards could deliver the greatest good for the greatest number.

Alongside the development of the police idea in the West ran a parallel history of colonial policing that is vital to understanding our topic.[75] Policing was central to the colonial system and imperial domination. It was used to impose European standards of legality although it frequently upheld certain aspects of traditional, native or customary law when it was convenient. European legal institutions of police and courts were used, along with other ideas, to impose modernity upon the globe. The cartographic effect of this was to project onto the world a patchwork quilt of legal jurisdictions that, after the colonial period, were chiefly configured as fictive nation-states. These jurisdictions did not necessarily conform to any local or indigenous sense of ethnic, cultural or historical identity.[76] A 21st-century example of the post-colonial legacy in policing is the role of transnational private policing in the oil-rich Niger delta and the way it transgresses the artificial state boundaries imposed onto the cultural geography of the West African region.

Policing was the lynchpin of the colonial project. Military authorities attended to 'constabulary duties' as well as being an 'army of occupation'. Very often colonisers encountered organised resistance to the imposition of outside rule and in such circumstances this was responded to with what would nowadays be called counter-insurgency operations. British colonial constabularies strove to elicit a degree of consent from the local population by being seen to conform to local legal customs.[77] Back home in the evolving liberal democracies, 'Rule of Law' rhetoric was an especially important legitimation device in order to rule *with* law. Concerns for the legitimacy of the colonial project were felt 'at home' in another way, since the metropolitan population would be vexed by having to pay for overseas possessions with blood and money. Simply put, the colonial constabularies aimed to install colonial social order sometimes in the teeth of armed resistance. The British approach viewed abiding contact with local populations as the essential condition for gaining intelligence, showing social solidarity and denying insurgents freedom of action. Towards the end of the British Empire, the doctrine of minimal force became – in theory – an important tenet of colonial policing. As Gandhi's use of passive resistance showed, military and police force *in extremis* tended to stoke the fires of resistance.[78]

Nonetheless, the colonial project in many cases involved bloody pacification including the use of military force in genocidal atrocities.[79] Especially in the early years of colonial expansion, policing often involved swift resort to deadly force, collective punishments and 'scorched earth' policies. Colonial police forces were charged with *imposing* imperial law and maintaining order among the 'lower orders' of the colonised populations. The model for British colonial forces was the Royal Irish Constabulary (RIC), a *Gendarmerie* that aspired to follow the civil policing model.[80] Members of the RIC and former soldiers were recruited to provide colonial policy leadership. Colonial policing practice was different from the model cultivated within the homeland, which was much more concerned with the appearance of legality, bureaucratic efficiency, effectiveness and policing by consent.[81] Whereas domestic policing was more firmly based on principles of minimal force and political independence, the explicitly paramilitary model of colonial policing assumed the *absence* of consent of the policed because, first and foremost, it was a mechanism to maintain domination.[82]

Colonial policing frequently involved selective enforcement in favour of dominant local groups, the criminalisation of indigenous practices and suppression of protest. A strategy of 'policing by strangers' ensured that police officers of all stripes were not policing communities where their own families lived.[83] Commissioners and senior officers of the British Imperial police were from England (the 'mother country'), or from Scotland, Ireland or other colonies of settlement, who were trained at British police staff colleges before being posted overseas or transferred between colonial forces. In colonial contexts, consensual policing was reserved for the settlement of disputes and investigation of crimes within the settler community. Insofar as Western powers could co-opt formal or semi-formal indigenous institutions of social control to their own ends, 'native customary law' could be incorporated into a consensual model of colonial policing. However, when colonial interests were threatened, the indigenous population could be subjected to coercive policing. As Paul Gilroy notes, the history of colonial power overflows with evidence of a destructive association of governance with military power and marshal law, which distorted every aspect of security governance in the colonies including medicine, schooling and public administration.[84]

There are parallels between colonial policing and the policing of the domestic class order of the metropolis in the contemporary 'global south'.[85] Although policing class order 'at home' always involved coercion, it seldom reached the same degree as in the colonial context. Still, the analogy is interesting, especially as things move beyond the immediate post-colonial period. Sivanandan, for example, referred to the militarised policing that grew up in Britain in the 1970s and 1980s as 'policing the domestic colonies'.[86] Twenty years later, the terminology had shifted to refer to policing the global south. For example, in the late 1990s, it was common for big city police departments in the USA to blend 'zero tolerance' with 'community policing' – metaphorically known as 'weed-and-seed'. Optimally from the police point of view, strategic community policing initiatives created the necessary legitimacy to allow the more coercive operations to be carried out with minimal risk or casualties. The weed-and-seed continuum is evidence of the contemporary 'internal colonialism' that keeps the global south down in the global system. Colonial policing in its contemporary manifestations of 'humanitarian assistance' to so-called weak, failing or failed states, works within a similar continuum of practice with 'peacekeeping' at the one end and 'counter-insurgency operations' at the other.[87] We show later in this book the various ways in which the legacy of colonial policing shapes contemporary global policing.

Types of transnational policing

The field of transnational policing comprises a complex inter-institutional nexus. The global system is not a rigid hierarchy but is complex and polycentric. Like politics, policing is 'local at all points'.[88] The importance of policing to global governance lies in its dispersal throughout the structure of power that it helps to constitute. The complexity of this system makes it challenging to describe. Ulrich Beck distinguished between 'globalisation rhetoric' and the actual political and social consequences of observable changes in the flows in capital, goods, services and information as markets become connected through advances in transport and communication technology. In separating the ideo-logical from the practical consequences of such shifts, Beck made subtle but important distinctions between 'globalism', 'globality' and 'globalisation'.

By globalism, Beck meant *neo-liberal* globalisation, or the 'ideology of rule by the world market'. This ideology – in Beck's words a 'haunting mega-spectre' in the world – reduces globalisation to a single economic dimension and, thereby, monocausally and economistically displaces other dimensions of social life, such as ecology, culture, politics and civil society. Globalism, according to this view, can only be enforced and cannot be legitimated. In contrast to the ideology of globalism, Beck uses the word *globality* to describe the contemporary and material reality of world society in late modernity, a reality of enduring patterns of 'worldwide interconnectedness'. This requires good policing in order to establish and maintain the conditions of social trust on which society depends. *Globalisation* was used by Beck to denote 'the *processes* through which sovereign national states are criss-crossed and under-mined by transnational actors with varying prospects of power, orientations, identities and networks'.[89]

A related distinction is between the 'inter-national' and 'transnational'; the former has been used to indicate relationships principally between sovereign states while the latter gestures at more fully globalised relationships where actions, activities and organisational structures transcend and transgress national boundaries. These ideas are vital to the study of global policing because they lift analysis beyond a state-centred understanding of international rela-tions and raise questions about contacts, coalitions, networks and interactions across state boundaries not controlled by the central foreign policy organs of governments.[90] The terminology itself indicates the importance of *non-state actors* (such as multi-national companies, organised crime groups or new social movements), *supranational actors* (such as persons working at UN or EU institu-tions) and *sub-state actors* (mid-level professionals operating within a variety of state-based agencies) in global affairs. This complexity is what we capture with the notion of a transnational-state-system, a set of assumptions applied within the context of a global market society.

Our next task is to sketch theoretically the institutional domain of policing within the global system. We do so first by making three analytical distinctions. To the concepts of 'high' and 'low' policing discussed above, we add the con-trast between 'public' and 'private' policing[91] and, drawing on work of Richard Ericson and Kevin Haggerty, we distinguish between the 'policing of territory' and the 'policing of populations'.[92] With these three analytical distinctions in mind, the typology shown in Table 1.1 can be used to describe the broad field of transnational policing.[93]

Low policing describes an array of roles, functions and work routines. Private security guards are very common in shopping malls, airports and other places of mass consumption or spectacle. Similarly, the visibility of a uniformed public

Table 1.1   Conceptual field of transnational policing

| | Police work aimed at securing territory | | Police work aimed at securing populations | |
	Private forms	Public forms	Private forms	Public forms
High policing	Corporate security guards	Guardians of the state apparatus	Corporate security specialists	State security and the public service
Low policing	Private security guards	Uniformed patrol officers	Private eyes and private spies	Police detectives and undercover cops

Source: James Sheptycki (ed.) (2000) *Issues in Transnational Policing*. London: Routledge, p11.

police patrol makes it the ubiquitous exemplar of the idea of state sovereignty almost everywhere around the world. Although highly visible to the public, the secret social world of the occupational subculture is obscure. Even more so is the manner in which 'private eyes' and 'private spies' operate. It goes without saying that the routine work of undercover cops is concealed by a veil of secrecy. Most of what people think they know about policing is filtered through widely spread fictional accounts and news story constructions found in the commercial media. If the workings of the most evident kinds of policing agent are, in fact, mysterious to most, those types indicated along the top row of Table 1.1 are even more so. The high policing functions, which guard the integrity of government installations and corporate institutions, are usually kept secret. The legitimacy concerns inherent in these practices are another reason why corporate and state-based high policing occupy the most secretive enclaves of the policing field. This typology itself reveals some of the difficulties of bringing policing, broadly conceived, to account.

To this flat picture of the policing field we can add a vertical dimension. According to the historical sociologist Michael Mann, in the contemporary global system there are five ideal-typical, socio-spatial networks of interaction: (1) local (sub-national), (2) national (bounded by the nation-state); (3) international (relations between nationally constituted networks) (4) transnational (passing through national boundaries unaffected by them) and (5) global (covering the world as a whole).[94] Mann recognised that empirically these networks blend into one another and that, as in any typology, there are fuzzy boundaries and grey areas. However, he maintained that it is useful to identify the ways in which long distance networks – national, international and transnational – have become denser and have assumed a greater role in the structuring of social life. Applying Mann's ideas to transnational policing, the spatial networks of policing power in Table 1.2 can be delineated.[95]

This configuration of policing 'levels' is in accord with the commonsense understanding of policing agencies as rank-structured bureaucracies. In fact, in the transnational knowledge society, hierarchical organisations are continuously

Table 1.2 A socio-spatial typology for transnational policing

Locus	Network	Examples
Global	Policing entities that have a global reach	Interpol, UNPOL, UN CIVPOL missions; World Customs Organisation (WCO); International Criminal Court (ICC Investigations Division); Egmont Group/Financial Action Task Force (FATF)
Regional	Regional security structures and associations	EUROPOL; Shengen Information System (SIS), Cross Channel Intelligence Conference (CCIC), the Association of Caribbean Police Commissioners (ACCP); Regional Security System (RSS – Caribbean)
National	National security structures created to be able to coordinate a national response and to work with international partners and liaison officers posted in overseas diplomatic missions	UK Serious Organised Crime Agency (SOCA), MI5, MI6, GCHQ, US national agencies such as FBI, DEA, Homeland Security, Treasury Department, State Department, Security Service; Netherlands KDLP; French Gendarmerie and Judicial Police; German Bundespolizei; Australian Federal Police (AFP); National Police Agency (NPA – Japan); Royal Canadian Mounted Police (RCMP), etc.
Glocal	Local policing agencies and units transnationally linked	Drug squad, counter-terrorism, criminal investigation departments, Operation Trident (London Metropolitan Police Service)
		Domestic inter-agency intelligence sharing systems linking police, customs, immigration and airport security

Source: Ben Bowling (2010) *Policing the Caribbean*. Oxford: Oxford University Press, p9.

cross-cut by networks of communication that bind them together. Institutions tend towards polycentric power, which is very often non-hierarchal.

Dick Hobbs and Colin Dunnighan argued that globalisation creates 'glocal' networks in 'local places and flexible spaces' linking the local and global into collaborations among criminals and law enforcement agents alike.[96] Maureen Cain described policing as 'indigenous but globally aware'.[97] This draws attention to local police officers – especially those in such units as drugs, counterterrorism and organised crime – who often understand the broader global political and economic context of their work. Big city police in Europe, North America and Australia respond to local cocaine and heroin street-dealing, for example, well aware that transnational supply networks extend back to South America and Asia. Glocal policing can be understood in terms of its global strategic effect that is comprised by multiple mid-range bureaucratic police co-operation practices across formal lines of jurisdiction.

Lashing together transnational multi-agency operations can be tremendously complicated because public and private security providers all have functionally delimited remits that differ in important ways. The FBI, for example, has a wider remit than the DEA, and the RCMP remit is wider still. The remit of private security providers is customer service so the functions of in-house security for multi-national corporate entities, such as Halliburton or Coca-Cola, are different to the functions provided by private security firms, such as the GEO Group or the private military company Blackwater (now known as Xe). All of these agencies could, in theory at least, become involved in a globally co-ordinated, multi-agency effort.

The transformative power of information communication technologies in the transnational-networked society is transfiguring highly rank-structured police organisations. Local police units in countries thousands of miles apart sometimes find themselves linked without any intervening central national authority. In an era of mobile phones and networked computers, local police needing information from far distant places can make instant contact as easily as they can with their colleagues in the same building. In many instances regional police co-operation enterprises are constituted precisely so that local policing functions can be networked across national borders without direct oversight by central national-state authorities. There is a good deal of complexity in how these various 'levels' co-articulate in practice. At the global level are institutions that are only loosely coupled to national states. As we show in Chapter 3, some of these organisations, Interpol first among them, are not at all constitutionally beholden to national sovereign interests, *they are fully supranational* and independent.

To understand how this complex system of global policing hangs together, this book advances a theory that pays specific attention to the occupational subcultures of policing.[98] This perspective holds that the core feature of the police occupation consists in its relationship to coercion, giving rise to a set of sociological and cultural expectations and adaptations that rests on the assumption that policing agents can be solutions to the predicament of authority.[99] Under conditions of globalisation, what then happens to the consent of the governed? Transnationally, police operate with law, if not under it, and around the world there is a sense that the social contract is being torn apart by competing claims. Policing subculture is a social space where agents actively create meanings of social order. We argue that the practices of transnational policing are essential to the maintenance of the transnational-state-system and serve to bolster it both symbolically and practically.

There are ancillary problems experienced within the occupational subcultures of policing, primarily to do with surveillance and the management of knowledge about policing power. The subculture of policing exhibits considerable local variation because knowledge relevant to policing is local knowledge. Nevertheless there remains a family resemblance among subcultures of policing around the world and this is what we mean by the transnational subculture of policing. Features of that kinship arise from common problems inherent in the use of coercion or the threat of violence as a means to achieve peace and security. Research on policing subcultures also empirically verifies that police agents around the world tend to adhere to cultural values associated with masculinity such as combativeness, suspiciousness, cynicism, pessimism, conservatism and a thirst for action.

As we will show in detail in Chapter 4, the idea that police subcultures around the world share some similarities is well established. But what is new is a *subculture of transnational policing* among an emerging occupational group memorably described by Robert Reiner as 'the new internationale of technocratic police experts', who travel the globe advancing the latest policing solutions.[100] Police agents of various stripes are increasingly prevalent in many settings in the system of global governance. They sometimes operate as liaison officers in an intelligence sharing and support capacity several degrees removed from the actual coercive use of force that is more often delegated to local units. Some are training local officers. Others actually assume operational control of local policing. The subculture of transnational policing shapes the global system in important ways. Decisions that these police agents take and the policies they make shape the transnational subculture of policing, which in turn shapes local policing around the world. The meanings and processes enacted within the policing field reflexively constitute the culture of global policing and thereby the destiny of world society more generally.

Conclusion: policing an insecure world

What would Derek Bond and his family make of this discussion? The media-made myth of the 'Man from Interpol' would have already been busted by their personal experience. Mr Bond had direct acquaintance with post-colonial policing and the South African prison system. His family personally endured the inner workings of the byzantine legal realm of cross-border policing. Their direct contact with the technological power of global policing illustrates the political complexity of the transnational-state-system of which it is a part. Those personal experiences plunged the Bond family into doubt about the nature of the social contract struck by transnational policing. Their story raises serious questions about the nature of the global policing enterprise.

This chapter has endeavoured to sketch out the components of a language necessary to establish a general theory of global policing. Our theory allows for subcultural adaptations of policing in different countries, organisational locations and occupational specialisms. Our focus is on the historical evolution of modern policing (a central component of the nation-state) as the transnational-state-system idea evolves and is superimposed onto the world system. The theory concerns the relationship between police and law and how the quality of the social contract shapes the legitimacy (or otherwise) of policing. It recognises the parallel history of colonial policing and foregrounds the coercive aspects of the police role in imposing social order domestically and transnationally. Our analysis emphasises that power in the global system is polycentric without an exclusive source of authority, and that the policing field is conceptually and organisationally fragmented. Global policing is the result of a complex overdetermination arising from multiple factors. The theory suggests that action on the policing field gains coherence as a result of the meanings engendered in the occupational subculture of policing around the world. As we explain in Chapter 4, this is strongly influenced by the newly emerging occupational subculture among specialist transnational police officers.

Theorising global policing is important because policework shapes the global system in crucial ways. Global policing theory is an opening into the global system and a microcosm of it. Transnational policing is a central mechanism in reproducing the transnational-state-system and constitutes the existing global system's most general characteristic. It is a synecdoche of globalisation. The occupational subculture of policing provides an interesting cast of characters for the global stage. The personal experience of the Bond family in their hour on that stage is emblematic of the way in which, to paraphrase C. Wright Mills, private troubles are transformed into global public issues.[101] Personal experiences of transnational policing indicate a general sense of crisis and the evidence that we examine in this book shows that policing subcultures are woven into the panic scenes of the global security-control society. To put it bluntly, bad policing creates global insecurity. It follows that global policing is, or should be, one of the crucial public issues of our time.

2

POLICING AND THE TRANSNATIONAL-
STATE-SYSTEM

The emerging transnational-state-system is profoundly affecting the jurisdictional sovereignty and functional diversity of policing in a globalised world. In
this chapter, we show how a variety of police actors have shaped the global
policing agenda focused on transnational organised crime and terrorism.
Security threats have, by and large, been defined in ways that reflect the
discourse of police agencies housed within powerful seigneurial states. The
chapter describes forms of bilateral and multi-lateral regional police and security
co-operation – for example, Mutual Legal Assistance Treaties (MLATs) and the
European Trevi organisation. Here we show that transnational policing is part
of a polycentric and fragmented structure of global governance. The chapter
questions the extent to which the world system can be governed by exclusively
tough policing methods and asks whether the observable trends in global policing
are contributing to the ungovernability of that system.

──────────────── **The changing morphology of the state** ────────────────

To understand policing in the context of a putative transnational-state-system
it is useful to take a step back and note how the state has been changing as a
result of globalisation. In the later years of the 20th century the rise of neo-
liberalism, the free flow of finance, the opening up of trade and economic globalisation generally, created fundamentally new conditions for the idea of the
state in the global system. The Keynsian state, most prevalent in Europe and
North America, has not withered away but has been 'hollowed out' with power
being pulled upwards into supranational organisations and downwards to non-
state actors including private corporations and non-governmental organisations. Importantly, this new state form is *post-national* 'insofar as the national
territory has become less important as an economic, political and cultural
"power container"'.[102]

Inspired by economists Milton Friedman and Friedrich Hayek and political theorist Joseph Schumpeter, a new form of state governance was propounded by Margaret Thatcher and Ronald Reagan. This new philosophy of state power was advanced globally through the IMF and the World Bank. The so-called Washington Consensus advocated the privatisation of state assets (de-regulation), and the liberalisation of investment and capital flows. At the cusp of the new century, the running down of public services for health, education and welfare were visible manifestations of neo-liberalism.[103] This trend operating, as it were, 'from below', contributed immensely to the changing morphology of the state.

At the same time as economic globalisation manifested the tendency towards the hollowing out of the state, the sovereign power of states was also drawn upwards into institutions of *supranational* governance. This was most obviously the case in Europe where the fast developing institutions of the European Economic Community and later the European Union added a layer to the system of governance 'above' the nation-state. The trend could also be observed more globally, although the effect of the transnationalisation of governmental power was uneven. For seigneurial states, rogue states and all the other sovereign-state constituents of the international system, the development of transnational platforms of governance as varied as the World Bank, the IMF, the Organisation for Economic Co-operation and Development (OECD), the Group of Seven (G7, later G8 and then G20), the UN and the Commonwealth Secretariat drew political power upwards. By the end of the 1980s, the high representatives of sovereign states were unavoidably interacting in a world system that included these supranational platforms of governance.[104] As a result of these transformations from below and from above, the idea of the international-state-system has morphed into a transnational-state-system.

These political transformations are reflected in dramatic changes in the global economic context.[105] Capital and labour markets have been integrated and world trade has increased. The volume of merchandise traded around the world quadrupled between 1995 and 2007 and in the same period the global market in commercial services increased sixfold. As an operating system of ideas, the transnational-state-system functions within this global market and in the mixed currents of global society and culture. This has had implications for how crime is framed and understood. The growth in legal markets has been accompanied by a concomitant growth of global flows of illicit agricultural and manufactured products (e.g. counterfeit medicines, narcotic and psychotropic drugs, counterfeits of brand-name products), professional and commercial services (e.g. sex work and money laundering) and of the people buying and selling them. Neoliberal policies adopted by governments, such as market de-regulation and the relaxing of trade barriers, were strongly associated with an increase in illicit commodity flows in a globally connected marketplace.

Neoliberalism also promotes certain kinds of human global mobility to meet the demands of globally mobile capital. Worldwide air travel grew 60 per cent between 1995 and 2007. The increase in world travel for business, the growth in tourism and the emergence of migrant, expatriate and diasporic communities created practical issues for policing, for example, managing the arrangements for when someone dies overseas, international missing persons inquiries, high profile diplomatic visits or lost and stolen identity documents.[106] In a globally connected and physically mobile society, policing is stretched so as to connect to similar organisations in other countries. One symptom of this is that international fugitive apprehension has become a police priority in many jurisdictions.

There has been a technological aspect to these transformations. The 'information revolution' suggests that new information and communications technologies (ICTs) are fundamentally transforming organisational working practice.[107] The capacity to communicate has radically increased through personal computers and mobile telephones. Globally the number of Internet users rose fourfold between 2000 and 2008 to 6.7 billion.[108] Worldwide there were four billion mobile phones in use in 2008, up from 2.7 billion in 2006.[109] The speed of international travel and telecommunications results in dramatically reducing the time taken to make connections between one part of the globe to another. This is what David Harvey calls 'time space compression'.[110] David Held and Anthony McGrew have noted that these processes increase the *extensity* of global networks, the *velocity* of global flows and the *intensity* and *impact* of global interconnectedness.[111]

The organisational change brought about by improved inter-continental communication includes the electronic connection of major economic systems and the creation of 'virtual money', the rise of global banks, multi-national corporations, the ubiquity of global brands, electronic advertising, social networking websites and 24-hour global commercial news media. The changes in the economy and society wrought by new technologies have changed the way all the major social institutions (including the state) work 'from within'. Growing global interconnectedness through telecommunications creates new opportunities for illegality and facilitates criminal collaborations, but it also opens up new possibilities for 'horizontal' communication and collaboration among police agents in the field, possibly reducing bureaucratic drag and political control. Advances in telecommunication provide new opportunities for the development of system integration and convergence between police and military forces.

With the idea of the transnational-state-system comes the hollowing out of the Keynesian welfare state to be replaced by a Schumpeterian 'workfare state'. This transformation is facilitated by the police and other institutions that deploy symbolic and practical coercive power for the purposes of social ordering. The changing morphology of the state has undermined the capacity of nationally based governments to ensure the welfare of the general population.

Such phenomena as environmental degradation, climate change, extreme poverty and mass migration are all issues that cannot be controlled by the traditional nation-state-system.[112] These processes create what criminologist Steven Spitzer called 'social junk' (people who have fallen through the cracks in the social system and become impoverished and dependent) and 'social dynamite' (people who have done the same, but have become potentially rebellious and violent as a result).[113] Consequently, policing and law enforcement agencies have increasingly adopted 'the strategy of colonial war', which according to Christian Parenti achieves 'peace through superior firepower'.[114]

The world has become more integrated economically, politically and socially, and a new set of problems and issues have emerged. The transnational-state-system is a set of ideas and practices that serve to 'containerise' insecurity. The 'waste products' of a globalised society (whether this is meant *literally* as in the case of toxic waste or *metaphorically* to describe desperately poor people) flow through the world system and therefore global hazards (rising sea levels, environmental damage, predatory crime) are not contained by national boundaries. The existing structures and mechanisms of policing are inadequate to the task of global governance because they are tied tightly to the idea of the nation-state. This goes right to the heart of the problem of governance and the global social contract: what form of governance is required to ensure that policing power is constrained, legitimated and held accountable when its social world lies hidden, often in the 'transnational space between' formally sovereign state powers? Theorists of global governance have grappled with similar issues for some time (see Chapter 1). Our interest is to illuminate the centrality of transnational policing subculture in the structure of global power.

Jurisdictional sovereignty and functional diversity in policing

The world system is polycentric. By this we mean that there is no hierarchical order to the structure of power that comprises it. Rather, there are many institutional centres of social power that animate the structure of the global system. The executive authorities of some powerful countries – which we call seigneurial states – are dominant but not determinant. The world system also includes a variety of non-state actors (such as corporations) and supranational centres of political power (such as the G8, NATO, UN, IMF, OECD and World Bank) that are relatively autonomous from specific states' interests and have effects of their own. The logic of the unitary state remains a prevalent assumption concerning political power within this system, but the power of 'the state' is transgressed, transfigured and ultimately transformed due to the cultural, economic, political and technological effects of globalisation.[115] That is why we make a distinction between the global system and the transnational-state-system. We are interested to foreground a particular type of institutional actor – transnational police officers – within the world system and demonstrate their special importance in shaping it. We think that policing is central to shoring up the idea of the transnational-state-system. In exploring the politics of policing in a global context and explaining how policing undergirds the transnational-state-system, two structuring principles need to be understood. The first is the notion of jurisdictional sovereignty; the second is the functional diversity and division of labour in policing practice.

Jurisdiction and the closely associated concept of sovereignty are important ideas in both criminology and international relations. The idea of state sovereignty was crystallised in the Treaty of Westphalia (1648), which codified the basic principles of territorial integrity, border inviolability and supremacy of state-law. Subsequently, Europe (followed by the rest of the world) was turned into a patchwork of competing states. The 1933 Montevideo Convention is a widely accepted codification of the rights and duties of states. Article 1 declares that the state 'as a person of international law' should possess the following qualifications: (1) a permanent population; (2) a defined territory; (3) government; and (4) capacity to enter into relations with the other states.

In the terms of critical geography, the history of modernity can be partly understood as the process whereby the principle of sovereign state jurisdiction was used to order the geopolitical cartography of world power. This gave rise to the 'billiard ball model' of international relations.[116] John Wear Burton's 1972 book *World Society* critiques the picture of the global system in which each state is represented by 'a government' and is seen as an entity in itself – a sovereign independent unit. Within this model it follows that what takes place within each unit is not the concern of other units. Because the state is supposed to have a monopoly on the use of coercive force and policing, above all aspects of government, is a matter of 'domestic jurisdiction'.

In this view of the global system, the only things that count as inter-national relations are the interactions between nation-states of differing sizes and power, interactions or contacts that are like those of differently sized billiard balls. Only the hard exteriors touch and heavier or faster moving ones push others out of the way. According to this model of international relations the points of contact are governments – because only governments interact internationally. To criminologists this model has some deficiencies since police are almost always sub-state actors, not the sovereign representatives of government. Similarly, non-state actors such as criminals and transnational security experts are not accounted for. We theorise about jurisdiction on the basis of a sociological account of the practices of policing found in a variety of institutional sites of power within a polycentric global system.

The second structuring principle affecting the way policing is enacted within the global system is functional diversity. Policing, including transnational policing, includes an array of tasks concerning the maintenance of public order, law enforcement, crime investigation, regulation and what sociologists of policing call 'social service functions'.[117] The latter may surprise readers who are used to thinking of policing exclusively in terms of law enforcement and crime control. Yet one of the most impressive and extensive transnational police missions in history came in the wake of a major natural disaster: the devastating effects of the Indian Ocean Tsunami of December 2004 that killed more than 200,000 people in 13 countries. The emergency assistance in this case involved more than 3000 police officers from 31 countries co-operating in providing disaster relief, helping with body recovery, using forensic science to identify bodies, repatriating victims, investigating victims' last-known movements and many other policing functions in various places across the region.[118]

Crime and related types of insecurity (problems such as piracy and drug trafficking) certainly form a central aspect of transnational policing. However, in Chapter 5 we also endeavour to show that other functions, like preventing environmental crimes such as toxic waste dumping, should also be understood as part of global policing service. These phenomena, and more, form the basis for police action that crosses the institutional boundaries of nation-states. The range of policing functions – from interdicting illicit drug shipments to identifying human remains in the wake of a tsunami, or the attempts to maintain order in the context of civil war – illustrate the diversity of the global policing mission. This raises a crucial question. Given the enormous range of competing security priorities, how is the agenda for transnational policing set?

───────── **Agenda setting and transnational policing priorities** ─────────

The concept of transnational organised crime first emerged in the 1970s and the subsequent evolution of the meaning of the term in official UN discourse offers a case study in global policy agenda setting.[119] Transnational organised crime was originally seen as a problem for developing countries vulnerable to white collar crime and corruption. In 1975, the final report of the Fifth United Nations *Congress on the Prevention of Crime and the Treatment of Offenders* concerned two associated concepts – crime as business and transnational crime. The former featured activities: (1) directed at economic gain involving commerce, industry or trade; (2) some form of organisation; (3) the use or misuse of legitimate forms and techniques of business, trade or industry; and (4) persons of relatively high social status or political power. The concept of transnational crime as spanning the borders of two or more countries was novel for its time. It is also interesting that the impact of transnational crime was originally conceived in terms of its trans-boundary economic and social effects, rather than in a language directly amenable to law enforcement criteria.

The vocabulary of 'crime as business' prevalent in the circuits of UN govern-ance was different from the language pertaining to traditional forms of wrong-doing. Transnational crime was seen to be particularly hard on developing countries and western transnational corporations (TNCs) were much criticised. The language called for more effective control over the abuse of economic power by national and transnational enterprises. Proponents of this discourse singled out for control the illegal, deviant and economically harmful behaviour of powerful and potentially monopolist TNCs operating where the state was relatively weak.[120] The original UN language for talking about transnational crime drew attention to terms like corruption and environmental destruction.

At the 6th UN Congress five years later, the terms of discourse concerning transnational crime remained much the same. Resolution 7 concerning the 'prevention of the abuse of power' showed the creeping influence of law enforcement discourse. Although transnational corporations were again men-tioned, the language was about the use of penal law. By 1981, the UN General Assembly expressed deep concern about crime and called for the forthcoming meetings of the Committee on Crime Prevention and Control to focus particu-larly on 'emerging trends'. Four years later at the 7th Congress the language concerning transnational crime was in flux fusing concerns about victims of crime with abuse of power. Discussions of business crime all but vanished. Economic crime was mentioned, but alongside a number of other issues includ-ing domestic violence and other crimes against women, the treatment of juve-niles and the exchange of prisoners.[121] Moreover, the new issues were articulated in terms of human rights whereas economic crime was not. Amid this shifting terminology was a renewed emphasis on the effort to control and eradicate illicit drug trafficking and the organised crime associated with it. The really new development in the transnational crime discourse of the 1980s concerned criminal asset forfeiture and confiscation which was articulated solely with regard to narco-trafficking but, curiously, not with regard to corporate elites.

By the late 1980s the transformation of the language of transnational crime was complete. The 1988 *UN Convention Against Illicit Traffic in Narcotic Drugs and Psychotropic Substances*, the latest in a line of such resolutions going back to 1970, entrenched the global drug prohibition regime. The language of trans-national crime prevalent at the 1990 Havana *Congress on Crime Prevention and Criminal Justice* showed the broader contours of the linguistic shift. The terms indicated that illicit traffic and transnational criminal organisations were 'pen-etrating' society at all levels. The insertion of the term 'organised' to trans-national crime was crucial. Transnational organised crime (TOC) was described in the terms of modern management and organised crime groups were pictured as being structured like corporations akin to IBM. The language was also largely spoken in law enforcement terms with large and complex criminal enterprises envisioned as 'targets'. Conspicuous by its absence was a concern with the ille-gal activities of multi-national corporations and, although the list of concerns associated with organised crime included things like environmental offences, corruption, crimes against cultural heritage, terrorism and economic crime, the priorities began and ended with drugs.

In the year 2000, TOC talk was codified in the UN Convention Against Organized Crime (known as the Palermo Convention). This development was important because domestic laws are introduced in the wake of international agreements, thus spreading the legal tools of the policing trade transnationally. The term 'organised crime', now central to the discourse, referred generally to groups of three or more people acting together over a period of time committing one or more serious crimes or offences in order to gain financial reward. The primary image invoked in the language was of drug cartels and differed fundamentally from that of 20 years previous. Out went talk of criminal collusion between corporate power and corrupt elites in developing counties. In came transnational organised crime, a script about criminal outsiders penetrating states and multi-national corporations for the purposes of money-laundering and the destabilisation of political systems. In Chapter 3 we examine the social and political significance of this new language in terms of a discourse of 'suitable enemies'.

A second case-study in transnational agenda setting concerns the prioritisation of terrorism and the distinction between 'ordinary law crime' and 'political crime'. This is fraught with difficulty because one person's terrorist is another person's freedom-fighter.[122] Article 2 of the Interpol Constitution, drafted and adopted in 1956, established the aims of the agency as being:

1 to ensure and promote the widest possible mutual assistance between all criminal police authorities within the limits of the laws existing in the different countries and in the spirit of the Universal Declaration of Human Rights;
2 to establish and develop all institutions likely to contribute effectively to the prevention and suppression of ordinary law crime.

Article 3 stipulates that it 'is strictly forbidden for Interpol to undertake any intervention or activities of a political, military, religious or racial character'.[123] There are many chapters in the history of Interpol illustrative of the tensions involved in making the practical distinction between political and ordinary crime. In 1959, the Interpol NCB in Havana issued a request for a Red Notice for former members of the Batista regime arguing they were 'really thieves and criminals pretending to be police [and] offenders against ordinary criminal law', but the request was refused by the General Assembly who were persuaded that the motive was political. To cite another example, after the Black September attacks at the Munich Olympics in 1972 – during which 11 members of the Israeli athletics team and a German police officer were killed – the Interpol Secretariat refused to be involved, again on the grounds of Article 3 of the Constitution.

By the beginning of the 1980s the distinction between 'ordinary law crime' and 'political crime' was breaking down.[124] The 1983 Interpol General Assembly in Cannes resolved to look again at acts committed by organised groups with multiple victims and 'which are usually covered by the general term "terrorism"'. The following year a resolution on *Violent Crime Commonly Referred to as Terrorism* was passed in Luxemburg which concerned organised groups engaging in violent criminal activities that are designed, by spreading terror or fear, to attain 'allegedly political objectives'. An additional resolution suggested that it was impossible to give a precise enough definition of 'political, military, religious or racial matters' and that each case had to be examined separately. In 1985, the General Assembly in Washington, DC passed a resolution creating the 'Public Safety and Terrorism' (PST) sub-directorate to coordinate and enhance co-operation in 'combating international terrorism'. This effectively ended any discussions concerning terrorism and the political prohibitions of Article 3. It also made international terrorism a standing agenda item for all future Interpol General Assembly and Executive Committee meetings and led to the development of training based on the 1986 *Guide for Combating International Terrorism*.

The General Assembly meeting in Cairo in 1998 issued a *Declaration Against Terrorism*, condemning the threat posed 'not only with regard to security and stability, but also to the State of Law, to democracy and to human rights'. The stage was thus set and not long after 11 September 2001 at the Interpol General Assembly in Budapest, a resolution was passed condemning 'murderous attacks perpetrated against the world's citizens in the United States of America' as 'an abhorrent violation of law and of the standards of human decency' that constitute 'cold-blooded mass murder [and] a crime against humanity'. The distinction between political and ordinary crime embedded in Interpol's constitution, which had historically been used to impede Interpol co-operation in counter-terrorism, dissolved entirely. Interpol freed itself from its own constitutional fetters and could participate in the worldwide 'war on terror'. The terrorist joined the organised criminal in the language of justification for global policing.

The agenda for the governance of transnational organised crime and terrorism was decisively shaped in slow increments over a 20-year period. We have used UN documents and the history of the interpretation of Article 3 of the Interpol Constitution to trace the evolving language of transnational policing and two of its most important objects: transnational organised crime and terrorism. This should not be read as implying that the UN or Interpol were responsible for driving the change. These institutions were merely vehicles. The shift in the language can be seen in a variety of other institutional sites comprising the transnational-state-system, including such entities as the OECD and the G8.[125] Obviously, this language was very common in large police agencies with global reach, from the AFP to the ZfV. Of course this language was also being advanced in a variety of other ways, including commercial news media and Hollywood movies. Before 9-11, the common parlance for transnational policing had already been established. That is why the UK-based newspaper the *Guardian* could point out in the immediate aftermath of the destruction of New York's twin towers in 2001 that 'before September 11 there was a very strong case for a global force to tackle the underground economy of laundered money including drugs, crime and the fruits of government corruption that is estimated to top £1,000bn. The unpaid taxes on these sums should alone be incentive enough for the global police.'[126]

Legal discourse and law-making in international police co-operation

'Laws', Peter Andreas and Ethan Nadelmann maintain, 'precede and define criminality'. It is through their law-making and law-enforcing powers that 'states set the rules of the game'.[127] This legal realism is contradicted by Andreas' and Nadelmann's own research findings and overstates the centrality of the state *qua* State in the embodiment of living law. We think that the idea of the state remains an important one in the global system, but there is room for much more awareness that non-state and sub-state actors influence the action on the global stage than is allowed by realist theories of law and international relations. In order to fully understand transnational law-making and law enforcement it is important not to overstate the importance of sovereign state actors and to give due regard to the effects of other players.[128]

A common assumption with regard to international legal assistance agreements in police co-operation is that they follow on from the 'recognition' by states of a transnational insecurity problem. According to this view, states' sovereign diplomatic representatives recognise problems and then create laws, bilateral or multi-lateral legal instruments or 'memoranda of understanding' that come to somehow direct international police co-operation. This assumption leaves the recognition of the problem in the first instance an unopened black box. As Jonathan Winer, US Deputy Assistant Secretary of State for International Law Enforcement from 1994 to 1999 explained, the harmonised legal standards expressed in the Palermo Convention were actually designed by technocrats at the mid-level of national and transnational bureaucracies. Moreover, these technocrats developed legal standards 'to meet the new demands of cross-border enforcement activities, with minimal interference by domestic political constraints'.[129] In other words, like most other transnational legal instruments for law enforcement co-operation the terms of the Convention were scripted by transnational policing actors themselves. The answer to the question, 'how do governments come to recognise problems for law enforcement that require transnational legal instruments?' is, in part, that law enforcement professionals create the grounds for such recognition.

Mathieu Deflem similarly observes the relative autonomy of police institutions from the states in which they nest and the 'relevance of [police] knowledge systems for the diffusion of police objectives and police technique in international partnerships'.[130]

In *Cops Across Borders*, Ethan Nadelmann sets out a detailed analysis of the use of undercover police techniques in the Benelux region in Europe.[131] Undercover policing was prohibited in most of Western European countries after the Second World War for obvious reasons related to the history of authoritarian policing during the period of fascism and Nazism. Policing agents acting as *agents provocateurs*, as instigators or facilitators of criminal acts, was therefore considered particularly abhorrent to late 20th-century Europeans. US law enforcement actors, such as the DEA, were much less squeamish and, indeed, were keen to promote undercover tactics developed in the United States to combat illicit drug trafficking around the world. A prime example of this was controlled delivery (a kind of *agents provocateurship*), but also included the entire panoply of new police surveillance methods.[132] In Western Europe at the time, these policing practices were all viewed as legally problematic from a fairly commonly held perspective on policing and civil liberties.

This had interesting effects in UK case law, for example in *Chinoy*. In this case a DEA wiretap was undertaken in France without the authorisation of an investigating magistrate in breach of French law and the European Convention on Human Rights. Yet evidence from this source was deemed admissible in an English court and the conviction was eventually upheld by the European Court of Human Rights.[133] This kind of entrepreneurship by the DEA had other consequences. In the mid-1990s, the politics of policing in the Kingdom of the Netherlands was convulsed by revelations about the undercover activities of the Inter Regional Team (IRT), which were made publicly known as a result of a Parliamentary Enquiry chaired by Martin van Traa.[134] The technique of controlled delivery, which entailed police officers taking an active role in the movement of drugs, looked to most members of the Dutch public like the acts of *agents provocateurs*. Dutch authorities were unable to interview agents of the DEA who took part in what was nominally an IRT operation. They had left the country and were purportedly no longer in any European jurisdiction. The scandal was a catalyst for subsequent law-making. Nadelmann concluded that 'not since the European powers trained colonial police forces has one nation's police agency exerted such a powerful international influence'.

The integration of DEA-style methods into European drug enforcement has required metamorphoses not just in the *modus operandi* of European police but in the laws regulating their behavior as well. Changes in the laws of criminal procedure can be seen as responses both to changing public demands on the police and to changing police practices. Courts, legislators and authors of internal police guidelines tend to respond to perceived police excesses by restricting the power and discretion of police, and to perceived inadequacies by expanding their power and discretion. In the later case, the pressures often arise from the need to legalise and regulate what the police have already begun to do 'extralegally' or illegally.[135]

These examples show that circumvention of the letter of the law by police authorities from one state on the territory of another do not necessarily entail legal consequences in the jurisdiction where the infraction took place. Decisions made in European courts do not reliably attach consequences to illegal behaviour by officials other than those of their own country. Extra-legal police action is easily conducted in the 'transnational space between' and these examples demonstrate such action has been used as a precedent to create new permissive rules for transnational policing.

To suggest that state laws precede and define criminality also neglects the actions and effects of moral entrepreneurs. The long history of drug criminalisation is the paradigm example of transnational policing.[136] Andreas and Nadelmann record that in 1898, when the Americans occupied the Philippines in the wake of the Spanish-American war, 'a pragmatic plan favored by Governor Taft to reinstitute the legal opium control system [...] was derailed when a leading antivice moral entrepreneur [...] mobilised vigorous opposition'.[137] The subsequent history of institution building has been long and fitful, leading to President Nixon's remarks to media executives at the Flagship Hotel in Rochester, New York, in June 1971: 'drug traffic is public enemy number one domestically in the US today and we must wage a total offensive, worldwide, nationwide, government-wide and, if I may say so, media-wide'.[138] Made during the Machiavellian moment of the Vietnam War, that statement helped to extend the power of the executive branch of the US government into new realms.

With regard to law-making facilitative of transnational policing functions we can see multiple actors in various institutional domains engaging in political actions. Within a world system that has grown increasingly complex, these multiple centres of social power – some in civil society (e.g. moral entrepreneurs), some at the executive level of seigneurial states and some at the middle ranges and front lines of police bureaucracies – exert power in transnational law-making and actual law enforcement. It is not the case that the state or system of states is an autonomous realm from which law is decreed. Law is a set of tools used in purposeful interaction and here we see it being used to constitute an important aspect of the world system by some of its most powerful actors from within the subculture of transnational policing.

When it comes to the articulation of policing functions, not all legal instruments that come into force afford equal effort. For example, consider the activities of Greenpeace (formed in 1970) and other groups of environmental activists and moral entrepreneurs to criminalise a range of deliberate harms to the environment. Perhaps these efforts will eventually result in changes, but so far crimes against the environment do not articulate well with law enforcement discourse or in quite the same way as drug traffickers and the other 'usual suspects' of transnational criminality. Perhaps the most significant international legal instrument to emerge thus far from the environmental movement is the Convention on International Trade in Endangered Species (CITES). This attempt to build a global regulatory apparatus to police the killing of wild animals and the harvesting of endangered plant species has created a considerable criminal opportunity structure.[139] However, environmental activists are more often redefined as 'ecoterrorists' and thus themselves become the object of police interests and control efforts. Indeed, they are more likely to be criminalised than those whose activities actually despoil the environment.[140] The mere existence of a legal tool (international or national) does not mean that it will be picked up and used. The decisions to use legal rules are always made by practical actors and those decisions are based on understandings that unavoidably draw on cultural meanings beyond those that the rules themselves articulate.

Another pertinent example of law-making is the Mutual Legal Assistance Treaty (MLAT). This is the basic mechanism used to facilitate police co-operation in investigation and evidence collection beyond jurisdictional boundaries in a form admissible in domestic courts.[141] Recognition of an emergent police requirement is followed by ad hoc semi-formal bilateral arrangements that are gradually formalised through the exchange of 'memoranda of understanding' (MOU). Policing practice may eventually even yield a fully brokered MLAT.

Systems for transfer of prisoners are an interesting example because of the idea of *habeas corpus* – the procedural device to examine the lawfulness of a prisoner's detention. Meaning literally 'you are to have the body' it is a legal action by which a prisoner can be released from unlawful detention. It depends on the 'writ of the sovereign' and is inextricably linked to the notion of sovereign jurisdiction. The idea of *habeas corpus* was already well entrenched in Common Law thinking by the 18th century and so it is not surprising to find that the British colonies (each of which was administered as a separate jurisdiction) required practical measures for transfer of prisoners between them – particularly in island regions. The current process of transferring prisoners between Commonwealth countries is based on the system for rendition between British possessions established in the 1800s.

The 1966 *Commonwealth Scheme for Rendition* served as a set of recommendations to guide the regulation of prisoner transfer between Commonwealth states. The 1995 and 1996 EU Conventions modify the 1957 European Convention on Extradition (ECE), which, as one of the first multi-lateral conventions for extradition, reflects many fundamental principles recognised as general concepts in extradition practice. The extradition treaty signed by the UK and US on 31 March 2003 and its implementing legislation the Extradition Act of the same year brings UK/US procedures more into line with arrangements with European countries by eliminating the need for *prima facie* evidence, but still requiring a detailed statement of the facts of the case to be provided.[142]

MLATs facilitating cross-border law enforcement by definition reify the abstraction of 'enforcement jurisdiction' and thereby the taken for granted conventions of the state-system. They are an example of how legal tools emerge from the practicalities of the policing task in the transnational context. They result when a functional or regional pattern of police collaboration becomes sufficiently entrenched through the inclusion of multiple institutional actors to warrant black letter law. Other scholarship has shown this same pattern with regard to global policing regimes to rid the high seas of pirates and slave traffickers during the 19th century, the imposition of a global drug prohibition regime during the 20th century and the subsequent transnational spread of undercover policing techniques.[143] This 'ground-up' process may be seen to interact with 'top-down' police policy pursued by actors working at transnational levels. Because of what Mathieu Deflem calls police 'bureaucratic autonomy' it is clear that the process is almost entirely articulated in the domain of the occupational subculture of policing.[144] Just as the classics of police scholarship show that police culture shapes police practice on 'skid row' and other neighbourhood beats, the same is true in the transnational realm.

Most academic studies concerning the legal instruments for transnational policing describe the content of the law without reference to a theory of law. The approach adopted here foregrounds 'law in action' rather than 'law in books'.[145] This highlights the relationship between formal rules (law) and institutional practice (policework), in light of inter-institutional political contestation and related systems of knowledge that provide the surface of emergence upon which these relations are conducted.[146] The policing discourse of law enforcement decisively shapes global policing practice, and thereby the world system. The polycentricity of power within the putative transnational-state-system gives rise to complex interrelations and it is not easy to say where the buck stops (or starts) and who or what institution is driving the changes. In sharper focus and detail, the next two sections take a contrasting look at developments in trans-border policing in Europe and the United States.

Developments in Europe

Since national policing jurisdictions in Europe are densely packed, bilateral transnational policing arrangements are long standing, especially in towns and cities close to or straddling borders. However, the perceived dangers of authoritarian policing in post-war Europe meant that, prior to the 1970s, there was no political will to establish significant national, let alone pan-European, police institutions. The exceptions to this rule were the various security and intelligence services that tended towards both national and international reach, but these were high policing functions, largely single-task oriented and secret, especially during the Cold War.

Between the Second World War and the end of the Cold War, the internal borders of Europe presented practical difficulties for local police. Even something as prosaic as household burglary took on added complexity when stolen goods were transported across national borders, a common phenomenon in the border towns and surrounding frontier regions. Consequently there were already many informal or semi-formal cross-border policing arrangements in Europe at the time of the first meeting of the so-called Trevi Group for intergovernmental co-operation on immigration, asylum, police and judicial co-operation in 1975.[147] The Trevi system operated in secrecy from its inception until 1989 after which a flurry of documents were published.[148] The creation of the Trevi group was preceded by a number of intergovernmental meetings on terrorism in 1971 and 1972. At a Council of Ministers meeting in Rome in December 1975, UK Foreign Secretary James Callaghan proposed, and the ministers agreed, to set up a special working group to combat terrorism in the European Community (EC). Later formalised in Luxembourg at a meeting of the EC interior ministers on 29 June 1976, the decision created the discretionary space for mid-ranking and senior police and security service officials to act in concert across Europe. The initial catalyst was concern about counter-terrorism and other matters of high policing, but the agenda was soon delegated to actors lower in the hierarchy of European governance and every aspect of policework came up for discussion.[149]

The Trevi structure was comprised of three levels: ministers of the interior (which met in June and December), the Trevi senior officials group (which met in May and November) and the working parties. The latter were numerous groups constituted of interior and home ministry officials, senior police officers, immigration and customs officials, and security service representatives. Active working groups met on a frequent and less structured basis to hammer out working practices related to a host of issues including terrorism, organised crime and illegal immigration. They considered police training and communications systems, contingency measures for safety and security at nuclear installations, transport of nuclear material and procedures for dealing with emergencies, disasters and fire fighting. The Trevi structure gave middle and lower ranking officials from interior ministries, police, immigration, customs and security services *carte blanche* to work together. A Scotland Yard officer who participated in the process explained how it worked:

> Once you get your proposal agreed around the individual working groups, you will get a ministerial policy decision at the end of the current six months. You must remember that the largest club in the world is Law Enforcement – and in Trevi you have that plus ministerial muscle.[150]

The 1989 *Palma Document* explained Trevi's emerging policies on policing, law, immigration and asylum as part of the ongoing development of the European political project. The following year's *Programme of Action* developed the projects of the European Information System (EIS, forerunner of the Schengen Information System [SIS]) and the European Drugs Intelligence Unit (which later became Europol). *The Declaration of Trevi Group Ministers* addressed the new requirements of a European area without internal borders and the need to co-operate on fighting terrorism, international crime, narcotics and illegal trafficking of every sort. The *Programme of Action* defined a synthesis of the arrangements between police and security services for consideration by the Trevi working groups in relation to terrorism, drug trafficking or any forms of crime including organised illegal immigration. The language in these documents shows the culmination of the development of the foundational ideas for new transnational policing structures across Europe, throwing light on the inter-relationships established between police, customs, immigration and security services agencies.

This process was capped by the signing of the Maastricht Treaty in 1992, which created the so-called Three Pillars of the European Union governance: first, economic and financial policy; second, military and foreign policy; and third, health and 'home affairs' including immigration, law, order and internal security. The move from ad hoc police co-operation to permanent institutions and agencies began with an enabling governmental framework but it was substantially shaped by prior practices defined by various working groups of police practitioners. This illustrates how important transnational policing was to the evolution of pan-European governance. The Trevi documents suggest that, in this governmental project, certain tenets of liberal democracy – the separation of powers between the executive, the legislature (backed by an independent civil service) and the judiciary – do not apply in the transnational realm (see Chapter 1). The structure for policing Europe was largely conceived by operational-level agents and passed up for senior government officials to agree. Although national parliaments ultimately ratified the conventions, they were not open to amendment. These conventions, resolutions and agreements had the effect of diminishing civil rights in almost every instance and included few democratic accountability or due process mechanisms to protect the citizen.

This largely bottom-up process of institutional development took place during the final years of the Cold War. During this period the threat of nuclear war and communist subversion waned, removing much of the pre-existing rationale for internal security policy. Police and security agencies undertook environmental scans and threat assessments. On the basis of police operational intelligence, terrorism, drugs and immigration emerged as the 'new security agenda'.[151] In place of the old justificatory logic of the Cold War, the new transnational policing system for Europe was deemed a functional necessity for new operational reasons.

The European Arrest Warrant (EAW) offers some more insights into this process and illustrates the ways in which police co-operation has been facilitated in Europe. The EAW effectively abolished formal extradition procedures between

EU member states and sought to make the arrest and transfer of suspects between them no more difficult than it was inside them. Pursuant to Title VI of the Treaty on the EU, the third pillar initiative required national judicial authorities from signatory states to recognise and directly execute requests for arrest and surrender. The new system sought 'to remove the complexity and potential for delay inherent in the present extradition procedures', with a view to establishing 'a system of free movement of judicial decisions in criminal matters, covering both pre-sentence and final decisions, within an area of freedom, security and justice'.[152] Terrorism was one of 32 offences not requiring 'double criminality' (i.e. the act needs only be considered an offence in the requesting state). The various offences listed include human trafficking, participation in a criminal organisation, laundering of the proceeds of crime, rape, arson, forgery, swindling, corruption and crimes falling under the jurisdiction of the ICC. EAWs may be issued for other offences, but their enforcement is subject to the requirements of the requested state, which infers 'dual criminality' (i.e. that the offence must be considered a crime in both jurisdictions) and is supposed to imply a potential custodial sentence of at least one year.

According to documentation from the Council of the European Union in 2007, EAWs were issued for offences including instances of possession of very small amounts of illicit drugs, the theft of two car tyres, impaired driving (where the measured alcohol/blood level [0.81 mg/l] did not significantly exceed the allowable limit [0.8 mg/l]) and the theft of a piglet. These examples raised concerns about 'proportionality' (a principle set down in Article 5 of the Maastricht Treaty) in the use of the EAW. This legal tool is not always used for serious crime and has other negative implications. According to *Fair Trials International*,[153] EAWs have:

- been used to move people across internal European borders for minor offences;
- been issued many years after an alleged offence was committed – in one case, 20 years later;
- no effective way of being removed, even after extradition has been refused;
- been used to move people across internal European borders to serve prison sentences on the basis of an unfair trial;
- been used to bring person(s) to trial on the basis of evidence obtained from police brutality;
- meant that some people spend months, or even years, in detention before an appearance in court can establish innocence.

Some civil liberties groups charged that in the emerging European policing system the rules were so enabling of police intervention that even reasoned opposition could itself be construed as a security threat warranting targeting and surveillance. Observing the power of mid-level bureaucrats and police agents to make policy and create transnational policing structures in Europe with so little democratic oversight prompted the view that the emerging European transnational-state-system:

> ... has all the hallmarks of an authoritarian state in which power resides in the hands of officials with no democratic or legal mechanisms to call them to account. An unaccountable and secret state, removed as it is from democratic pressures, public debate and legal restraints, operates in an arbitrary and author-itarian manner. The lack of public awareness is not just due to the secrecy with which this state has been created. It has been aided by the collusion of the media which has failed to invigilate on behalf of the citizen, and by an almost total absence of critical political interest, liberal or otherwise. The absence of account-able executive action does not bode well for Europe's future and recalls Europe's past.[154]

In Europe we see police subculture adapting legal rules and shaping enforce-ment jurisdiction to suit operational requirements. In rather undemocratic ways police have decisively shaped the EU regional-state-system.

Developments in the United States

The US has an extremely large number of enforcement jurisdictions within one large federal state. Historically, most policing capacity in the USA was invested in city and county police forces, so with an estimated 14,000 local and 50 fed-eral police agencies it is difficult to generalise about American policing. The extension of federal police power is largely a 20th-century story, although in the 19th century the federal government did have some policing capacity through various branches of the military, the Customs Service, the Postal Inspection Service and the US Marshals service. After the passing of the *Posse Comitatus* Act 1878, the military's role in both domestic and international policing matters was restricted. The US Secret Service (established 1865) was probably the leading US federal police-type agency until 1908 when the 'Bureau of Investigation' was created (FBI, the word Federal was added in 1935). The Federal Bureau of Narcotics (FBN) was created in 1930. The modern Bureau of Alcohol, Tobacco, Firearms and Explosives (ATF, a branch of the Internal Revenue Service) was a relative latecomer. It arrived on the federal scene in more or less its present form in 1972, out of mergers and re-organisation that began with the establishment of the Bureau of Prohibition within the Bureau of Internal Revenue in the 1920s.

Sometimes people favour the fragmentation of policing power along jurisdic-tional lines on the grounds of a kind of constitutional separation of powers. This is faulty logic. In the US, overlapping federal and non-federal criminal jurisdiction creates accountability difficulties for multi-agency task forces, which are routine in certain types of operation such as large-scale public order, counter-drug or illegal immigration operations. More often, the lack of a rational basis for delineating functional and geographical jurisdiction inhibits strategic planning for evidence-based, effective and efficient policing. The sociology of policing literature has shown substantial 'incentives and disincentives to communication, co-operation, coordination and collaboration [the 4-Cs]'.[155] In the US, the major incentive to the 4-Cs are 'multijurisdictional offenders' and the lure of acquiring forfeited criminal assets. The major disincentive is 'institutional turf'. When President Bill Clinton flirted with the idea of merging the DEA and FBI in 1993 (both under the Department of Justice) it was on the managerial grounds of efficiency, economy and effectiveness. The attempt to end problems of inter-agency rivalry foundered because of the predictable difficulty in 'trying to meld two rival agencies with vastly different cultures'.[156] Institutional rivalry, overlapping functions, sometimes operational failure, unintended negative consequences and overall lack of co-ordination are the hallmarks of institutional fragmentation. This is certainly not a good alternative to a reasoned separation of political powers.[157]

To the organisational sociologist, the myriad law enforcement agencies that make up the policing system in the US are each institutions of social power in their own right. Competition between agencies partly explains the freewheeling aggressiveness of the occupational subcultures of law enforcement in the USA. The huge federal institutions already mentioned and the large municipal police forces like the New York City Police Department (NYPD) sometimes act across international borders. From the early 1970s the FBI took an increasing interest in international organised crime and terrorism and increased the posting of liaison officers overseas. The 1971 crime film *The French Connection* (starring Gene Hackman as 'Popeye' Doyle, a ruthless and bigoted lead officer from the NYPD's narcotics squad) helped normalise the idea of US cops abroad for an American public. From around this time, many US agencies began cultivating networks of overseas liaison officers in earnest, including Customs for smuggling guns and liquor; the Immigration and Naturalization Service (INS) for immigration crimes and trafficking in persons; ATF for gunrunning and smuggling; the Secret Service for international counterfeiting and financial crimes; and, most aggressively, DEA to enforce global drug prohibition. The trajectory of the established US policing system was on course to a future in the transnational realm. Founded in geographic and functional jurisdictional fragmentation but with tendencies toward the centralisation of specific law enforcement functions in institutions based in Washington DC, the internationalisation of a fragmented US law enforcement system extended outward into the polycentric system of global power.

The no-holds-barred occupational subculture of policing is symbolically and practically evidenced in the 1992 legal case of *US* v. *Alvarez-Machain* (1992).[158] In this case, rather than making a formal request for extradition, in April of

1990 a number of armed men (privately hired to do the job) broke into Machain's office in Guadalajara and abducted him. DEA agents took custody in El Paso Texas and he was subsequently extradited to Los Angeles to stand trial where he was eventually convicted. Like the earlier case of *Verdugo-Urquidez*, the court's decision side-lined customary international law and the terms of the existing US–Mexico Extradition Treaty. In doing so, it reached back into US legal history, to the frontier society of 1886. Citing the *Ker-Frisbie* doctrine, US courts agreed that forcible abduction is not a sufficient reason to prevent the party in question from answering charges brought within the jurisdiction of a court that has the power to try him for the alleged offence. As would be expected, there was a series of inquiries and much criticism in US legal circles and a treaty prohibiting trans-border abductions was concluded in 1994. The subsequent effort to use counter-law to provide a break on transnational law enforcement excess may have provided some temporary respite. Less than a decade later, however, the initiation of a massive worldwide system for secret 'extraordinary rendition' again demonstrated the laissez-faire style of US international enforcement practices, this time under the auspices of the war on terror.[159]

By 1994, there were approximately 2000 US federal law enforcement agents based in US embassies around the world. They were not accountable to any specific central authority, but worked as local representatives of their respective parent agencies under a miscellany of arrangements varying from formal government-to-government bilateral agreements to ad hoc agency-to-agency exchanges operating outside the context of any legal instrument or written agreement. This was engineered in an uncoordinated and largely secretive fashion.[160] Absent transparent accountability to a public authority there was often little or no co-ordination of intra-agency planning. Accordingly, due to the many concurrent and uncoordinated operations, friction between the US enforcement agencies operating internationally was common. These could concern a variety of intelligence, enforcement, policing and diplomatic activities relating to overlapping topics, persons and incidents. The Iran-Contra scandal of the 1980s, for example, showed elements of the US military and security apparatus working at cross-purposes to the missions of the DEA and ATF in Central America.[161]

We argue that each US law enforcement agency capable of operating transnationally on a sustained basis should be regarded as only loosely coupled to the state *qua* state. They are in fact independent institutions acting transnationally. Enforcement institutions publicly funded by seigneurial states are among the most powerful transnational actors in the global system. Moreover, in the American case there is an additional complexity, since private forms of policing have long outnumbered public ones.[162] Private transnational policing exists in many parts of the world but the United States has had a long established market. Indeed, the most effective US law enforcement organisation – and the first that could be characterised as a police organisation capable of operating transnationally on a sustained basis – was the Pinkerton Detective Agency established at the beginning of the 20th century.[163] One hundred years later the studies of private contract security companies attest to the continuing importance of the private security sector in the transnational realm.[164]

By the end of the 20th century, police and security agents working at varying levels across the transnational-state-system had interwoven a policing capacity housed in a complex and ramshackle institutional architecture built from a concatenation of pre-existing organisations. While the USA developed its modern transnational policing capacity in the early 20th century, in Europe the history of transnational policework was punctuated by two wars. There the tradition of policing was much more tightly bound to *raison d'état*, and strict notions of legality prevailed, whereas in the USA governance was much more *laissez-faire*, leading to a more unrestrained police occupational subculture and giving more opportunity for private forms of policing to develop.[165] There are many other differences of detail because various policing-type agencies are involved. Partly because this system is so difficult to render visible, it grew up with next to no public discussion about the ramifications of these transnationalising power structures. Concealed behind the façade of 'suitable enemies', the general public could only assume that the agencies' response was necessary, appropriate and focused on the most harmful practices.[166]

Multi-agency co-operation; the military, security and private sectors

One strand of research in the sociological study of policing concerns multi-agency co-operation. Alice Sampson, Harry Blagg and colleagues demonstrated that local crime prevention initiatives and other police intervention projects intended to impact on local crime are shaped by power differentials between different agencies in a multi-agency setting.[167] They observed that when co-operating with police, other actors such as social workers and teachers found that the ability of police divisions to call on material and human resources could lead to undue influence. With the hollowing out of the Keynesian 'welfare state' and its gradual replacement with a Schumpeterian 'workfare state', as noted in Chapter 1, the effects of power differentials in police multi-agency settings operating at local-municipal, national, regional or global scales became even more evident in shaping the global system.[168] Even the term 'co-operation' is a loaded one. These field studies revealed that often participants on all sides felt it more as multi-agency co-ordination. The questions were: who is doing the co-ordination, who is being co-ordinated and who holds the power in inter-agency relationships?

It is with these thoughts in mind that we turn our attention to tactical police co-operation with other institutions. One of the most important of these is the military. Peter Kraska has superbly documented the militarisation of the American criminal justice system.[169] He showed how the Posse Comitatus Act 1878, which had previously prohibited military involvement in police or internal security matters, was eroded and how a co-operative relationship at all organisational levels has enabled technology transfers and information sharing. He explained how small arms firepower and expertise in Special Weapons and Tactics (SWAT) was transferred from the military to the police and how this was normalised. Kraska also charted a growing tendency of police and other segments of the criminal justice system to absorb war rhetoric in formulating operational tactics and control rationale for crime, drugs and terrorism. Research on policing public order showed paramilitary policing in a slightly different variant, but the influence of military language, tactics and strategy was clearly evident there too.[170] The 'technostructures' of the military had been mapped onto policing.[171]

Another very powerful kind of institution that is important in considering potential imbalances in multi-agency transnational policing tie-ups are the security services. The intelligence nexus that connects policing and a variety of high policing agencies (e.g. MI5 and MI6 in the UK; the CIA and NSA in the US) has been examined in considerable detail by Peter Gill and Mark Phythian.[172] Their work on the secret security services forms a double helix with research on intelligence-led policing.[173] That is to say that the intelligence and information handling systems used to co-ordinate policing and security services activities closely mirror each other. The effects of this are quite visible in big city police departments across the US, which have prioritised the intelligence function by re-engineering organisational structures and processes around a shared vision of the terrorist and criminal threat.[174] Current policies require information collection, reporting and dissemination (under strict access regulations) and local city chiefs are encouraged to ensure that their departments are proactive in acquiring intelligence relevant to international organised crime and other security threats. A whole new language has developed in the policing occupation concerned with integrating community policing and enhanced systems of centrally co-ordinated command (such as CompStat) around the task of intelligence sharing with other agencies, both federal and non-federal. This literature focused on advanced information communication technologies and encouraged police executives and managers to adopt the new discourse of intelligence-led policing as a management device.[175]

Loch Johnson's encyclopaedic *Strategic Intelligence* reviews the intelligence studies literature from many different disciplinary angles. According to him, 'the overall conclusion reached by most studies on intelligence accountability is that oversight is often overlooked by lawmakers'. The end result is 'an absence of checks and balances on the secret agencies, which can result in intelligence failures'.[176] Stimulated by the perceived intelligence failures of 9/11, many US studies reveal a drive towards centralisation of the intelligence function and advocate a strong office of director of national intelligence:

> America's intelligence agencies must work together more closely to share information about threats facing the United States, eschewing their cultural proclivities toward parochialism. In a phrase, intelligence consolidation must replace the current dispersal of authority.[177]

In all states, both the military and the security services are strongly oriented around the language of national security. The influence of these institutions on the transnational-state-system is considerable. Their workings in the world system help to perpetuate a cycle of insecurity based on ideas of inter-state competition. National security discourse operates on the basic assumptions of the 'billiard ball' model of the global system, with states being the primary, if not only, actors (see Chapter 1). That this is fiction is clear from the substantial literature on private military companies and private security providers at the high end of the policing spectrum.[178] In *Blackwater: The Rise and Fall of the World's Most Powerful Mercenary Army*, Jeremy Scahill explains how this private military company (described as the 'Fedex of national security policy') was in fact the Bush Administration's 'praetorian guard'.[179] The state and its attendant 'national security discourse' remains an important organising principle in the world system, hence our use of the term transnational-state-system. However, we hasten to add, in our view the problems of global social ordering render *national* security discourse rather atavistic.

Probably the most innovative research on multi-agency thinking in transnational policing is the theoretical work developed by Clifford Shearing and colleagues, focusing on questions about how 'security nodes' of state-based and private security actors might be co-ordinated. Here the term 'nodes' refers to specific institutional sites (police agencies, customs agencies, private security companies, community action groups, NGOs, etc.) where governmental resources and knowledge relevant to security and social order maintenance are concentrated. These nodes are understood as linkable together like a spider's web in a network of nodes. This web provides the structure of 'security governance'.[180] The nodal governance literature has focused specifically on relatively weak social actors in these networks and has fore-grounded concerns about social justice. Theoretically it works well alongside the human security paradigm and within a human rights discourse predicated on the Rule of Law.[181] Altogether this is a very hopeful paradigm for security governance, but keeping in mind the perennial questions we raised earlier about the imbalances of power in multi-agency partnerships and the implications of rule *with* law, there is plenty of room for scepticism. The mixed evidence about the network of security nodes for corporate resource extraction industries operating in peripheral regions of the global system does not dash all hopes for equity, justice and safety; but the signs are not encouraging.[182] The multi-agency inter-relationships in play that undergird the functional ideas of the transnational-state-system tip the balance in favour of a discourse of militarisation and securitisation of policing intelligence. The resulting cycle of insecurity ends up undermining the well-being of the global social body and preventing a thriving global state of prosperity.

Conclusion: policing the new world order

The world system of nation-states and colonies that existed at the start of the 20th century was fundamentally transformed by the dawn of the new millennium. The emerging transnational-state-system is a complex of powerful agencies acting above, beyond, within and below the state *qua* State. The world system is polycentric and its policing is characterised by functional diversity and cross-cut by formal lines of territorial sovereignty. Agenda setting is largely in the hands of technocrats working supranationally, nationally, locally or at the middle range of the putative transnational-state-system and sometimes working simultaneously at multiple levels. Most often the work is done away from public scrutiny, or at least out of the limelight. Agenda setting in policing policy is not particularly democratic, but it is certainly political. The theory advanced in this book suggests that it is the social quality of politics, and not the letter of the law, that moulds the contours of policing (globally or otherwise). That is why our theory places so much emphasis on the cultural meanings imbued in these processes.

Our reading of the literature suggests that global policing is shaped not by a global social contract but by the norms, values and meanings inherent in the subculture of transnational policing. National societies are no longer what they were when state structures and their attendant policing and security apparatus were constituted at the dawn of modernity. Alongside states, transnational corporations, the transnational capitalist class and the cultural ideology of consumerism are fundamental aspects of the global system. Richard Sennett argued that the combined effects of these disparate phenomena on social life are corrosive of the social contract and are therefore inherently criminogenic and productive of widespread insecurity.[183] This raises profound questions about the governability of the whole system, because efforts to 'keep the lid on' by aggressive policing methods can only work for so long.[184] Our inter-disciplinary theoretical perspective suggests that global policing is, for better or for worse, highly influential in the world system. Whatever form the system of global governance takes in the future, we predict that Robert Reiner's 'new internationale of technocratic police experts'[185] or Fenton Bressler's 'policeman's club'[186] will be part of it.

3

THE GLOBAL POLICING ARCHITECTURE

Understanding global policing requires a careful examination of its architecture – its institutional framework and the component parts that hold it all together. Developing our socio-spatial and functional typologies set out in Tables 1.1 and 1.2, we describe the various layers in the structure of transnational policing: *global* and *regional* police organisations constructed 'above the state', '*national* policing hubs' and the intelligence silos that feed them. Under each heading we describe the relevant institutional structures, their functions, powers, and the legal and political frame within which each works. This chapter also describes the important role of *private security* actors in the global policing architecture and concludes with an examination of *glocal* policing – the result of re-wiring local police structures into the transnational-state-system.

Global police agencies

It was not until the latter half of the 20th century that institutions for transnational policing began to take shape and only towards that century's end that a truly global policing capacity was created. Today, a number of global policing agencies exist. Most are rooted in 'parent' organisations including the UN or the WTO, while Interpol is a freestanding supranational entity. The significant feature characterising these agencies is that they are constituted 'above' the nation-state and are not beholden to any single national government.

Interpol

Interpol is the most widely recognised 'brand name' in transnational policing.[187] It is the only truly supranational policing institution funded with taxpayers' money.[188] With 188 members, Interpol is probably the second largest global public institution after the UN. It is not treaty-based nor does it have police powers of arrest and detention. According to Article 4 of Interpol's Constitution 'any country may delegate as a Member to the Organisation any official police body whose functions come within the framework of activities of the Organisation'.[189] But it is not widely known or understood that police forces, not states, comprise its membership.

Despite the ambiguities in Interpol's constitution, it has acquired customary status as an intergovernmental organisation (IGO). The academic literature and Interpol documentation on its constitution shows that the agreements made with the government of France in 1972 and 1982 consolidated Interpol Headquarters as being free from external accountability giving the organisation and its personnel full diplomatic immunity. On 16 June 1983, US President Ronald Reagan signed Executive Order 12425 designating Interpol 'a public international organisation entitled to enjoy the privileges, exemptions and immunities of the International Organisations Immunities Act'.[190] In 2006 the Interpol General Assembly welcomed the fact that its independence had been confirmed by the courts and that tribunals in member countries had recognised the organisation as having an existence separate from their membership. In particular it embraced the International Labour Organisation Administrative Tribunal (ILOAT) ruling that Interpol is an independent international organisation not subject to any national law. It further welcomed 'recognition of the Organisation as an international legal person by other intergovernmental organisations, particularly by the United Nations'.[191] In this and many other respects, Interpol is genuinely a supranational institution.[192]

One way to read Interpol's history is to see it as an institution successively 'captured' by different states' interests. According to this reading the most significant moments were when the 'captive status' was transferred.[193] When it was first established in 1923 Interpol acted as an informal arm of the Austrian State Police. The period of the Second World War saw its 'Nazification' and Interpol HQ moved from Vienna to Berlin.[194] After the war, the organisation moved to France and entered a prolonged period of French domination, which ended in 1986 when a stage of Anglo-American hegemony commenced. Under Secretary General Raymond Kendall (a UK national), the organisation underwent a wave of modernisation, especially of its communications infrastructure. Technological modernisation accelerated when Ronald K. Noble (a US Treasury Department official and former head of FinCEN) became Secretary General in 2000. As well as introducing the agency to counter-money-laundering practice, Noble oversaw numerous organisational changes. In 2003 the new Command and Co-ordination Centre came online allowing worldwide intelligence dissemination, emergency and disaster management. In 2004 the agency inaugurated the office of Special Representative to the UN and in 2008 a Special Representative to the European Union was appointed. Under Noble's watch, Interpol cemented its importance in the global policing architecture.

Interpol's primary role is to facilitate transnational police-to-police communications. The quickest method is to send a 'diffusion' issued by member countries and circulated without formal review by Interpol HQ. Frequently these are followed up with a 'formal notice', but diffusion can be used to request immediate assistance on virtually any police matter. Interpol has historically used a formal system of coloured 'notices': Red Notices amount to the worldwide circulation of national arrest warrants; Blue are specific requests for information on named persons of interest in relation to a crime; Green circulate information and intelligence on suspect individuals and activities; Orange relate to hazardous materials or other potential threats to public safety; Yellow relate to missing persons; and Black Notices report unidentified dead bodies. In 2005 the UN-Interpol 'Special Notice' was introduced. These notices, issued jointly by the UN Security Council and Interpol, pertain to a list of groups and individuals associated with Al Qaeda and Taliban affiliates targeted for UN sanctions and it reflects the organisation's new focus on terrorism (see Chapter 2). The people named in a Special Notice may be subject to arrest, asset freezing, travel ban or arms embargo.

Notices are circulated to member organisations through a system of National Central Bureaux (NCBs). According to an official audit of the US Interpol NCB by the Audit Division of the US Department of Justice, in early 2009 there were approximately 25,000 active notices circulating worldwide, the majority of which were Red and 20 per cent of which were generated by US law enforcement agencies.[195] From the standpoint of public international law, Red Notices are elusive administrative measures. They are a kind of 'soft law' since authority is assumed and delegated 'at a distance'. In socio-legal terms either the Red Notices go 'under the radar' because they are not 'hard law', or they become 'hard law' in which case the accountability mechanisms to national states would render the whole Interpol enterprise impractical. Nonetheless, a Red Notice – interpretable in practice as an international arrest warrant – is what landed Mr Bond in a South African prison for three weeks, as we saw in Chapter 1. Soft and under the radar Red Notices may be, but they are also legal powertools.

The communication system is only one example of the ambiguous legal autonomy achieved by Interpol. That independence undoubtedly contributed to the growing technological sophistication of the organisation. With regard to data protection, an appendix to the 1982 Headquarters Agreement created a five-member board, only one of whom is not directly appointed by Interpol or chosen from a list pre-selected by Interpol executives. Interpol maintains separate databases relating to stolen and lost travel documents, stolen motor vehicles, finger prints, DNA, 'habitual criminal offenders', child sex offenders, all with virtually no external oversight. As well as facilitating police-to-police communications, Interpol provides three other basic functions: database maintenance and intelligence analysis; operational support; and training. In all respects, Interpol functions as a legally autonomous transnational organisation. Despite not having direct operational policing powers, Interpol is in a position of global influence.[196]

The Interpol network extends globally, but the NCBs in the global south operate at a lower level of technical sophistication. In 2000 only about half of the NCBs worldwide had access to Internet-based communications, but this rapidly expanded under the umbrella of the I-24/7 system giving online access to Interpol databases on a continuous basis. At the time of writing, four principal databases were in use: the 'nominal database' (containing over 150,000 names); the DNA database (almost 100,000 DNA profiles from 55 countries); the Automated Fingerprint Identification System (100,000+ fingerprint sets) and the 'Fusion Task Force' database (with records pertaining to over 12,000 persons suspected of being linked to international terrorism).

Outside Europe and North America, the Caribbean sub-regional bureau centred on the Interpol NCB in San Juan, Puerto Rico is reputedly the best developed. The Interpol network for this region underwent substantial upgrading in the 1980s. Ostensibly financed by the UN, the creation of an Interpol-based police telecommunications network in the region expanded the presence of US law enforcement. The UN fund that paid for the network upgrade was itself primarily underwritten by US money, an example of transnational police 'financing at a distance'. In this instance the Interpol network might best be looked at as a way for branches of US law enforcement institutions to extend into the region under the Interpol flag.[197] However, this is not simply another instance of the Americanisation of international law enforcement, but rather an example of how relatively powerful member organisations within the Interpol structure can influence its agenda. Eventually concerns about such influences arose within the organisation itself as evidenced by the *Resolution Statement to Reaffirm the Independence and Political Neutrality of Interpol*. This document explains member countries' concerns about measures affecting their freedom to compose delegations to statutory meetings, the independence of the staff members seconded to the General Secretariat and the Executive Committee and concerns about deciding on the venues for Interpol meetings.[198] Even supposing it were possible, preventing direct effects on Interpol policy and operations by the central organs of the states whose police institutions make up the organisation's membership would not make the institution politically neutral. When it comes to global policing, it is simply not possible to talk of neutrality in the absence of neutral consequences.

Considering its liquid relationship to the global system, it is perhaps not surprising that Interpol came bottom of the league table in terms of overall accountability of the 10 IGOs surveyed in the *Global Accountability Report* for 2007. That report also commented on Interpol's lack of transparency, noting that the organisation is involved in crime control, a 'generally closed and secretive [activity] traditionally dominated by states and not open to civil society involvement'.[199]

World Customs Organisation

No discussion of global policing would be complete without including the World Customs Organisation (WCO). Customs agencies make up important building blocks in the global policing architecture despite a common assumption that they play only a minor support role in policing. The work of customs officers is generally confined to key transport nodes such as ports and airports, but they have very extensive administrative and criminal law enforcement powers. These are often wider than that of 'blue uniformed policing' including powers to gather secret intelligence, search people and premises, arrest suspects, freeze bank accounts, and seize cash and other assets. The modern customs organisation will typically have investigation and intelligence units, run covert investigations and have extensive land and maritime policing capabilities. Moreover, many customs officers self-identify as cops or detectives and as being part of a shared law enforcement subculture.[200] We could call them close cousins within the 'police family'. The traditional role of customs has been to collect import and export duties at borders and to protect states' revenue by controlling the movement of goods and people through ports and airports, checking cargo and luggage to ensure that all taxable goods have been declared. Customs duties have historically been a significant financial resource for states. However, customs organisations worldwide are undergoing massive structural change stimulated by the rapidly increasing volume of world trade encouraged by neo-liberal policies emphasising the freedom and flexibility of the market, the free flow of goods across international borders and the removal of fiscal barriers to trade.[201]

The blueprint for modern customs operations is the 1973 Kyoto Convention that sought to facilitate legitimate trade and travel and, by implication, define and control illegitimate trade and travel.[202] As markets were de-regulated, customs agencies became less concerned with collecting revenue at the borders and instead came to feed off the revenue streams of global trade itself. As the number of participants in world trade increased, regional agreements proliferated and trade rules became complex. A shift towards manufactured goods with increasing use of shared- and component-parts-production changed the types of transactions handled by customs administrations.[203] Rather than being concerned with import control and excise duties, customs co-operation meant global monitoring and total surveillance of the supply chain. This is beneficial for large multi-national corporations who manufacture and ship products between markets.[204] In the corporate world of production, the introduction of 'just-in-time' distribution, low inventory retention and multi-modal transport facilitated new ways of organising resource acquisition, manufacture and distribution. This put new pressure on transnational supply chains. Automation, risk management and intelligence gathering were among the techniques adopted by customs agencies to separate licit from illicit goods and interdict the latter. The effort to create the capacity for the global 'total surveillance' of all goods in transport has yet to be fulfilled, and arguably never can be. The reorientation of customs around the principle of transnational customs co-operation is nevertheless a revolutionary idea.

The World Customs Council grew out of the Customs Co-operations Council, which itself was a response by the European Community member states to the General Agreement on Tariffs and Trade (GATT) established in 1949. It adopted its present form as the WCO when the GATT mutated into the World Trade Organisation (WTO) after the conclusion of the Uruguay Round of trade negotiations in 1994. The WTO has 153 members who collectively account for about 97 per cent of world trade. It is a forum for settling trade disputes and implementing trade rules. The WCO is like the enforcement arm of its parent organisation, the WTO. Its stated objective is to promote the efficiency and effectiveness of member institutions, the customs agencies in member states. It enforces standards through a number of 'soft law' instruments, the International Convention on Harmonized Commodity Description and Coding (ICHCDC), the International Convention on the Simplification and Harmonization of Customs Procedures (ICSHCP) and the SAFE Framework for Standards to Secure and Facilitate Global Trade. The WCO enforces rules on its members by the threat of exclusion by import authorities invoking WTO requirements. The SAFE Framework is a non-binding instrument that contains supply chain security and facilitation standards. It enables integrated supply chain management across all modes of transport. The aim is to eventually provide total surveillance over a seamless movement of goods moving through secure transnational commodity supply chains.

Because the function of customs surveillance has been transnationalised in this manner, the WCO and its member agencies are involved in a variety of policing functions. Perhaps a less obvious one concerns corruption. The introduction of advanced information and communications technology (ICTs) to manage the transnational flow of goods also created a way of conducting anti-corruption surveillance. Information management systems enable compliance management, and so offer a way to police against corruption.[205] Through the WCO, the work of customs agencies is transnational, but they also retain a role as 'first line of defence' for border protection and people are most apt to think of these functions when they think about customs agents. Security threats, including organised crime and terrorism, disease and environmental threats are among the risks in which customs agencies co-operate in controlling. Customs organisations are useful in this regard since they have police powers on land and sea under the rubric of enforcing prohibitions and restrictions on particular goods (including alcohol, prohibited drugs, infected goods, indecent and obscene articles, and counterfeit products). Customs organisations are also drawn into ancillary policing tasks such as the enforcement of immigration controls in small ports, airports and of laws relating to fisheries. The Convention on the International Trade in Endangered Species (CITES) and the Basel Convention on Hazardous Waste are also policed by customs agencies. The

WCO has been active in coordinating a global effort to police intellectual property claims. Behind the banal language of global trade – the Uruguay Round and the Doha Round, etc. – a considerable infrastructure of transnational policing has been put into place.

The WCO's importance as a building block in the architecture of global policing was cemented in 1998 when the organisation signed a Memorandum of Understanding (MOU) with Interpol. The MOU concerned co-operation between police and customs in the fight against transnational crime.[206] It was premised on Interpol's mandate to promote the widest possible mutual assistance between police authorities and all institutions likely to contribute to the prevention of crimes, and the WCO's mission to enhance compliance with trade regulation and protection of society. The MOU emphasised the two organisations' shared competence in combating, '*inter alia*, illicit drug trafficking, money laundering, illicit diversion of precursors and essential chemicals, counterfeiting, traffic in human beings, intellectual property fraud, firearms trafficking and smuggling, and environmental crime' and stressed the need to avoid the duplication of effort. In the MOU it was also agreed that the two organisations should consult on developments in their fields and exchange information relevant to transnational crime. It noted the need to ensure the accuracy and validity of information, to safeguard confidential information and observe restrictions in communicating information. It agreed that there should be reciprocal arrangements to attend each others' meetings and to make arrangements for implementing joint projects on matters of common interest. To support this initially, a German customs officer was appointed as a full time WCO attaché at Interpol Headquarters in Lyon to establish all the protocols, memoranda and letters of agreement between the two organisations.

The WTO lies at the centre of the administrative architecture for governing the global economy and the WCO is a key building block in the global policing architecture. These agencies are quite strictly intergovernmental and unambiguous in their constitutions. The WCO does not have the extensive independence enjoyed by Interpol and in this respect it is tied more tightly to the states that make up the transnational-state-system. Yet its policing function is particularly facilitative of corporate interests by virtue of the free flow of trade that it oversees. The disciplines on trade that it helps to ensure affect the lives of millions.[207] Eliminating quotas has consequences for the structure of production and employment in the jurisdictions they apply to.

The Caribbean island of St Vincent, for example, was drastically affected by a 1994 WTO decision ending the preferential marketing of their bananas in Europe.[208] Although its contribution to world trade was less than 1 per cent, 70 per cent of the population worked in banana export. The social effects of the changes were devastating: the number of farmers directly employed in growing bananas fell from approximately 3600 in the year 2000 to about 1300 in 2008 – this in a country with an estimated population of about 115,000. The labour disruption and social conflict was considerable and the marginal change in the worldwide trade of bananas was of benefit only to large-scale corporate producers. In 2009 the representative of St Vincent and the Grenadines informed the 64th session of the UN General Assembly that the social changes and dislocations wrought in the wake of the changes in trade quotas for bananas had a direct effect on the island's vulnerability to transnational criminal enterprise.[209] The place of the WCO in the architecture of global policing and its connections through the WTO to global governance generally, illustrate the priorities inherent in the idea of the transnational-state-system as it concerns global markets. As the banana trade example suggests, policing global trade is facilitative of markets and corporate interests, but not necessarily attentive to the well-being of local communities that are the foundation of the global system.

The Financial Action Task Force

The Financial Action Task Force (FATF) was born in a basement office located in the OECD headquarters after a meeting of the G7 in Paris in 1989.[210] It is an intergovernmental institution that acts as a policymaking body but without the benefit of an independent constitution. The FATF mission is reviewed every five years in a process undertaken by ministry representatives from the member states and organisations.[211] The FATF was instrumental in the construction of a transnational infrastructure for police surveillance in the global money system. It is therefore a building block of the global policing architecture, but a curious one because it had subsequently to facilitate the construction of other subordinate building blocks at state-jurisdictional level (called financial intelligence units [FIUs]). Unlike the WCO and Interpol, its basic organisational units were not already in existence when the FATF was created. Like many other parts of the global policing architecture, the one established to police the money system had imperfections but it still provided important cross-ties of multi-agency support bridging state and non-state actors in the transnational-state-system.[212]

FATF developed and promulgated a list of '40 recommendations' defining policing countermeasures against money laundering. This list is 'soft law' and does not have the formal backing of any state authority per se. Using a system of mutual evaluations, participating jurisdictions 'enforce' the standards and practices of financial surveillance onto each other and thereby the global banking system. The FIUs were the new institutions for orchestrating this surveillance. A partial list of these institutions includes the following:

AUSTRAC   Australian Transactions Reports and Analysis Centre
FIC   Financial Intelligence Centre, South Africa
FinCEN   Financial Crimes Enforcement Network, USA
FINTRAC   Financial Transactions Reports Analysis Centre, Canada

STRO	Suspicious Transaction Reporting Office, Singapore
TRACFIN	Traitement du renseignement et action contre les circuits financiers clandesins, France
ZfV	Zentralstelle für Verdachtsanzeigen, Germany

All of these, and many other FIUs around the world, are co-ordinated via membership in the Egmont Group, which is an informal group with a system of membership that is as arcane as Interpol's. Like Trevi before it (see Chapter 2), the Egmont Group originally met in secret when it convened in 1995 at the Egmont Arenberg Palace in Brussels. The list of attending FIUs has never been published but on its website, US FinCEN claims leadership in setting up the first meeting[213] and FIUs in Britain, France, Belgium and Australia have all stated that they were part of the initial effort. The Egmont Group emerged as a result of the challenges to practical co-ordination of information exchange between FIUs.[214] Institutional friction required an operational level solution to the information-interface problem.[215] FATF and the global FIU structure comprises a massive multi-agency surveillance infrastructure, but as we shall see in Chapter 5, it is far from clear that it has achieved the operational goals expected of it, much less provided a good set up for policing the global money system.

United Nations Police

The UN has a policing capacity and this too is an important building block of the global policing architecture. The Police Division (UNPOL) is embedded within the 'rule of law and security institutions pillar' of the UN and has its own Assistant Secretary General. [216] It has a small headquarters staff that manages the Division and a 'standing police capacity' comprised of police officers from around the world who are deployed for short periods to any UN mission that asks for their expertise on issues relating to policing including public order, border control, police reform, criminal investigations, intelligence management or any other aspect of policework. Technically, the UN does not have a police force of its own but the Security Council has the power to deploy what are called 'formed police units' drawn from member states to different peacekeeping missions. This deployment, best known as the Civilian Police Programme (CIVPOL) has provided police support to UN peacekeeping operations since the 1960s.[217] Shortly after the first CIVPOL deployment in Congo in 1960, then UN Secretary General U. Thant predicted that the world would 'eventually have an international police force which will be accepted as an integral and essential part of life in the same way as national police forces are accepted'.[218] Fifty years after this 'visionary statement', a true world police force has yet to be created but the UN CIVPOL system has served as a substitute for this building block of global policing governance.[219]

The most significant UN policing effort is the support provided to policing in weak, failing or failed states and those undergoing reconstruction. In 2010 policing was the fastest growing component of UN peacekeeping, deploying more than 17,500 UN police from 98 countries in 18 missions around the world.[220] The UN policing function is defined with reference to a catch-all category of peacekeeping but this extends to tackling organised crime including targeting gangs in Haiti, heroin trafficking in Afghanistan and arms trafficking in the Democratic Republic of Congo. According to UN police adviser Andrew Hughes, collaboration between UNPOL and Interpol 'brings the combined weight of a majority of the world's States to bear on organised crime networks'.[221]

The CIVPOL designation grew out of a need to distinguish between the military police and the civilian police elements of peacekeeping missions. Military police are police tasked with the function of controlling military personnel and are part of the military chain of command. CIVPOL are units constituted from UN member states' police forces operating under a UN mandate. They wear the official uniform of their home country while operating in the field, in addition to the UN blue beret and badges. They usually operate unarmed but can carry batons and firearms in some circumstances. Notwithstanding the uneven qualities in training and experience they bring into the field, the UN has been making increasing use of civilian police in responding to a perceived 'security gap' in unstable regions where indigenous police and security forces are insufficient to 'maintain law and order'. In addition to functions such as monitoring, advising and training indigenous police organisations, UNPOL operations have also included force re-organisation and riot control.[222] Generally, UNPOL missions seek to shore up the 'fragile states' of the transnational-state-system of which the UN organisations form a part.[223] These 'weak', 'failing' or 'failed' states lie at the opposite end of a spectrum from that of the seigneurial states. We look at UN policing in practice in more detail in Chapter 5.

International Criminal Court police

The newest institutional building block of the policing architecture that has a fully global mandate is the International Criminal Court (ICC) investigative division. The ICC came into being in 2002 when its founding treaty, the 1998 Rome Statute, entered into force. At the time of writing, 116 states are parties to the Statute of the Court and a further 33 countries have signed, but not ratified, the Rome Statute. It is a permanent tribunal created to prosecute individuals for the crimes of genocide, crimes against humanity, war crimes, and the crime of aggression, all of which are formally defined in the founding treaty document. The ICC is strictly a court of last resort, investigating and prosecuting only when competent national courts have failed or declined to act.

Many of the Court's advocates argued for universal jurisdiction, which would have allowed the ICC's prosecutors to arrest persons charged with the above crimes anywhere in the world, but US representatives, among others, objected.[224] Hence the more limited powers and jurisdictional purview. The ICC's prosecution division is staffed by lawyers, investigators and analysts, as well as police officers, many with experience of investigating human rights abuse. Its investigative policing function is comparable to the *Police Judiciare* working for investigating magistrates in continental Europe. Just as a district attorney's office in the USA or the prosecutor's office in Argentina may set out to investigate serious crime, so may the ICC's prosecution division. This investigative policing function – undertaken 'in the field' – includes interviewing suspects, witnesses and victims, recording evidence and providing expert advice on investigative procedures and techniques. ICC police are also required to facilitate existing international networks among local and national police authorities co-operating in the investigation of the crimes listed in the Rome Statute. Prior to being seconded to the ICC, investigators are expected to be trained and qualified in criminal investigation and to have at least five years' experience in criminal or financial investigations or intelligence handling, with a special focus on complex, large-scale cases. In 2010 the head of investigations was a former officer from the Belgian *Gendarmerie* who had responsibility for a budget of €21 million for investigation and analysis and 165 staff employed in investigation teams.[225]

Before the ICC was established, academic lawyers called for a police investigation section comprised of police officers of member states screened and selected by the court.[226] Investigative police working on behalf of the ICC challenge the doctrine of national sovereignty, which is one reason why the USA, China and several other countries declined to sign the Rome Statute and become party to the ICC. However, it is important to stress that the ICC prosecutions division lacks the power of arrest. It is empowered to issue an arrest warrant but must rely on state parties – i.e. domestic police agencies – to execute such warrants.[227] For example, on 28 September 2010, the French police arrested Callixte Mbarushimana, suspected of war crimes and crimes against humanity allegedly committed in the Democratic Republic of the Congo (DRC). The limits of this approach were exemplified in March 2009, when the ICC issued the first ever arrest warrant for a sitting head of state, Sudanese President Omar Hassan Ahmad Al Bashir, for war crimes and crimes against humanity. As long as Al Bashir remains President of Sudan and travels no further than those states that have condemned the ICC's action, this warrant will remain unenforceable.

As Zhou argued, although international criminal justice may never attain the full set of legal competences enjoyed by its domestic equivalent, in order to achieve its objectives the ICC requires 'an efficient and predictable law enforcement system' capable of using 'appropriate force to bring to justice indicted persons'.[228] Extending the power of arrest to the ICC investigative division as officers of the court would be an unprecedented extension of global law enforcement power and may never come to pass. National sovereignty is the barrier, but the sentiment that this should not be absolute or invoked to protect 'state criminals' echoes remarks by former Prime Minister of Canada Brian Mulroney in considering UN intervention for cases of humanitarian crises and human rights abuse:

> ... quite frankly, such invocations of the principle of national sovereignty are as out of date and as offensive to me as the police declining to stop family violence simply because a man's home is supposed to be his castle.[229]

This conjures up a powerful image of global police as a band of uniformed blue knights stopping violence in the home and ending conflicts in weak states. The image suggests one of tough, masculine enforcement tactics and boots on the ground. The reality, insofar as the ICC was concerned during the first decade of its operation, has been far less robust.

Regional police agencies

In the previous section we looked at a number of policing agencies situated 'above' nation-state in the global system. These institutions were shown to be intertwined in complex ways with the states' interests, particularly those of seigneurial states. Yet a degree of institutional autonomy from states *qua* states was also demonstrated. In these next two sub-sections we describe two more building blocks of the global policing architecture that lie above the nation-state, but whose geographical spheres of influence are confined to specific regions. Here we look at Europol and, less well known, ASEANAPOL.[230]

Europol

Europol is perhaps the second best known transnational police *marque* after Interpol. It would be wrong to suggest that the creation of Europol was due entirely to the perceived deficiencies of Interpol or the rise of Anglo-American hegemony during Raymond Kendall's time at the helm. However, by the late 1980s the consensus view was that Interpol was wholly insufficient for the evolving transnational policing needs of the European Union as it broadened and deepened the scope of its governance and sphere of influence.[231] Academic observers were perplexed about claims that Euro-crime was rising (in the absence of any reliable statistics about the phenomenon, or even an agreed operational definition of what it might be), but still noted the rise of the trope of transnational organised crime.[232]

Europol was established in the wake of the Maastricht Treaty in 1992 as part of its 'third pillar' on justice and home affairs. The Europol convention was drawn up in 1994 and the Europol Drugs Unit started working straight away. When EU member states ratified the convention in 1999, Europol was ready to commence functioning across the full range of its policing competences. Because Europol is a treaty-based, state-backed supranational policing body, its activities are legally bound to certain areas of investigation and are framed within the European Convention on Human Rights. The actions of Europol are ultimately accountable to the political and legal machinery of the European Union and its constituent member states. However, the governance machinery of the EU is highly complex and some observers argue that Europol suffers from a democratic deficit due to weaknesses in national accountability mechanisms and the limited role of the European Parliament.[233]

Monica den Boer and Willy Bruggeman characterised the governance of Europol as one of 'Euro sclerosis'. According to them, while the agency is politically accountable to the EU Justice and Home Affairs Council (JHA) and each of the ministers who take part in the JHA are themselves accountable to their own national parliaments, national parliaments face considerable obstacles in overseeing the activities of Europol due to limited or late briefings from the JHA. The organisation lacks transparency and informal working practices – referred to as the 'old boys' network' – have been sustained within the interstices of the formal structures.[234] Formally, Europol has a management board, comprised of one representative from each member state and from the European Commission, which exercises day-to-day control. There is oversight of the agency's various databases under the auspices of a joint supervisory body (JSB) composed of representatives of the national data protection authorities, which review Europol's data-gathering and analysis.[235] The European Court of Justice has authority to exercise its jurisdiction in the interpretation of the Europol Convention. In view of their 'operative capacities', when acting in support roles and in joint investigation teams, Europol officials are legally accountable to the Court and can be called to testify in criminal proceedings.

Ethnographic studies of cross border policing showed a variety of organisational dilemmas and operational solutions for policing the internal security of Europe propelled by an already embedded subculture of European police technocrats (den Boer's and Bruggeman's 'old-boys network').[236] Thomas Mathiesen observed that 'while governments and other authorities emphasise the struggle against traditional, serious, international crime [...] all of the empirical and documentary material available clearly shows that the goal is to be found at the crosspoint between the shutting out of aliens and the protection of vaguely defined public order and State security'.[237] The practical service capacities of existing trans-border policing were incrementally transformed through the gradual introduction of a language concerning serious organised crime and intelligence-led policing. Malcolm Anderson and his colleagues at Edinburgh

University noted a 'gradual transfer of internal and external security control [...] from the nation-state to international institutions'. They suggested that, if the high policing functions come to dominate European policing, 'the more secretive and elitist ethos of the security services would gain ground and the ideal of a transparent, rule governed and politically neutral system would become no more than a remote possibility'. Writing in 1995 it was already clear that intelligence services across Europe were 'increasingly penetrating fields which used to belong to the realm of "ordinary policing", such as organised crime and right-wing extremism, while the police services also started beginning to shift their priorities away from local crime and to the use of proactive (i.e. clandestine and undercover) methods'.[238] Observing this incrementalism we are reminded of the words of former US Supreme Court Justice William O. Douglas:

> as nightfall does not come at once, neither does oppression. In both instances, there is twilight when everything remains seemingly unchanged. And it is in such a twilight that we all must be most aware of change in the air – however slight – lest we become unwitting victims of darkness.[239]

ASEANAPOL

At a superficial level, the development of the Association of Southeast Asian Nations (ASEAN) region is similar to the European Union, but it would be a mistake to see too many parallels. The 1967 Bangkok declaration between the governments of Lee Kuan Yew (Singapore), Ferdinand Marcos (Philippines), Suharto (Indonesia), Abdul Rahman (Malaysia) and Field Marshall Thanom Kittachorn (Thailand) is considered the founding moment in the establishment of ASEAN. It was followed by the 1976 Treaty of Amity and Co-operation in South East Asia, which, more or less, consolidated the boundaries of the regional transnational state order. Its history is a complex mix of post-colonisation, as the European powers withdrew substantial military presence from the area in the aftermath of the Second World War while, at the same time, the region came under the shadow of Cold War politics. The fundamental principles agreed in the 1976 Treaty reveal the concern to establish a stable set of states. These included, among other things: the renunciation of the threat or use of force, non-interference in the internal affairs of one another, and mutual respect for the independence, sovereign equality and territorial integrity of each. Suharto in particular was associated with the movement of non-aligned states, an effort to articulate an alternative discourse to Cold War bifurcation.[240]

The motivations for the birth of the ASEAN project lay in the interests of the governing elites of the sovereign states that it comprised. It was also substantially shaped by the broader currents affecting state formation in Asia more generally during the period.[241] However, the overriding factor in shaping the region was the relative power of certain specific indigenous ethnic and clan based groups in strategically located geo-spatial locales. One obvious spur to regional co-operation was Malaysia's and Singapore's nervousness about Javanese expansionism beyond their hegemony in Indonesia.[242] Consequently the ASEAN project is substantially about peace and inter-state stability, and historically has been the product of close interpersonal contacts among highly placed political and social groups. There has been a concordant reluctance to institutionalise and legalise co-operation that might undermine elite control over the regional-state-system. Since its inception, ASEAN has broadened to include more regional states (Papua New Guinea, Brunei, Vietnam, Laos, Burma, Cambodia) and by 1997 had grown to include so-called 'ASEAN Plus Three' (Japan, China, and South Korea). Aside from a stable and peaceful regional transnational-state-system, another ASEAN focus has been on securing the region's economic competitive advantage as a production base geared towards world markets. Whereas the European Union started as a common market nested within a regional-state-system based on a compact of welfare states, the ASEAN region is the land of the 'Asian Tigers' and has been more geared to the rigors of unfettered capitalism.

It is against this background that the system of transnational police co-operation in the region should be understood. Although nominally committed to the prohibition of certain drugs under the provisions of existing UN Conventions reaching back to the 1970s, the regional compact did not organise around transnational policing issues until the mid-1990s when it brought anti-organised crime policy to the forefront of multi-lateral concern and there was a deepening of security ties. The Manila Declaration on the Prevention and Control of Transnational Crime (1998), the Yangon Plan of Action to Combat Transnational Crime (1999) and the Vientiane Declaration Against Trafficking in Persons Particularly Women and Children (2004) are indicative of the security dialogue that took place at the top levels of the regional system. All of this was co-ordinated centrally through the framework of the ASEAN Ministers Meeting on Transnational Crime, supported by meetings of relevant senior officials responsible for 'drug matters', customs and immigration and meetings of ASEANAPOL (the Chiefs of National Police). The latter functioned particularly usefully as a point of contact with Interpol and the UN, especially for the purposes of high profile media events.

The growing literature on crime and crime control in the region often took as given the difference between organised crime and terrorism. Organised crime is concerned with accumulating the aggregation of illicit wealth, whereas terrorism is primarily political. On this view there may be symbiosis between the two, but they are distinctly different.[243] The ASEAN region had concerns with both, but close examination of these taken for granted differences reveal the politics intrinsic to the designation of illicit economies. Nicholas Dorn and Michael Levi showed a glimpse of the politics of illicit market designation when they compared ASEAN and EU perceptions about priorities for counter-money laundering and anti-terrorist finance.[244] While the EU perceived risks for money laundering, illegal timber trade and terrorist finance as essentially an 'Asian Problem', the ASEAN's primary concern was for tighter control mechanisms around small arms and light weapons and they regarded representatives of Western governments as lacking appropriate enthusiasm. Similar differences of opinion were also revealed about informal banking and value transfer systems (in which Asian-run businesses have a competitive advantage).

Ko-Lin Chin's tales from inside Southeast Asia's drug trade provide an ethnographically thick description of heroin trafficking from the frontier regions of the 'Golden Triangle' – where China, Burma, Laos and Thailand meet on the ethnic ancestral lands of the Wa people – to the metropolitan capitals of Asia and beyond.[245] He provides a criminological account of the core and periphery of the regional transnational-state-system and the inter-connections between licit and illicit markets that run through it.[246] His account continually stresses the importance of 'grey' business in the supply of drugs and their micro and macro political connections. The convergence of grey business, geopolical instability, improved communications and transportation, rising global demand and the weak guardianship of international, regional and national law enforcement agencies provided the grounds for 'an epidemic of drug consumption'.[247] A broad analysis of crime control rhetoric in the region concluded that it exhibited all the cultural expectations of 'high crime societies', a term originally coined by David Garland,[248] who referred specifically to Europe and North America. In Asian societies, strategies of criminalisation and harsh punishment are increasingly normalised and 'the emerging patterns seem eerily similar to the now typical American strategy of "governing through crime"'.[249]

There are similarities in the language of crime and crime control across the global system as a whole, but these intersect with other discourses – 'Asian values', human rights, trade and finance, and environmental issues for example. The ASEAN regional state compact does not have the system of independent courts, parliament, commission, council and the vast bureaucracy of the European project, nor does it have anything comparable to the European Convention on Human Rights. Whereas the transnational policing subculture in Europe thrives behind an official façade of 'Euro sclerosis', in the ASEAN region transnational policing subculture evolved partly in the 'grey' areas described by Ko-Lin Chin.[250] The building blocks of the global policing architecture quarried in the ASEAN region, so to speak, exhibit their own cultural, economic, political and social hallmarks.

National policing hubs

National policing hubs are the mainstays that connect the struts of global policing to the transnational-state-system. A study of organisational change in the policing sectors of 15 west European and Scandinavian countries revealed no standard model for these institutional hubs, but it did show that the 'new security agenda' had significant repercussions for the structure of the police sector across the continent. The Netherlands reorganised its 148 police constabularies into an integrated national and regional structure in 1993. Sweden created a National Criminal Intelligence Service in 1995 and Denmark did the same in 1998. In both instances these were modelled on the British example. Luxembourg merged its two national police forces into one in January 2000. In Belgium the *Gendarmerie*, the national Judicial Police and the Municipal Police, were integrated into one police force structured on two levels (federal and local) in April 2001. This is not to over-emphasise the degree of similarity emerging in European policing; for example, the French police system – which has always had a high degree of centrally controlled policing including the *Gendarmerie* and *Police Nationale* – was resistant to structural adjustment. Meanwhile, Germany's established federal policing architecture devolves most policing functions to the 16 *Länder* (federal states) with a *Bundeskriminalamt* (BKA) and the *Bundeskriminalpolizei* (BKP) each having an overarching federal mandate. The federal model required fewer internal structural changes in order to facilitate pan-European policing co-operation. Transnational pressures to fit into the intelligence-led policing paradigm did not exactly force different countries' policing structures into a single mould, but the information and communications technology revolution that propelled it shaped them in distinctive ways.[251]

The idea of a national police force along the lines of the 'continental model' has historically been resisted in Britain. As of this writing it had 43 territorial 'Home Office' forces in England and Wales, eight in Scotland, the Police Service of Northern Ireland and a number of national specialist forces such as the British Transport Police and armed Civil Nuclear Constabulary. The first major step towards a centralised system was the creation of the National Criminal Intelligence Service (NCIS) in 1992 and the National Crime Squad (NCS) in 1998. The role of the former was strictly confined to intelligence management, but the NCS was a national law enforcement agency with a structure of regional crime squads whose detectives worked with local police to carry out arrests.

When, in the early years of the 21st century, the UK created the Serious Organised Crime Agency (SOCA) out of the previously existing NCIS and the NCS – as well as law enforcement intelligence units from HM Customs & Excise and the Immigration Service – agents transferred from security and intelligence agencies took up key leadership positions: David Bolt (former MI5) 'director of intelligence', Paul Evans (formerly MI6) 'director of interventions' and Sir Stephen Lander (former Director General of MI5) as Chair of the Board of Directors. These individuals, together with Bill Hughes, Director General of the Agency and former head of the NCS, were responsible for implementing SOCA's overall approach, its relationship with ministers and for oversight of its operational performance. As such they were in key positions of influence to shape the occupational subculture of the newly constituted UK national policing hub and to act as an important influence on the transnational subculture of policing. This raised troubling questions about the development of a combined national secret intelligence and police force with a transnational reach.[252] Viewed from a global perspective, SOCA and its successor the National Crime Agency, is a *de facto* UK national police force.

The US security apparatus was radically transformed by the creation of the Department of Homeland Security (DHS) in 2002. This involved the integration of all or part of 22 federal agencies into what was intended to be a 'single, unified and integrated' cabinet department. At the time of writing, the DHS employed more than 230,000 people doing such jobs as aviation and border security, cybersecurity, chemical facility inspection and emergency response. Although the DHS has yet to undergo sustained academic scrutiny, early signs are that it suffers from a lack of democratic accountability and questions have been raised by some media sources, notably the *New York Times*, regarding the costs of privately contracted security consultants working for the organisation and the apparently consistent failure of the organisation to meet targets it has set for itself. Homeland security rhetoric in the United States is heated, raising a smokescreen that blocks the view of the workings of this organisation and operates as a justication for increased securitization. This, we argue, has the paradoxical effect of increasing insecurity.

A Rand Corporation study *Reorganizing US Domestic Intelligence: Assessing the Options,* published in 2008, described the complexity of the federal structure of intelligence-led policing in the USA. In so doing it provided a description of the US national policing hub, subsequent to the 2001 Patriot Act and 2002 Homeland Security Act.[253] According to this report 'if the arrangements for domestic intelligence in the USA were considered as an enterprise, what would be most obvious about it is that it is complex and dispersed'.[254] Included in the description of US domestic intelligence apparatus were not only the FBI and other 'three-letter agencies' (a euphemism for the major federal police and intelligence agencies), but also Border Patrol, Transportation Security Administration (TSA) and the Coast Guard (see Chapter 5). Beyond these federal agencies were the thousands of local police agencies and hundreds of thousands of local police officers portrayed as the 'eyes and ears' of domestic police intelligence. In the Rand study, several metropolitan police organisations were credited with large and sophisticated intelligence capabilities – with the NYPD singled out as being in a class of its own. It found that private security guards were three times as numerous as public law enforcement officers. Since most of the 'public' infrastructure in finance, transportation, information and the like was in private hands, those private-sector managers were accounted for as a significant part of the overall police intelligence system.[255]

The parallel rise of intelligence-led policing and national policing hubs in Europe, and the evolution of communications hubs or 'fusion centres' in North America and elsewhere makes the architecture of the police surveillant assemblage look seamless.[256] This is to mistake description for actuality. The US Department of Justice audit of the Interpol NCB in Washington DC, for example, revealed extensive difficulties in co-ordination from the levels of top management down to the networks in the various law enforcement agencies. The extensive list of difficulties included linkage blindness, institutional myopia, and other organisational communications problems.[257] A review of intelligence-led policing in Europe also exposed an extensive catalogue of organisational pathologies.[258] The idea of these communications hubs is an important one for the global policing architecture, but looking closely at police institutions reveals not building blocks but a network of (sometimes crossed) wires.

We concur with Robert Reiner that some form of policing is required in any social order.[259] New social institutions are made up from materials recycled from existing ones. The problem is, and here lies our concern, that the national policing hubs that we see as holding together the structure of global policing are ad hoc and narrowly focused on a small range of enforcement concerns – chiefly to do with terrorism and organised crime. The institutional complexity and narrow law enforcement vision contribute to the many 'false positives' (exemplified by the case of Derek Bond) where the damaging effects of arrest and detention are inflicted on innocent people without any prospect for accountability or redress. The secrecy protocols of national security discourse assumed within a global policing infrastructure welded to these national policing hubs is antithetical to transparent and democratically accountable policing. For these reasons we think there are reasons to be fearful.

Private transnational policing

The relative dearth of empirical research on the role and functions of private policing providers in the transnational sphere perhaps explains their neglect in theoretical discussions about transnational policing.[260] According to Philip Stenning 'there is virtually no research which tells us, in a comprehensive and balanced way, about what private transnational policing actually involves, who benefits from it (and how), and what the problems and challenges with it are'.[261] Without that basic empirical knowledge an inclusive theory of transnational policing is difficult, but we think that recent detailed and theoretically sophisticated work on private transnational policing is substantial enough that it has become possible to properly locate it in a theory of global policing.[262] The existing literature converges on one point: private security forms a large and growing part of the global policing system. What is less clear is *how* privatised forms of security provision fit into the architecture of global policing.

The global private security market is worth over US$139 billion, and is forecast to grow 8 per cent each year to reach a value of US$230 billion by 2015. Rita Abrahamsen and Michael C. Williams argue that the 'quiet revolution' in security provision has gone global.[263] Their whirlwind tour of the global security market in the early 21st century makes the point. In the UK the ratio of private to public police was nearly two to one and in the USA nearly three to one. The number of private security companies in Russia had gone from an estimated 4000 one year after legalisation in 1992 to 6775 (not including 4612 in-house security operations) by 1999. In India the private security sector employed 5.5 million people, 1.3 million more than the country's combined police and armed forces. Similar indicators show much the same patterns in many other jurisdictions. Moreover, after Walt Disney's master-planned community *Celebration* was established in 1996, public–private partnerships in the security field became ubiquitous and taken for granted. We agree with Abrahamsen and Williams that, when it comes to policing, the strict line between public and private is blurred, which raises interesting questions about the centrality of 'the state' in the global system of governance.

In Chapter 1, we established that the blurred boundaries between 'public policing' and 'private security' permeate the global policing architecture from top to bottom. Our discussion of global multi-agency policing looked at inter-institutional effects arising from interaction between policing and military organisations (which may also take place under public or private auspices). Peter Kraska showed how the 'growth complex' of the publicly administered domestic criminal justice apparatus in the USA was facilitated by merging privatised military contractors with national armed forces.[264]

The transnational-state-system, in its vast domestic, intergovernmental and supranational complexity, provides the architecture in which the many private actors reside, act and influence the character of the world system. Moreover, the states that make up the transnational-state-system are themselves disaggregated. Its principal actors are the various *sub-state* institutions of which they are comprised. Transnational linkages at the middle-range of the system and in the grey areas between private and public are crucial juncture points in the global policing architecture. With respect to matters of policing and security, the meaning and logic embodied in the transnational subculture of policing stretch across both the domestic–global and public–private divides. Abrahamsen and Williams insist that the theoretical distinction between public and private is not empirically steadfast because of the shifting networks that feature in the policing and security sector worldwide. They point to the emergence of 'security assemblages' from within these networks to show that understanding the emergence of global security requires an approach that is simultaneously global and local. They also raise questions about the effects of the de-centering of the state in the processes of global governance. Theories of nodal governance tend to suggest that this de-centering does not need to be replaced by some other sovereign, but rather that it is relational and contingent.[265]

We have a number of thoughts on these ideas. First, the logic of these 'security assemblages' reflects taken for granted assumptions about the transnational-state-system as a container for insecurity which is reflected in continuing discourses about 'national security' in the context of *privatised* 'high policing', for example where 'industrial espionage' and 'traditional' (i.e. political) espionage intersect.[266] Second, as we discuss elsewhere in this book, privatised security in urban contexts evidently reflects social class differences patterned into the mixed geography of the global south in the global north. Third, we think that studies of private security companies, private military companies, and in-house security in the corporate resource extraction industries show not relationality and contingency, but rather a bias towards private corporate interests in capital accumulation.[267] This brings us back to some considerations raised in Chapter 1. Readers will recall that Bertrand Russell's belief that a global social contract was necessary, but required re-thinking because late modern society is built around organisations rather than individuals. The transgressive effects of corporate power in a global system predicated on neo-liberal ideas makes the transnational-state-system fundamentally different from the nation-state-system that preceded it. This has implications for how we articulate a global social contract and the local governance of insecurity.

The tie-ups between private and public security actors into 'security assemblages' function as 'air ducts' in the structure, figuratively speaking, helping to oxygenate the system by circulating professional knowledge and ideas about the governance of insecurity. This circulation happens horizontally across the interstitial spaces between public and private institutions. It also happens vertically from the central recesses of the transnational-state-system to the remotest local communities. However, it is not all hot air. Extending the architectural metaphor to include private actors requires that we also bear in mind that security assemblages which include private transnational policing institutions contribute in practical ways to securing territory and to the surveillance and control of suspect populations (see Chapter 5).

Glocal policing

The architecture of global policing has its foundations in the neighbourhood 'precincts', 'divisions' and other 'basic command units' of the local police. The foundations of modern domestic policing were laid on the grounds of civil society in the 18th and early 19th centuries. In the next chapter we outline how the subculture of liaison officers co-articulates with local subcultures of policing and helps to make the total architecture of global policing a social world of its own. We now round out our discussion of the architecture of global policing by providing a sense of what is, in operational police parlance, happening 'on the ground'. The evidence is that the re-organisation of policing at the national and transnational levels has had important effects within the foundational structures of policing in local communities. This is certainly the case in the UK where, in 2003, Prime Minister Tony Blair commented, amid much speculation by media commentators about the establishment of a 'British FBI', on the need for an 'historic overhaul' of the UK policing architecture. Talk about police force re-organisation in the UK had historical antecedents going back at least to the early 1960s,[268] but the establishment of the SOCA had implications for policing at the local level. By 2004 senior British politicians were voicing plans to amalgamate the existing 43 police services of England and Wales into approximately 20 larger force areas, a suggestion that was politically contentious and proved impossible to deliver at the time. But even without something as obvious as forced amalgamations of the existing police services, policing at the divisional level was being re-wired.[269]

Speculation about large-scale police re-organisation in the UK arose again in 2011 when the hitherto secret National Public Order Intelligence Unit (NPOIU) was revealed to have been controlled by the Association of Chief Police Officers, a privately registered company.[270] The scandal exposed the interconnections between privatised high policing and the state and there were calls for change. The scandal involved police undercover operatives infiltrating various ecological campaigning groups, but any subsequent organisational changes to the architecture of UK policing should be understood as part of a long-term historical trend and not simply as a reaction to circumstances.[271] The re-configuration of local policing is certainly not unique to the UK. Policing in many countries, especially but not exclusively in seigneurial states, exhibited similar tendencies. For example, a study of the governance of organised crime in Canada concluded, in part, that the trends and processes underway were a microcosm of global developments, 'as the information processes of the Canadian police sector were re-engineered [...] so to was it in other countries. The result was a change in the architecture of the police sector across the globe'.[272]

Decisions made in far off centres of the global policing architecture have affected the wiring of local police divisions. The Interpol I-24/7 telecommunications system is being made available in police control rooms and customs agencies around the world and has penetrated right down to street level officers who have become adept at using global systems to facilitate local policing.[273] According to the Interpol website, in 2010 a co-ordinated fugitive apprehension programme 'Infrared' was launched involving 50 officers in 29 countries acting in concert to detect and arrest 450 long-term international fugitives (of whom 160 were arrested within a year). Within the European theatre, specialist fugitive apprehension officers have started to travel overseas with mobile pass-port and fingerprint readers to pursue the evidence gathering and apprehension processes enabled by the European Arrest Warrant.

The re-wiring of local policing and its transformation into glocal policing is the result of the effects of advanced information and communications technol-ogy on organisations generally,[274] neo-liberalism and the general shift from the nation-state to the market-state,[275] and the rise of the discourse of transnational organised crime and security. In addition to the influence of technological advance, the commercialisation of policing and the rise of the language of transnational organised crime and security, the fads and fashions of policing rhetoric also furthered the process of re-wiring local policing structures. 'Zero tolerance', 'broken windows', the 'Compstat paradigm' and the 'New York miracle' were terms that found special favour in the vocabulary of policing around the world at the turn of the millennium. The concept of zero tolerance, it will be remembered, was first deployed in the policing context in New York in the early years of the 1990s. It was not a new concept then and had been previously used in, among other things, campaigns against domestic violence. In New York the phrase coalesced around a criminological theory and a set of technological practices, as well as the pluralisation of policing.[276] The techno-logical innovations were impressive, especially in a society used to being awed by the 'scientification of policework'.[277] The pluralisation of security provision happened in tandem with the adoption of zero-tolerance public policing, which was widely credited with the New York 'crime drop', even though both the theory on which it was based and evidence of its effectiveness were unconvinc-ing.[278] A new kind of 'hybrid-policing', 'plural policing' or 'networked policing' had been configured in NYC.[279] The Compstat paradigm was shown to be effica-cious in the coordination of multiple policing and security agencies around core goals thereby effectively re-wiring the organisational structures of pre-existing police institutions.[280]

'New York Style' zero-tolerance policing, and the Compstat paradigm were among the most successful exports in the history of policing. Former NYC Police Chief William J. Bratton was able to brag in his book *Turnaround: How America's Top Cop Reversed the Crime Epidemic* (published in 1998, two years after he got his picture on the cover of *Time* magazine), that New York-style policing was being sold in the UK, Germany, Italy, Japan, Norway, Brazil, China, Hungary, Switzerland, Portugal, the Netherlands and Israel.[281] Bratton had done something quite amazing: he had become the number one global policing celebrity. Along with a host of other police 'entrepreneurs', he helped to reconfigure local policing in a variety of places around the world. On the same ticket, former New York City mayor Rudolf Giuliani was invited to lead a high-profile delegation to Mexico City, with his newly formed security-consulting firm Giuliani Partners in October 2001. In the aftermath of 9/11, he was invited to Mexico City to sell the Compstat model solution to urban problems by a consortium of Mexico's City's powerful political and economic elite.[282] 'Plan Giuliani' cost Mexican taxpayers US$4.3 million and his tour in 2003 prompted jeers from Mexican news-media for touring 'hot spots' in a convoy of 12 armoured sport-utility vehicles, surrounded by 400 police officers with a helicopter whirring overhead — he warned the plan needed four years to achieve significant results.[283]

The 'New York miracle' appealed to business interests in Mexico City worried about the 'chaotic environment' of the city. Concerns included things such as informal commerce, inefficient tax recovery, urban disorder and decadence, public insecurity, serious organised crime and a lack of legality. Plan Giuliani was an off-the-shelf model of Compstat policing re-packaged for local consumption. It appealed because the combination of hybrid public–private policing together with the rhetoric and practices of ZTP, aimed to remove problematic populations and activities from downtown areas. The objective was to improve the city centre so that it would suit upper-middle class consumers of housing and services, foreign tourists, management executives and global investors. It was a property developer's bonanza. Most of the hi-tech policing capabilities recommended by Giuliani were eventually installed in central downtown areas of historical and cultural interest. In 2007 it was reported that Mexico's federal government had tried to respond to crime by installing 'urban security systems' – networks of outdoor cameras monitored by computers – in 16 of the country's 31 states.[284] Half a decade later, the war on drugs and crime in urban Mexico had intensified and things, except in specific exclusive zones, have become worse.[285]

The significance of techno-policing in Mexico serves an example of the re-wiring of the local structures of policing and security. In Mexico City and elsewhere around the world, local policing institutions have been reconfigured due to the ICT revolution, privatisation and insecurity discourse. These same influences operate at every level of the transnational-state-system and connect local with global centres in the policing architecture. From New York to Tokyo, the patterns of policing are being transformed by global changes. One way to envisage these complex processes is to look at the 're-wiring' of the local command posts of policing. The recurrent pattern in glocal policing is producing a worldwide *City of Quartz*.[286]

Conclusion

This chapter has sketched an outline of the global policing architecture. It is far from a complete description but sufficient, we hope, for the reader to envisage how the structures of global policing have developed over the fairly recent past. None of the forms of policing described in this chapter existed one hundred years ago; most have sprung up since the end of the Second World War; some were created at the turn of the millennium. It is now possible to think of global policing in institutional terms and the extended architectural metaphor has helped us to do that. Policing institutions and their personnel have a significant presence in the global architecture of governance. In this chapter we have shown that building blocks of policing power located at strategic points in the transnational-state-system are wired to police buildings at the local level. The architecture of transnational policing has been put in place without public discussion or political dissent. Transnational police actors have decisively moulded the architecture of global policing and consequently have shaped the character of the global system more generally. In the next chapter we turn our attention to an analysis of the occupational subcultures that form within the institutional structures of global policing.

4

THE OCCUPATIONAL SUBCULTURES OF GLOBAL POLICING

We now turn to cultural criminology in order to explore the distinction between the *transnational subculture of policing* and the *subculture of transnational policing*. First, this chapter provides a short explanation of the role of international liaison officers (ILOs), the 'global cops' who inhabit the architecture of global policing. They are 'knowledge workers', who can sometimes reach right down to police divisional levels helping to create a new glocal policing subculture. The chapter provides a substantive discussion of subcultural theory and explains how this is useful in attempting to answer the question: 'who are the global cops?' Using the dramaturgical metaphor, we set out the cast of characters that inhabit the architecture of global policing and work in the transnational policing theatre of operations. We identify eight archetypal roles: *technician, diplomat, entrepreneur, public-relations expert, legal ace, spy, field-operator* and *enforcer*. Drawing on empirical research evidence from the sociology of policing, we show how each of these actors plays their role out in the field. Having set out the cast of characters we then consider how cultural approaches to understanding policework connect to a theory of global policing and the politics of the transnational-state system more generally.

──────── **Police liaison officers and the transnational space between** ────────

The French political sociologist Didier Bigo described the work of police liaison officers as creating a global 'security archipelago'. According to him, ILOs are marginal to their respective police organisations and yet integral to a profound change in global security. Liaison officers are a primary means of circulating knowledge through the global system. Acting within and between police organisations, they are like 'station-masters' directing and shunting information as quickly as possible to where it is needed.[287] In the European sphere, police liaison officers have been much studied.[288] One professional label used to describe the liaison role is 'intelligence officer'; one who is more or less devoted to pure police knowledge work. According to Bigo:

> The principles of free trade and free movement have made the liaison officer role crucial for policing in Europe, because it is they who manage the flow of information between their respective agencies. Indeed, police customs and immigration agencies have all sought to develop specialist liaison officers and the development of various bilateral and multilateral agreements have more or less codified these emergent networks. The resultant interconnections of the various agencies involved (including security agencies; *haute polices*) has served to reinforce the power, status and influence of all.[289]

The informality of ILO networks allows policing agencies to exchange confidential information without leaving a paper trail.[290] This role in information-sharing has unique importance in transnational policing. Normally, police agents rarely gain access to intelligence files from other agencies, especially ones in other national jurisdictions. Secrecy and the 'need to know' principle are axiomatic in policing and information hoarding is standard practice. The barrier of secrecy ironically contradicts another central axiom of intelligence-led policing which sees efficient information sharing as essential to effectiveness.

Often working on specific cases and, strictly speaking non-operational, ILOs do sometimes partipate acvitely in investigative work on the ground outside their legal jurisdiction, defined formally by the boundaries of the nation state.[291] In all cases, the ILOs seek to influence policing outcomes in pursuit of their organisational objectives. In the case of Derek Bond (see Chapter 1), the FBI liaision officer – in this case termed a legal attaché – was able to influence the South African police in Durban to arrest and detain Mr Bond and also belatedly provided the information that authorised the Durban police to release him three weeks later. This case shows how seigneurial state policing power extends overseas through the auspices of the ILO and through employing coervice powers provided by a foreign police force.

The activities of liaison officers in the developing world have not been the subject of a great amount of empirical research. Although such officers can be found in all corners of the globe, we elaborate again on material from the contemporary Caribbean because it provides in microcosm a more general view of the ILO in a post-colonial setting. The entire spectrum of liaison officer work can be found in this region from surveillance and intelligence gathering right up to the assumption of operational command. The West Indies are home to a significant number of British ILOs who, historically, have been associated with enforcement units from HM Customs, NCIS and subsequently SOCA. There is a strong continuity with British colonial policing in the mid 20th century that included a network of MI5 agents and Security Liaison Officers sponsored by the Foreign and Commonwealth Office. In 2010, UK liaison officers were permanently based in Jamaica, Trinidad and Barbados, with extra teams rotating in to provide additional support at ports-of-entry and ad hoc visits concerning specific inquiries. As well as British, there are also liaison officers from the US DEA, Treasury Department and the State Department Diplomatic Security Service posted throughout the region. NYPD, Miami Dade PD and the ATF routinely send officers and the US Federal Marshals Service regularly deploy a Fugitive Apprehension Team to render suspects to face trial in the US courts. French policing officials are frequent visitors as well as Germans, Dutch, Brazilians, Canadians and Columbians.[292]

Contemporary transnational policing in the Caribbean region echoes its past. Just as the region functioned in the 19th century as a testing ground for innovations in governance and security that could then be cycled between metropole and periphery of empire, in the post-colonial period technologically savvy transnational liaison officers facilitate similar circuitry, only much faster!

The inter-connections between officers from the London Metropolitan Police Operation Trident and the officers based in Kingston Jamaica in the early 2000s illustrate the strategic depth that liaison relationships can achieve. Operation Trident was a sustained Metropolitan Police operation investigating gun crime within the Jamaican diaspora communities in London. A major figure in this was Mark Shields, a veteran UK police officer with more than 30 years experience, much of it in Special Branch. Shields' career is an example of life at the cutting edge of transnational policing. During his career he spent time as a liaison officer in Germany and as an investigator on the City of London Police's fraud squad. As a detective in the London Metropolitan Police's serious and organised crime unit in 2001 he managed investigative teams concerned with gun crime that had links to Jamaica. This brought him into contact with the Caribbean liaison officer network and eventually to lead an investigation in Jamaica into an extra-judicial killing, known as the Kraal shootings. This was a messy affair, since it involved allegations of extreme police brutality and cover-up in the actions of several Jamaica Constabulary Force (JCF) officers after they shot dead four persons – including two women – in the town of Kraal in May of 2003. The shootings were the subject of a gripping trial when several officers from the JCF stood in court accused of murder.

This case is worth dwelling on for a moment because it reveals how transnational expertise circulates through the social world of transnational policing helping to consolidate it further. During the eight-week trial, the Crown called 43 witnesses many of whom portrayed the Kraal shootings as a case of extra-judicial execution. Evidence presented at the trial included analysis of cell-phone signals by a British expert. Forensic evidence supported by other UK-based experts also included analyses of projectile trajectories and gun residue on participants' bodies and clothing. The scientific evidence strongly supported the case for the prosecution. In December 2005, the jury found Senior Superintendent Reneto Adams (aka 'Saddam') and his colleagues – corporals Shane Lyons and Patrick Coke – not guilty. The case divided the country. On one hand, Adams was greeted on the steps of the Kingston court house by jubilant crowds of supporters and on the other, the outcome was roundly condemned by Jamaican human rights advocates.

Mark Shields was subsequently given long-term secondment from Scotland Yard and appointed Deputy Commissioner of the JCF, a formal position with responsibility for crime investigation with Jamaican officers under his command.[293] Shields retired from his post in the JCF in 2009, not before achieving public notoriety on several more occasions, once in a case involving 500 trucks of stolen white coral beach sand and another as lead investigator into the sudden death of Pakistan team coach Bob Woolmer during the 2007 Cricket World Cup. Shields subsequently took up employment with a private security firm in Jamaica. His career offers unique and intriguing glimpses into the subcultural world of transnational policing.

Liaison officers play major roles in the subculture of transnational policing. Whether on the level playing field of the European Union or in a more lopsided post-colonial setting like the Caribbean, South Africa, or Indonesia, liaison officers are in position to transmit key cultural meanings through the occupational subculture of policing. They are one important way that local policing is globalised. Officers on secondment establish outposts of their parent institutions. Individually they establish lines of communication between different agencies and between different levels of organisational hierarchy within their own institutions. Collectively and individually they move around the global policing architecture transferring knowledge about what the practical tasks of policing consist of. Without liaison officers, the intelligence-led policing model now found in Interpol, UNPOL, Europol, SOCA, the FBI, and the DEA and within the major national hubs of the global policing architecture, would grind to a halt. The information would not flow, the models would not transfer, the intelligence would not be analysed and the threat assessments would not be operationalised. In the subcultural world of transnational policing, liaison officers are the connection between the 'trapeze artists and the ground crew'.[294] They move throughout the architecture of global policing and epitomise the subculture of transnational policing. They are the main players in Robert Reiner's new police internationale.[295] Through them, specific subcultural norms percolate within policing institutions at every level of the global system.

Subcultural theory and policing

The preceding discussion raises questions about how to delineate the occupational parameters of policing so as to define the role-types that fulfil its dramaturgical requirements. That is to say, how can we best convey a sense of the secret social world of the policing occupation? Our general theory of global policing draws inspiration from subcultural theory and cultural criminology.[296] In this chapter we lay out a specific theory of the occupational subculture of policing and show how it is related to a generalised global culture of insecurity. This interrelationship produces the security control paradox: the 'pervasive sense of insecurity that exists amidst, and in spite of, the multiplication of tactics for ensuring security'.[297]

According to Peter Andreas and Ethan Nadelmann 'a cop is a cop, no matter whose badge is worn, and a criminal is a criminal regardless of citizenship or where the crimes were committed'.[298] In earlier work, Nadelmann cited a variety of cultural attributes including loyalty, insularity, authority, instrumentality and conservatism as common aspects of police culture. Above all, the police occupation is driven by a sense of mission.[299] 'What making a profit is to businessmen, regardless of nationality, so catching the criminal is to cops all over the world.'[300] This common-sense view of police subculture lacks sociological perspicacity, but the above list of the norms and values associated with the occupation does resonate with the extensive literature in this field.[301] Observing this surface appearance can be both important and illuminating because, as the early 20th-century American sociologist W.I. Thomas put it, 'situations defined as real are real in their consequences'.[302] Momentarily we will discuss further these common-sense aspects of the occupational subculture of policing, since they are part of the system of meaning that is implicated in the character of global policing.

Before that we must stress some general principles of subcultural theory. First, as David Downes contended, it is not very helpful to label a discernable group as 'subcultural', unless the concept is given some explanatory work to do.[303] In his general formulation, subculture is understood as the 'solution to a problem'. Subcultural theory posits that groups of social actors encounter problems and possibilities in common and, to the extent that they develop collective responses, they can be meaningfully said to have constituted a subculture. Generally speaking a subculture can be defined as *a set of learned problem-solutions and a repertoire of perceived possibilities held in common by a social or occupational group*. The essence of subcultural theorising is the ability to explain the sociological basis of a particular group's problem-solutions in ways that lay bare the meanings held within that social world.

Research on police organisations around the world has found striking similarities in some of the meanings imbued in the occupation. Of course, policing in Australia differs from in Zimbabwe to the extent that the police officers and how they police in each place reflects the demography, history, law and culture of the societies within which they are embedded. Nonetheless, it is a staple finding of police research that certain values, experiences, expectations and behaviours are to be found among policing agents working in very different circumstances around the world.[304] In this sense the 'culture of policing' is usually understood to be a consequence of the unpredictable outcomes of police intervention. The routine experience of being lied to and being on the receiving end of unpredictable violent behaviour, for example, induces some members of the occupation to be suspicious, pessimistic and cynical.[305] A not uncommon aphorism heard in the world of policing is 'the job's fucked!' reflecting the everyday experience of 'on the job' and 'in the job' trouble.[306]

Another aspect of this 'cop-sided view' of the occupational culture emphasises attributes such as loyalty to colleagues, insularity and detachment from 'civilians'. These attributes are held in place by their opposite, which are the projected characteristics of villainy. Culturally, the policing occupation is constructed in dualistic terms, as a force for good in a world of insufferable evil or as the 'thin blue line' that stands between order and chaos. This has ramifications at a general cultural level, but it is not much help in the study of the lived social world of the policing occupation. That is why sociologists of policing have, through further terminological refinement, sought to sharpen up the analytical power of the subcultural approach.

The classic work in the sociology of policing subculture is Jerome Skolnick's study of policing a Californian city *Justice Without Trial*.[307] In his book, Skolnick describes how the police officer's 'working personality' is forged within the confines of 'the job' by three related factors: danger, authority and the need to get something done. These aspects of the police workplace give rise to particular ways of thinking, Skolnick calls them 'distinctive cognitive tendencies' in the occupational group and this thought-style is part and parcel of the occupational subculture. It is the nexus of authority and danger and the need to 'produce results' that is the classical root of the problems and possibilities held in common by police officers. This gives rise to a kind of collective response that we find in the occupational subculture of policing. In this classic formulation the workplace culture was primarily understood with reference to police patrol officers. For example, the requirement for local municipal police officers to undertake road traffic patrol can bring them into fairly frequent conflict with the public, creating a sense of isolation from the 'civilian population' and a sense of solidarity with, and loyalty to, work colleagues. The demands of police patrol work generally establish a dynamic where officers soon learn the desirability of 'covering each other's backs' both on the streets and with respect to the stories colleagues tell superiors in the context of 'on the job trouble'. This is related to the 'blue wall of silence' that prevents officers from informing on colleagues' corruption and misconduct.[308] Subculture in this sense is a set of learned problem-solutions and a repertoire of perceived possibilities held in common by uniformed patrol officers.

Egon Bittner, another foundational thinker in the sociology of policing, located the essentials of the occupational subculture of patrol officers with reference to their presumed 'monopoly of coercive force'.[309] According to him, 'the role of the police is best understood as a mechanism for the distribution of non-negotiable coercive force employed in accordance with the dictates of an intuitive grasp of situational exigencies.'[310] The coercive transaction is held to be the defining core of the police occupational subculture because particular problem-solutions unique to the policework arise out of it. Applications and permutations of these foundational thinkers' ideas continue to the present.[311] As William Muir explains, the subculture of policing draws attention because the exercise of coercion 'seems on first acquaintance mean and barbaric [and the] human qualities which appear to be required for the practice of coercion seem incompatible with any civilized notion of the good'.[312] Policing is a tainted occupation, but the distinction between 'street cops' and 'management cops' shows that there is more to that social world than the danger–authority nexus.[313] As many observers have documented, the sociological study of the occupational world of policing is versatile: the craft knowledge of mounted police who spend their days riding horses differs greatly from bicycle cops, dog handlers, traffic patrol, firearms units, Special Branch and financial crime investigators. When sociologists of policing documented the occupational routines of private security and private policing, it became even more difficult to generalise about policing subculture.[314]

In looking for subcultural commonality within the complex division of labour of the policing occupation, it would be a mistake to confuse the idea that police subculture has certain common elements with the claim that policing is the same everywhere. It clearly is not. A police public order unit in Durban, South Africa will have a different subculture from the police on skid row in Edinburgh or Vancouver.[315] The complexity of policing documented in this book points to the ways in which a putative subculture of global policing is shared among a wide range of professions. This includes customs officers, immigration enforcers and others in the security sector including coastguard captains, airport security officers and soldiers carrying out constabulary duties in war-torn areas or providing support for their blue uniformed colleagues, all of whom are being drawn into the discourse of policing. In what follows we sketch out a number of parameters of the policing occupation that set the form for collective responses in subcultural terms. In our view, these parameters principally shape and define the learned problem-solutions inherent in the subcultural world of policing.

The parameters of policing subculture

There is an intriguing difference between 'transnational subculture of policing' and the 'subculture of transnational policing'. The former refers to the norms, values, attitudes, beliefs and routines shared among police officers around the world. The latter refers to the subculture of specialist transnational police officers. For us this distinction opens up a space of theoretical inquiry and thinking. We take it as a given that, in general, police are required to respond to situations defined as problematic to good social order and the organisational response may include the proportionate use of force.[316] In earlier chapters we defined policing broadly as a set of technologies and practices which aim to help maintain the health of the social body. We emphasise that considerable discretion in policework often means that it is policing agents who define what is problematic for good social order, how the health of the social body is determined and whose prosperity is to be preserved.

In all cases the ability to use coercion to 'get the job done' is a fundamental factor shaping the organisational life-world of the police occupation. This parameter corresponds closely to the concerns highlighted by Skolnick, Bittner and the other early pioneers in the sociology of policing who have typically analysed it in terms of the operational problems that street patrol officers encounter. What interests us is how this parameter of policing (the general expectation that it is about intervention – forceful if necessary – to preserve social order and keep the peace) forms the occupational worldview of the new policing internationale, but this needs to be appreciated in an overall organisational context because other existing conditions also shape the subcultural life of policing. Simply put: it is the police themselves who decide which laws are to be enforced against whom and how.

A widely recognised parameter common to the policing occupation everywhere concerns the information environment and its organisation.[317] Information is considered the 'life-blood' of policing. The need to manage knowledge flows, and the way people respond to and resist those demands, is an important determinant of the occupational subculture in any organisation. Owing to common features of technological innovation, the same trends can be found in universities, hospitals and major corporations, all of which now institutionally 'think through' the mediated means provided by advanced computer systems.[318] Advances in information technology have been at the forefront of organisational change in policing institutions around the world. However, progress has been uneven.[319] While advances in information and communications technology appear to enable action, the opportunity costs that result from the large-scale organisational transformation (which is implied by the term 'information revolution') may actually retard action.[320]

A significant proportion of contemporary professional policing literature is concerned with the ways in which advances in, and training requirements for, technology can be managed more efficiently.[321] Since a variety of advanced ICTs provide the essential pre-requisite of the intelligence-led policing paradigm, 'informationalisation' is a taken for granted parameter within the occupational subculture.[322] There is even a recognised vocabulary of organisational pathologies in intelligence-led policing that forms part of the subcultural argot concerning problems and possibilities involved with information policing.[323]

There are other important parameters in the police occupations that require collective problem-solutions. We have previously emphasised the role that law plays as part of the tools of the trade, and the double-edged qualities of counter-law. It follows that how to 'do things with rules' provides a key aspect of the police occupational subculture. Law in relation to policing forms a vastly differentiated array of instruments and, because of jurisdictional fragmentation and functional specialisation, this parameter may have many different specific effects. At an abstract level, law creates both problems and possibilities in policing and is a central feature of the occupational subculture no matter where it is manifested.[324]

Management is another important parameter felt by actors in police institutions at every scale.[325] Economy, efficiency, effectiveness, agency-related performance criteria and personal performance review all form aspects of modern police management.[326] The way that policing institutions 'think' creates boundaries for both the formal and informal methods of 'getting the job done' and therefore places another kind of parameter on the occupational subculture.[327] Alongside management and law, the political framing of policing must be considered because politics provides a complex parameter of action that circumscribes occupational subcultural solutions to the problem of 'what is to be done'.[328] Sociologists thinking about the subculture of policing also bring in broader cultural parameters such as masculinity and racism that have demonstrable effects in shaping occupational subcultures.[329]

All of these factors need to be borne in mind when framing a general understanding of the transnational subculture of policing. Although there exists a broader matrix of problem-solutions than is indicated by the danger–authority nexus of classic police subcultural theory, that idea remains crucial. The difference is that the global networked society creates additional parameters that condition this core feature of policing. For example, policing institutions are dominated by the rationalisation of surveillance. Police use advanced technologies to conduct surveillance on suspect populations and one of the ironies is that police themselves constitute a suspect population. Since police-law (governing *with* law) is already structured to give control agents access to legal, scientific, electronic and personal knowledge about suspects and suspect populations – in Richard Ericson's turn of phrase 'system rights have displaced suspects rights' – the only way to control the police is to turn surveillance back on the surveillance system.[330] This has complex ramifications for the policing subculture.

These considerations are all acutely felt within the police because, as shown in Peter K. Manning's ethnographic work, policing is a 'tainted occupation'.[331] One of the most telling ramifications of this is that, like very few other workplace subcultures, in policework people get hurt when things go wrong and fatalities are part of the job. This tainted quality results in a certain detectable defensiveness when its participants are exposed to outside scrutiny. Built around a core sense of mission to get the job done, by coercive means if required, the police occupational subculture is shaped by a number of obvious, yet subtle, parameters which we identify as being technology, law, management and politics. Police workplace subculture is enacted within a highly complex institutional matrix, as we have conveyed in earlier chapters. This makes the task of succinctly describing the life-world of these actors quite challenging.

Meet the global cops

Before explaining the sociological effects of policing subculture we first introduce the characters that routinely act it out. Making use of the dramaturgical metaphor we sketch out eight archetypal policing agents who carry out the roles policing globally requires. These are 'ideal types' and, if the drama of global policing is a sociological play on a stage set by history, then the following cast of characters is intended to explain a bit more about how each one plays their part.[332]

The technician

The technician role arises from the dependence in modern policing on advanced information and surveillance technologies.[333] It is the lynchpin of contemporary knowledge-based or intelligence-led policing.[334] The technician is the name for a role that is broadly concerned with the efficient gathering and management of data. This role is an appendage of the surveillant assemblage.[335] It is not exclusively tied to police CCTV, but that is certainly an important aspect. A typical scene in a contemporary police office – in an airport for example – would be a team of technicians in a room with a bank of video terminals, scanning footage with the aid of automated face recognition software.[336] Photographs of particular people may be isolated from all of this data, collated and disseminated to officers in the field in the form of 'spotters books' – small handheld booklets of 'mug shots' for use at airport transit stations, ports-of-entry and 'mega-events'.[337] In this way, the technician contributes to the functioning of the coercive capacities of the organisation. Technicians may also be involved in using ICTs to monitor the work of police agents in the field.

A variety of crime analysis techniques are used by the technician, including analysis of hot spots, suspicious transactions reports, telecommunications data or information contained on confiscated computer hard drives.[338] The technician is also involved in crime investigation undertaking aspects of evidence gathering and analysis.[339] There is a temptation to invoke the image of an Orwellian state here, but this should be tempered by the recognition that surveillance and intelligence systems, like any other kind of system, are imperfect.[340] Organisational difficulties, flaws in analysis and equipment failure are the most obvious reasons ensuring that the technicians do not have total control and that, ultimately, system-reach is limited. Such flaws may underlie a certain capriciousness found in policing action from time-to-time and account for many of the 'false positives', 'failures to identify' and 'wrongful convictions' that occur under the aegis of intelligence-led-policing.[341] Nevertheless, this policing role raises concerns about crime control technologies and their implications for liberty and freedom of movement.[342]

The diplomat

The diplomat is a useful role in the complex architecture of policing but has not been the object of much scholarly attention.[343] The police diplomat should be attuned to the nuances of legal, bureaucratic and political difference found in the multi-institutional settings in which policing takes place. The diplomat might be of use in a joint investigative team or joint task force helping to facilitate a multi-agency action plan. Echoing Didier Bigo, diplomacy is *le cri d'honneur* of the ILO. The prestige of the diplomatic role often brings with it the requirement to speak several languages as well as hold knowledge of different legal and criminal justice systems. They need to understand MLATs and other legal instruments described in Chapter 2 as well as the issues concerned with working across jurisdictional boundaries.

In certain respects, this is the most difficult and demanding role and rarely found in the world of policing. It entails much more than a wide-ranging understanding of how to 'get things done' and a smooth use of bureaucratic and legal rules. It also requires a sociological skill: the capacity to step outside one's own narrow world-view and frame of reference in order to see things from another's perspective. The capacity for 'reflexivity' is hard to achieve and perhaps a little bit at odds with a police mission so often construed in one-dimensional law enforcement terms. Nevertheless, policing organisations require members who can play the diplomat role because not everything can be orchestrated by issuing commands.[344] Often they will be required to provide 'leadership beyond authority'.

The entrepreneur

The rhetoric of sales has deeply permeated the police subculture. Whether it is William J. Bratton selling zero-tolerance policing on a consultancy basis or a group of enterprising police officers and analysts selling partner agencies abroad the idea of an innovative software solution for serial homicide investigation,[345] the entrepreneur is an important and well-recognised role in policing. It is important to distinguish between different types of entrepreneur. Bratton's consultancy is *on the job* entrepreneurship. Selling innovation *within* the job is a different kind of enterprise.[346] The heads of Interpol NCBs, for example, see themselves as having to market Interpol's 'global policing mission' within their own domestic police force.[347]

Given the 'invitational edge' to corruption inherent in policing illicit markets, the entrepreneurial role can involve shady dealings.[348] The distinguishing feature is often said to be the degree to which the entrepreneurship is in pursuit of institutional goals or the benefit of the concerned individuals. Sometimes these converge, which could either be an invitation to individual and systemic corruption or an opportunity to practice a virtuous circle of guardianship. The latter is less common since the entrepreneur is expected to sell to the highest bidder.[349]

The entrepreneur is an agent of institutional change. If the diplomat is interested to make sure that the system is in smooth working order, the entrepreneur is busy advancing the next big idea. The technical wizardry of scientific policing needs to be sold to users and to the paymasters who finance the acquisitions. The entrepreneur is by nature an innovator who sees change as opportunity. This sometimes includes aspects of moral entrepreneurship.[350] When Harry J. Anslinger was appointed first commissioner of the newly formed Federal Bureau of Narcotics in the 1930s, he sold the idea of marijuana prohibition as a means to advance both personal and institutional ends.[351] In so doing he fundamentally shaped the institutional terrain of US law enforcement. In present times, the dominant narrative of police leadership and, by extension, police culture is articulated through entrepreneurship, giving rise to worries that formerly important skills like criminal investigation might have lost importance.[352] Dick Hobbs charted the habits of police entrepreneurship in great detail; one of his police informants is worth quoting at length:

> Of course I am like a businessman. Put it this way, out there you got the punters, taxpayers and regular civilians, they pay me wages and they want a service from me. Then there's the villains. For me to provide a service to the punters I nick the villains. But if I do deals with some villains I can nick those that really need nicking. So I do a deal here, a trade there, somebody goes down and I keep paying my mortgage.[353]

The public relations expert

The ability to sell is amplified by the art of public relations. Once policing agencies reach a certain size they usually include a media liaison office.[354] The PR-guru at HQ is an obvious personification of this role, but even the successful patrol officer must be able to do good 'community relations'.[355] It is several generations since the craft of PR was synthesised out of the lore of social psychology and the ad-men of Madison Avenue to create the skill set for engineering public consent, appetite and mood.[356] In a televisual society where a significant amount of political communication is undertaken via electronically mediated means, PR has become ubiquitous in corporate life. The Internet web pages of Interpol, Europol, the AFP, RCMP, FBI and the typical Big City police departments are all exercises in PR that project a legitimating image of the global policing enterprise.

Notwithstanding their sometimes crude nature, people are susceptible to police public relations exercises. For example, Peter Manning showed how 'the police funeral' functions as a moral drama in the interests of policing legitimation.[357] People are persuaded of the value of policing performances only to the extent that the performance is compelling. Police PR acts to repress and circumvent some dilemmas in policing and dramatise others. To a remarkable extent, the management of perceptions about global insecurity has shaped the contours of the global policing mission. The hidden persuaders of policing PR, perhaps more than anyone else, have marked the practices of transnational policing.[358]

The legal ace

Policing with law requires practically every agency in the policing field to have at least one legal ace in the hole.[359] Taken together, the double-edged quality of law and the creativity that legal rules allow make this role indispensable. In some jurisdictions, police departments need to have legal teams on hand to handle civil actions for malpractice.[360] Legal tools in the hands of police outsiders prompt counter-law manoeuvring from the inside. The legal ace is obviously essential in the construction of criminal prosecutions. Then too, they increasingly emphasise on disruption tactics against 'serious organised crime', so legal beagles are just as likely to be looking at ways of using civil, administrative and regulatory law as tools of disruption.[361] The legal ace is an important card in the deck of transnational policing, even if the actions recommended by actors playing this role sometimes seem questionable.[362] To cite an example from the policing of geopolitics, a legal ace can – from the comfort of his study at Harvard Law School – create a plausible reasoning on the basis of the 'ticking bomb scenario': for instance justifying intensified police interrogation or a pre-emptive lethal strike on the grounds of reasonable suspicion. The overwhelmingly political and ideological emphasis on managing law enforcement 'effectiveness' in the occupational subcultures of policing – transnational and otherwise – means that the use of legal expertise for policing is sometimes antithetical to ethically encoded norms such as due process, legality and human rights.[363] In policing law, the double-edged nature of legal rules and the uses and abuses of counter-law give pride of place to the legal ace.

The spy

Ever since Gary Marx undertook his ground-breaking work on undercover polic-ing and the use of covert techniques, the role of informant-spy has been exposed as a main player in the occupational subculture.[364] Marx's view has been that this role is a 'necessary evil' that can be regulated and controlled in order to minimise unintended consequences and individual excesses.[365] The informant-spy role is about managing secrecy and deception. The role has been normalised and deceit has become routine in policing.[366] While democratic societies may once have been extremely suspicious of secret police, they are now seen to be necessary, justifiable and indispensable.[367] In this role, police 'cut deals' with criminals and rule-breakers with the aim of longer-term law enforcement results.[368] If policing is key to governance, the rise to prominence of covert techniques may indicate something about the corrosion of character and broader civic virtues brought about as a result of subcultural work routines in policing. The initial idea of the democratic police officer was as a visible symbol of social order on the street.[369] From this view point, police spies are anathema in a democracy. However, sociologists have shown how lying, deceit and crafty persuasion are integral to social life and so it is hardly surprising to find police actors doing just that in situations and places that lie at the edges of social order.[370] From this perspective, lying and secrecy must be judged prag-matically with respect to overall social welfare. However, because most contem-porary undercover policing produces a population of suitable enemies rather than sustaining notions of the general good, this role creates insecurity.[371] The police informant, the spy and *agents provocateurs* further colour the legitimacy of an already tainted occupation.[372]

The field-operator

The field-operator is the workhorse of policing. This is where politics hits the pavement[373] and policing meets the public.[374] A range of functions may be undertaken by officers in this role. Shepherding crowds of people away from a scene of danger, perhaps during a life-threatening human stampede at a global 'mega-event', is an example of the indispensability and centrality of this role in policing. The field-operator's duties (in addition to and apart from law enforce-ment) involve securing the life and well-being of a community, institution or territory. Skilful field-operators are able to solve problems rather than simply react to them. They manage both immediate issues of public safety and aim to avert future ills. It was the virtuous field-operator whom Herman Goldstein lionised in his theory of problem-oriented policing.[375] Field-operators have been major players in multi-agency policing, neighbourhood policing and commu-nity policing experiments in many jurisdictions.[376]

Successful field-operations can manage social conflicts and harness positive pro-social impulses in the building of community.[377] When successful, the field-operator proves the claim that policing is centrally about facilitating the building up of civil society and fostering the conditions under which liberal democratic society can function.[378] The parameters placed upon policing through political use of 'war on crime' rhetoric greatly constrict this role. Indeed, because the language of crime fighting as 'real policework' is so redolent within the occupational subculture that field-operators, despite their skills, most often play a support role to the leading actor.

The enforcer

In the contemporary drama of policework, the enforcer usually takes a starring role.[379] Predicated on a firm belief in the efficacy of coercion, the enforcer maximises the assertion that the use of force is the core task of policing. In so doing, the role foreswears the caveat that the real skill in policing lies in finding ways to avoid the use of violence. The masculine attitude of the typical enforcer is clear in the words of a DEA agent describing the puny efforts of his agency against might of the drug cartels: 'think of an ant, crawling up an elephant's leg [pause] with rape on its mind.'[380] The enforcer role, in its purest manifestations, is symptomatic of a loss of contact with the complexity of reality and a tendency to grow even more reliant on the exercise of force.[381] For Kleinig, the 'crime fighting' enforcer is a punitive role, which often sees suspects treated as guilty until proven innocent or even as enemies.[382] When enforcers take the lead role, illegal and harmful practices such as the abuse of force and extra-judicial executions become more likely. In the transnational realm, it is the enforcer who is associated with kidnap and extraordinary rendition. When the idea of restraint is jettisoned, all that is left is a standing temptation to use violence first and ask questions later.[383]

Good policing is impossible when the enforcer role dominates. But because policing has been fragmented into a number of different law enforcement functions, there is scant attention paid to how it all adds up to policing for the general good. In the context of the militarisation of policing as well as a plenitude of war metaphors, the enforcer is very often centre stage in what is characterised as a fight against global crime.[384] Few subjects make more exciting television (if ultimately disturbing viewing) than scenes of riotous disturbance filmed safely from behind police lines, or of SWAT teams preparing to enter a building or of security officers (guns or tazers drawn) rushing to neutralise a misbehaving airline passenger.[385] The enforcer role-type has been normalised and is no longer seen as exceptional. The normalisation of the exceptional has consequences for the aspiration to create a culture of human rights and civil liberties in policing.[386]

The varied occupational character of global cops

This is the principal cast of characters who act out the roles of policing on the world stage and down on the local street-corner. They offer a range of adaptable styles observable within the occupational subculture of policing. They are roles, ideal-types and abstractions; real individual social agents inevitably blend these styles. They may also act 'egotistically' or in 'bad faith', or be an 'empty uniform', be 'on the take' or 'married to the job'. The list only partially captures the life of this social world but these typifications provide a vocabulary for understanding the drama of contemporary policework. While one officer may on the whole play the diplomat role, circumstances may prompt him or her to wear an entrepreneurial cloak. When it comes to illicit drugs, a particular officer might habitually adopt an enforcer role but play the role of a technician in dealing with financial investigations. The spy can easily switch to a PR role when it becomes necessary to spread dis-information in order to cover up malpractice or errors of judgment. The characteristics of the legal ace and the field-operator can be constructively blended so as to solve social problems before they manifest in social harm. The diplomat and the field-operator, together with the technician, could all be called upon in the context of community capacity building programmes.

Since police organisations are rank-structured, even when they are not paramilitarised, the resultant 'command and control' style simultaneously underpins and complexifies the subcultural aspects of the occupation.[387] Holding it all together are definitions of 'real policework', which are supported by the subculturally defined sense of mission and an emphasis on crime fighting – rather than a focus on service provision and helping people. They gain further importance because of the masculine ethos of the occupation, the so-called 'cult of masculinity'.[388] Altogether this produces a criminalised 'other'. Theories that concern the interaction between policing-controllers and criminalised-others developed by cultural criminologists provide a vocabulary for talking about labelling, folk devils, moral entrepreneurs, crime panics, suitable enemies and deviance amplification.[389] As the evolution of the terminology of transnational organised crime in the UN context shows, this new official category is a 'social construction'. The idea of transnational crime started as a somewhat vague gesture towards the activities of multi-national corporations, but a decade-and-a-half later drug cartels had become 'Public Enemy Number One'. For cultural criminologists the resulting crime wave reportage, 'moral panic' and 'deviancy amplification' were all predictable.[390]

This critical perspective on policing suggests that the apparent functional logic of policing – there are bad people who do bad things and therefore we need 'the police' to go after them – disguises a deeper logic concerning a more general crisis of social order. Policing-related panics can be read as symptomatic of a wider crisis of hegemony.[391] The insecurity discourse of global policing is not so much a response to real problems but rather indicates a generalised cultural crisis resulting from factors such as unemployment, racial tension and economic inequality. In the febrile political atmosphere of so-called post-modern or late-modern age the global projection of a cast of 'suitable enemies' serves as an ideological smokescreen. While not fully subscribing to the theory of false consciousness, we see the interaction between policing subcultures and their objects as critically important in shaping the confines of the global system. The Manichean world-view of good-guys and bad-guys forms the staple of the common-sense understanding of cop culture. This world-view tends to reinforce a global sense of insecurity and props up the notion that the transnational-state-system can containerize security.

Global policing, subculture and accountability

The significance of the occupational subculture in shaping global policing becomes clear when it is placed in the context of the relationship between policing and other institutions of governance. It is through democratic mechanisms of accountability and control that policing practice becomes responsive to public welfare concerns and the general social good. Gauging the extent of officers' autonomy in the transnational realm is therefore crucial to understanding how subcultural norms and values fill the transnational space within which policing decisions are taken. As we discussed in Chapter 2, the laws governing policework are permissive and much policework takes places in a context of wide discretion and low visibility.[392] In this context, there is 'considerable leeway for police culture and the social and situational pressures on officers to shape police practice'.[393] The question: 'how far should the police be independent from direct political control?' is a staple of liberal democratic thinking.[394] Philip Stenning argues that 'there is very little clarity or consensus [...] about exactly what 'police independence' comprises or about its practical implications' and this lack of clarity about the political answerability of democratic policing can be found internationally.[395] According to Kent Roach, '[t]he idea that the police are a law unto themselves is unacceptable in a democracy', but the thought that police can be 'directed by the government of the day [...] raises concerns about improper partisanship'.[396]

Conventional legal positivist accounts of the governance of the police start with the contention that the police should, first and foremost, be accountable to the 'law of the land'.[397] The kinds of law are many, but include the substantive criminal law that defines specific behaviours as crimes which therefore become the objects of policing. Formally, the police are permitted to act in ways that intrude into an individual's liberty or use coercion if there is 'reasonable suspicion' that a criminal act has been or is going to be committed. Procedural law – also known as criminal procedure – sets out a framework within which the criminal law may be enforced, specifying the rules under which police may arrest, how long they may hold a person in custody, the rules for interview, interrogation, etc. Formal legal institutions – such as the criminal courts, the office of the prosecutor, attorney general, etc. – all play a role in policing the police, that is seeking to ensure that the police abide by the rules and do not act beyond their powers. The civil law also plays a role since police actions going beyond what is permitted by law – abuse of force, wrongful arrest, etc. – are torts for which citizens might seek compensation in the civil courts. Instance of gross misconduct by the police can of course lead the police to be subject to the full force of the criminal law (although it is rare for police to be convicted of wrongful acts committed in the course of their duty). The problems in translating the language of police accountability articulated in the domestic sphere into the field of transnational policing become obvious immediately – if police acting beyond national boundaries are to be accountable to the law of the land, one might ask: 'which land is that?'

A mechanism of accountability, articulated more or less strongly in different places, is some form of *democratically* elected political authority. Seeking to ensure that the police are properly accountable to the law, political figures of various sorts – elected politicians such as a government minister play a political role in holding the police to account. In the UK, for example, the home secretary is the most powerful figure in setting police priorities and has the greatest control over law enforcement budgets. In other countries, similar powers are held by ministers of national security or of justice. In federally decentralised systems, such as the USA, political figures holding the police to account include state governors or the mayors of big cities to whom such forces as New Jersey State Troopers or New York Police Department are accountable. The tensions between politics and law come into clear view and are resolved in a variety of different ways – in some places, elected representatives have the power to hire and fire police chiefs, while in other jurisdictions, the police are insulated from direct political control.

Roach identified four ideal-type models of police–government relations.[398] First, full police independence, in which the police are immune from government intervention on a wide variety of matters, including things like the policing of political demonstrations. Second, quasi-judicial police independence, which restricts police independence to the process of criminal investigation. Third, democratic policing, which restricts police independence but places greater emphasis on the responsible minister's accountability and control over policy matters in policing. Fourth, governmental policing, which minimises both the ambit of police independence and accepts the greater role of central agencies in coordinating government services including policing.[399] Scholars in this area have drawn a distinction between accountability and control of the police. According to Geoffrey Marshall, police accountability may either be 'subordinate and obedient' or 'explanatory and co-operative' to governing authority.[400] While accountability of the subordinate and obedient variety shades over into control, the latter clearly aims at ensuring that police agents act (or refrain from acting) in specified ways, regardless of expectations to give accounts after the fact.

In all of these debates, both 'the police' and 'the government' are implicitly conceived of as unitary and monolithic. We have already shown (in Chapter 3) that the policing field is a fragmented institutional terrain, broken up into a complex division of policing labour, and (in Chapter 2) that the transnational-state-system is disaggregated and polycentric. One answer to the dilemmas posed by the fragmentation of the policing field is the idea of 'policing commissions' that could hold all providers of *policing*, rather then just 'the police', to account. This idea has yet to be put into practice and we doubt that it will be effective in the field of transnational policing. Our doubt arises at least partly because of the observable influence of paramilitary and security imperatives in policing subcultural discourse that provide considerable cover of secrecy.[401] Nevertheless it is widely understood that, in order to govern policing and security institutions and to safeguard the public interest, states should regulate, audit, facilitate, influence and control action across the wider field of policing and not just with respect to blue uniformed police.[402] Advocates of this perspective also foreground the interests of relatively weak social actors in the constitution of nodal policing.[403]

In addition to the most formal mechanisms of accountability to the law and to a democratically elected political authority, a range of other institutions and processes are employed to hold the police to account. In some places, independent bodies have a role in investigating complaints against the police – such as the Independent Police Complaints Commission in London or the Northern Ireland Ombudsman's Office. In many countries there are also neighbourhood-based monitoring organisations – such as Community Police Consultative Committees or Civilian Review Boards – which have a role in ensuring that police act in ways that are acceptable to local communities and meet their expectations. Other kinds of 'soft' mechanisms for policing the police include the role of investigative journalists, police monitoring groups, human rights associations and so on.

Some scholars argue that the police reporting systems arising from the new information technologies have created conditions for enhanced police accountability. Use of force and other critical incident reporting systems together with CCTV surveillance, early warning and early intervention systems have improved the capacity of police organisations to scope officer conduct and for ordinary citizens to carry out *sousveillance* of police misconduct. Together with accessible citizen complaint procedures and structures for civilian oversight, these surveillance mechanisms arguably provide powerful tools for enhancing individual officer accountability, unit accountability and overall organisational accountability.

And yet, reflecting on the difficulties of bringing the tens of thousands of public police agencies in the USA to systematic account, Sam Walker observed that:

> Candor requires that we emphasise the *promise* of the new accountability, as distinct from an achieved reality. By the prevailing standards of social science research there is only limited evidence that the tools and strategies described ... in fact achieve their intended goals.[404]

Obviously devices such as digital cameras, mobile phones, and voice recorders enable greater visibility of interactions between police and members of the public. The tragic death of Ian Tomlinson (a passerby at the G20 protest in London in September 2009) at the hands of a police officer was broadcast over the Internet. This was not only surveillance footage obtained from public security CCTV cameras, but from the moving images of the events captured by members of the public on their own handheld devices. While some incidents of officer wrongdoing are brought to public attention in this fashion, at the same time police officers and police agencies in advanced technological societies also use the ubiquity of video surveillance as defensive measures in managing the threat of attacks on police officers as well as to manage citizen criticisms and complaints about officer conduct.

Thomas Mathiesen has made the theoretical distinction between *panoptic* power (where the few overlook the many) and *synoptic* power (where the many overlook the few). In a society where the power of surveillance is the power of the watcher over the watched, both panoptic and synoptic surveillance forms will likely converge along the lines of master statuses concerning gender, class, ethnicity, age and the like; meaning that surveillance power tends to recreate existing social hierarchies.[405] Like law, the 'technological fix' is a double-edged sword. We concur with Walker that it is not certain that it can provide the mechanism for maintaining public confidence in the policing system.[406]

The governance of the policing field is dwarfed by the complexity of the governmental field more generally, especially when looked at in a global context. Ideas that protect seigneurial states' interests tend to dominate political institutions of the world system, while populations grounded in weak, failing or failed states are particularly vulnerable. The theory developed here side-steps the 'sovereignty trap' in thinking about the current evolution of policing power within the global system. Under conditions of transnationalisation, conceptions of sovereignty and law have become fluid. The transnational-state-system is polycentric and the states that comprise it are disaggregated into a variety of sites of institutionalised power. Since the police were the keystone of the nation-state-system symbolically representing sovereignty, the transnational subculture that has grew up among ILOs prompted Bigo to acclaim that national sovereignty has become a myth.[407]

Writing in the mid-1990s Malcolm Anderson was sceptical that the problem of governing transnational policing could be attended to through strict adherence to the principle of national sovereignty (defined in terms of the 'law of the land'). In an age of advanced communication technologies he argued that it had become anachronistic to think that central governments could police the police because the speed of communication made it impossible for states to maintain a *monopoly of information*.[408] Where policing resources are fragmented, nationally-based central authorities cannot dominate all external relations. In places where there is limited governmental capacity – in so-called failed states, oceans, cyberspace and border zones – state sovereignty is difficult, if not impossible, to assert in any meaningful way. An open market in policing information, according to Anderson, 'represents an erosion of sovereignty and control, unacceptable to virtually all the advanced industrial democracies.'[409] At the millennium, the transnational subculture of policing had gained more than relative bureaucratic autonomy from the state. Taking into account that at least half of the global policing field is, in one way or another, privatised, the degree of autonomy that agents in the policing field have must also be reckoned in terms of market relations.

Political scientists are apt to provide solutions to these problems that emphasise different forms of qualified centralisation/decentralisation in policing control.[410] From a socio-legal standpoint this emphasis on pragmatic regulation is problematic. Even in the limited sense of beat cops studied by the classic police subcultural theorists, empirical evidence showed clearly their wide *operational discretion* in invoking the law. Understanding *why* and *how* policing agents act requires, therefore, an understanding of police subculture – the recipes for action, rhetorical forms of 'real policework' and the lexicon of 'suitable enemies' that articulate it.[411] The sociology of policing has recognised the phenomenon of rule *with law* for a long time, but in an era when the idea of the sovereign state has been thoroughly transgressed under the pressure of globalisation, the ability to rule with law belongs to those who occupy central sites of policing power in a polycentric global system. The transnational subculture of policing has been (or is in the process of being) cut loose from the systems of legal sovereignty that initially gave rise to the idea of the police institution. Through the global interactions emanating from within the subculture of transnational policing, the language of 'suitable enemies' has come to dominate discourses of security.[412] In our view, this is a formula for bad policing and fosters insecurity. The security–control paradox hides behind the fiction of national security interests, which are predicated on obsolete notions of national sovereignty. The language of national security amplifies worries about the official folk devils, which are themselves socially constructed within the subcultural world of policing and through the interaction of that subculture with the wider society around it.

Looked at from the perspective of the global system, policing organisations enjoy differences in their degree of independence from institutions of governance but the main actors in the occupational subculture inhabiting those

institutions largely write their own script. The expectation that formal democratic mechanisms of accountability and control can make policing practice
reflect public welfare concerns and uphold notions of the general social good is
exceptionally difficult to fulfil. In the heat of insecurity discourse, one impul-
sive reaction is to either license some punitive Hobbesian Leviathan or to
embrace a primitive punitive populism. The tug-of-war between these two
impulses is just the sort of situation we described in Chapter 1 as a 'Machiavellian
moment'. The beginning of the 21st century is a historical point at which the
dissolution of one social system (the nation-state-system) gives over to the possibility of a new system of social power (a global society) – the tensions thus
created give rise to the opportunity for a power grab. The ideas and practices of
the transnational-state-system are dominating the historical moment of which
policing agents are the primary bearers. All of which prompts us to ask: what is
going on behind the mythology of national sovereignty and the façade of folk
devils, and who benefits?

Conclusion: occupational policing subcultures – global thoughts/local acts

Figuratively speaking, the global policing architecture – designed and built
largely by police – houses the rapidly developing subculture of transnational
policing. The policing script gains general cultural currency by virtue of successful truth claims about the nature of threats, risks and harms broadcast globally
through television news and entertainment media. We have explained the roles
played out in the drama of policing from the local precinct to the global beat
and how the closed social world of the police occupational subculture has been
transnationalised. Multiple vertical and horizontal networks configure global
policing and act to shore up the transnational-state-system. This default pattern
arises from two structural principles: functional diversity and jurisdictional
sovereignty.

The hubs of global policing constitute the backbone of global governance, a
polycentric power system with a myriad of policing tasks spread across a patchwork quilt of imagined sovereign jurisdictions. The script of global policing
accounts for the security–control paradox: the pervasive sense of insecurity that
exists *amid, in spite of* and sometimes *because* of the multiplying of tactics for
ensuring security.

Each member of the cast of policing character-types described in this chapter
plays a specific role in the theatre of police operations. Technicians capture and
disseminate knowledge of suspect populations and manufacture images of official targets on that basis. Entrepreneurs sell the discourse and practices of security, sometimes using fear to do so, further amplifying insecurity. Shaping the

transnational drama of global policing is the public relations expert who, in vocalising the 'police mission', provides a compelling rhetoric of legitimation that forms perceptions of global insecurity. The legal ace provides an essential skill-set for ruling with law, but it is a form of rule already scripted by a set of taken for granted dualistic assumptions built around the pursuit of the bad guy. Thus the legal ace can be found deploying law to normalise exceptional practice, even when paradoxically those practices run counter to espoused norms such as due process and the protection of fundamental human rights and freedoms. This corrodes trust, but few practices are more productive of insecurity than those associated with the increasingly prominent role of the informant-spy in the policing occupation. Democratic police are important symbols of order and therefore routinising forms of deception inherent in espionage into policework is bound to be corrosive of a broad culture of civic virtue. Peaceful communities must be based on trust, but undercover operatives and secret informers rely on deception and therefore betrayal. The enforcer is most often centre stage in the drama of policing. No policing role more clearly projects the core occupational cultural expectations – the play of cops and robbers, good guys and bad guys – better than this one. This role is also most susceptible to the invitational edge of paramilitarism and therefore the use of deadly force, extrajudicial execution, illegal rendition and torture.

Lest we be accused of undue pessimism, we should say that the subcultural drama of policing can be shifted. Among the available role-types the diplomat and the field-operator offer the greatest promise. The diplomat has a wide skill-set and the ability to see things reflexively from others' points of view. The field-operator has skills including the ability to think creatively and solve problems. If the language of global policing was not so fixated on rounding up the usual suspects then, instead of acting out a script as supporting actors to the enforcer's lead, more imaginative problem solving could perhaps be developed. The language of suitable enemies arises out of the interaction between active agents within the occupational subcultures of policing and receptive audiences. These interactions are shaped by the politics of global policing accountability that define the transnational-state-system and shape the global social order. In this chapter we have introduced the characters who animate policing occupational subculture and showed how they play their parts. Our final task is to describe and explain what transnational policing looks like in practice 'on the ground'.

5

GLOBAL POLICING IN PRACTICE

Having set out a theory of global policing, its architecture and occupational subculture, this chapter examines policing in practice and looks in detail at its effects on the ground. We have observed that policing is shaped by jurisdictional sovereignty and functional diversity and that policework involves the control of territory and the surveillance of suspect populations. The theory pursued here delineates the boundaries of the global policing field distinguishing between 'high' and 'low' policing and 'public' and 'private' security. This perspective challenges taken for granted assumptions about 'national sovereignty', the conceptual glue of the transnational-state-system. Here we provide an analysis of the transnational policing of territory and global flows.

Among the many interesting objects of territorial policing, we have chosen four – borders, oceans, cyberspace and mega-events – to illustrate our more general theoretical claims. In terms of flows, several objects for policing stand out as useful illustrations of our theory: people, money, drugs and weapons. In all cases, our goal is to derive an understanding of global policing as a set of practices in order to reach some normative conclusions. In one final example we look at policing humanitarian assistance in a so-called failed state, which shows how the policing of territory and flows manufactures the conditions of the 'global south' in the 'global north' and creates black holes in the world system. We retain the term policing (rather than law enforcement) because it captures the normative meaning inherent in the science of police and extend the dramaturgical metaphor developed in the previous chapter to show how the transnational cast of policing characters interact.

Policing transnational spaces

Police secure territory in a number of ways (see Figure 1.1). Patrolling on foot and in vehicles is the traditional 'backbone' of policing and is intrinsically concerned with control of the ground. Static guarding outside critical national infrastructure, 'access control' for buildings, transport hubs such as railways, ports and airports are all examples of the police role in defending places. Territorial policing is also backed up by defensive technologies including locks, bolts and walls and in some places fences backed with electricity and razor wire, armed guards and watchtowers stretch for hundreds of miles. Not all the spaces that the police seek to patrol can be conceived of as sovereign territory. Most obviously, international waters, airspace, cyberspace and outer space are beyond the control of any single nation-state, although attempts have been made by seigneurial states to claim control over them. Some places – border zones, airports and other ports-of-entry – take on a transnational quality as travellers move through the liminal space of the departure lounge. Other places become transnational at specific moments, such as the locations of 'mega-events' where states' claims to the domestic monopoly of coercive force are temporarily overridden. These transnational spaces create special problems and possibilities for policing.

Policing border zones

The border is often conceived of as a thin line on a map that separates nationally sovereign territories. People who cross borders have become accustomed to a variety of technologies of control as they encounter police, immigration, customs and private security. The frontier border zone has been likened to a complex filtration system.[413] It is there to select, eject and immobilise.[414] What Karine Côté-Boucher calls a 'smart border' extends inside and outside sovereign territory, as well as being a strict line of demarcation. The border is constituted through a diverse array of legal, administrative and technological procedures such as refugee containment, counter-terrorism and information sharing. Forward intelligence gathering by police, customs and immigration officials 'outside' the sovereign jurisdiction combined with the practical ability to use surveillance and coercive powers 'within' provide depth to the frontier region. This diffuse border is constituted by policing technicians for enforcement purposes; its fluid control measures are based on information and communication technologies, but also include coercive facilities such as detention centres, prisons and other forms of confinement.[415] Figure 5.1 illustrates the diffuse border with layers of external, boundary and internal controls.[416]

In some places, border zones constitute containment areas, known as 'growth triangles' or 'export processing zones'. The *Malquiladoras* along the US–Mexico border show how zoning technologies formalise economic and political action at specific scales across national borders.[417] Policing practices provide the mechanisms for creating or accommodating an archipelago of distinct islands

GLOBAL SURVEILLANCE AND ENFORCEMENT				
Carriers' liability	Harmonisation of asylum policy	European border agency	Interpol travel documents database	Fugitive apprehension squads
PRE-ENTRY CONTROLS				
Immigration liaison officers	Extraterritorial borders control		Watch lists/No fly lists	Pre-entry clearance
	Border posts	Border patrols	Fences	
BORDER PROTECTION				
Immigration officers	Customs	Serious Organised Crime Agency	Special Branch	Military
IN-COUNTRY ENFORCEMENT				
Immigration service enforcement	Police enforcement	Joint snatch-squads	Special Branch	Private security
Employer sanctions	Entitlement cards		University student surveillance	Public 'dob in' hotlines
DIFFUSE LOCAL SURVEILLANCE				

Figure 5.1   The diffuse border

Source: Weber and Bowling (2004) see fn 416

of 'governance within', generating a pattern of variegated but linked sovereignty. This archipelago is an important interstitial space within the frontier border zone constituting 'free enterprise areas' within the transnational-state-system. In areas along the US–Mexico border there has been a notable failure to consolidate peaceful social order in the spaces surrounding the *maquila* industry giving rise to a variety of 'security practices' by private actors and moral entrepreneurs.[418]

Another example is the Sijori triangle between Singapore, Indonesia and Malaysia. Mainly funded by government-linked Singaporean corporations and Indonesian conglomerates based in Jakarta, the Sijori enclave excluded local populations who had lived on the territory for generations. The triangle surround is a reconfigured frontier characterised by squatter housing, prostitution, crime and general community disintegration that came into existence after an influx of people in search of jobs overwhelmed local governance capacity. This entailed the formation of new boundaries within Indonesia. The simultaneous development of manufacturing and tourist resort expansion attracted mass migration from across the region resulting in a sharp segregation of industrial parks and tourist compounds. Housing developments sheltered in a 'landscaped biome' were developed for managerial and professional elites commuting from Singapore and visiting tourists. Shantytown was for the destitute labourers working in the industrial park. Techno-enforcement, in the form of security checkpoints and armed guards, divided the 'haves' from the 'have-nots'.[419]

The Sijori triangle and the *Malquiladoras* are examples of more general features of the frontier border zones of the global system. Like the infamous Sangatte refugee camp near Calais these 'abject spaces' demonstrate how transnational policing *grounds* population flows.[420] From a political science viewpoint, this is a 'border game' played on the assumed basis of the Westphalian doctrine of national sovereignty (see Chapter 2). High policing rhetoric leads to secrecy about border policing, which is normalised on the basis of the dramatic assumption of danger. The results can be fatal, as in the case of Robert Dziekanski who was killed by a police taser in Vancouver International Airport on 14 October 2007.[421] In a globalising world, the logic of border control also has to be sold. It is the product of entrepreneurship. As Peter Andreas has observed, a US advertising agency coined a catchy slogan to recruit border guards: 'A career with borders, but no boundaries.'[422]

Policing the oceans

Attempts to exert sovereignty over the oceans extend back to early modernity. The 1703 Hague Convention declared that a nation should be sovereign over those waters that it could defend from shore, defined as the distance reachable by cannon – which was then 3 miles.[423] The history of the Law of the Sea illustrates the slow accretion of individual states' territorial claims overlapping with the extension of multi-lateral attempts to govern the oceans. Neither the assertion of sovereign states' territorial claims over the maritime environment, nor more recognisably supranational efforts have been successful in creating a comprehensive system of oceanic policing. In a well functioning world system, the oceanic ecosphere would be policed on the understanding that it is a global commons.[424] Instead, the global maritime 'security agenda' is symptomatic of the tension and conflicts inherent in the transnational-state-system.[425]

Contemporary maritime policing is rooted historically in attempts to control piracy, slavery and smuggling.[426] Following abolition of the transatlantic slave trade in 1807, Britain signed numerous bilateral treaties to suppress trafficking and eventually a relatively weak treaty among the 'great powers' of Europe was agreed in 1815. Following the rejection of a British proposal in 1818 for a multilateral treaty, Britain made bilateral treaties, starting with Portugal, to accord a carefully limited reciprocal right of 'visitation' (the maritime term for stop and search) of ships suspected of carrying slaves. With the signing of the Quintuple Treaty for the suppression of the African Slave Trade in 1841, slave trafficking was declared a crime of piracy subject to universal jurisdiction under customary international law, which European powers had previously agreed on. Not until the 1862 Washington Treaty was a mutual right of interdiction agreed. Until then, the USA opposed a non-treaty right of visitation so many slave traders would hoist the American flag when confronted by the British navy. The essential choice was then, and still is today, between a system of law *above* individual states and a system of law *between* states. In the main, contemporary policing of the high seas is based on bilateral treaty arrangements that secure the interests of seigneurial states.

The 1982 UN Convention of the Law of the Sea (UNCLOS) created the contemporary framework for multi-lateral maritime policing including responses to crimes at sea such as piracy, armed robbery, illicit traffic in drugs, guns and ammunition and weapons of mass destruction.[427] It codified 'territorial waters', over which the coastal-state has full sovereign rights, at 12 nautical miles, beyond which are the high seas which are 'open' to all ships without hindrance.[428] Ships may travel through territorial waters on 'innocent passage' where they are subject to the enforcement powers of police marine sections and coastguards.

In some countries – such as the UK – the coastguard is a civil force concerned largely with search and rescue but also with enforcement of maritime laws concerning pollution, port security and the safety of navigation. In other countries, the coastguard is a military agency. For example the US Coast Guard (USCG) is a branch of the United States Armed Forces, which answers to the Department of Homeland Security during peacetime, but which is considered part of the Navy during wartime. During the earlier years of the 20th century a major task for the USCG related to enforcing laws against alcohol smuggling in near waters. Today the USCG is an important player in counter-drug trafficking operations and maritime law enforcement in extended US coastal waters.

Flag state jurisdiction applies on the high seas.[429] This means that outside territorial waters, coastguards and naval ships may ordinarily stop and search only those vessels registered in the state flying their own national flag.[430] A ship may be forcibly boarded on the high seas under article 110 of UNCLOS if it is reasonably suspected of engaging in piracy or the slave trade, broadcasting illegally or lacking a flag. The 'flag state' can grant permission to foreign coastguards to search suspicious vessels through assigned duty officers where bilateral security agreements exist (see below).[431] The power of visitation on the high seas cannot be enforced by most countries since their boats are only suitable for coastal waters. Only the police, coastguards and naval forces of powerful seigneurial states have the capacity to undertake extensive policing on the high seas.

Maritime drug enforcement

US drug law enforcement has transformed maritime policing since the 1970s when drugs first became an issue in the Caribbean and in the countries of Central and South America. From that time, the war on drugs brought interdiction efforts to areas further away from the USA and closer to foreign coasts.[432] The 1980 US Comprehensive Drug Abuse Control and Prevention Act created a new legal basis for high seas interdiction. It drew on previously existing US bilateral arrangements originally related to policing alcohol prohibition, thereby effectively ruling with law by re-tooling a historically obsolete legal instrument.[433] Under this Act, US Customs Officers and Coast Guards may board any vessel within US customs waters to conduct a search using force where necessary.[434] The term 'customs waters' refers to jurisdiction over any vessel flying the flag of a foreign government with whom they have a bilateral arrangement.[435] In the wake of the new Act, a treaty was signed with the UK to permit US authorities to board British vessels in search for drugs in a vast area of sea comprising the Gulf of Mexico, the Caribbean Sea, the Atlantic Ocean west of longitude 55° West and south of latitude 30° North and everywhere within 150 miles of the Atlantic coast of the United States.[436] Essentially the USA staked out a territorial claim over the massive area of the Atlantic Ocean projecting its 'third border'. Vessels and property seized in this area can be labelled criminal assets and forfeited to US authorities, and the crew can be expeditiously rendered to the US in order to stand trial. This is a significant departure from the customary rule that jurisdiction follows the flag on the high seas. As Siddle points out, 'there is no *quid pro quo* for the new agreement, beyond the satisfaction for the British Government that it is protecting the good name of the British flag and co-operating in the suppression of a trade which is part of a universal problem'.[437]

In international waters the discretionary power of USCG and Navy captains licenses the use of force. In 1990 the US Coast Guard cutter *Chinconteague* chased a Cuban owned but Panamanian registered freighter *The Hermann* for 24 hours before opening fire causing significant damage to the vessel but failing to stop it. At port, Mexican officials conducted the search at the request of US officials but reported to have found no contraband. Diplomatic complaints from the Cuban government about the use of force on a vessel in international waters were defended as 'legal law enforcement activity' by then Secretary of State James Baker III.[438] The US frequently searches vessels in international waters, sometimes with the use or threat of armed force including 'sharp-shooters on helicopters to disable the engines of drug smugglers' boats with rifle fire'.[439]

The main legal tools enabling transnational maritime policing are the 'shiprider agreements'. These legal understandings extend the sovereign powers of seigneurial states into new waters. The US has 30 such agreements, including one with the government of the UK relating to the waters of the Caribbean and Bermuda and one with China for the purposes of fisheries protection. These bilateral treaty arrangements give US officials – a designated Law Enforcement Detachment (LED) or 'shiprider' – powers to embark on the vessels of the signatory country to assist in boarding suspect vessels, to enforce the country's laws and enforce US law outside territorial waters. These treaties also allow the partner state to designate its own 'shiprider' to travel on US vessels for the purposes of authorising pursuit, search and seizure of vessels flying the partner's flag in territorial waters and allow US ships to enter the signatory state's territorial waters to investigate, board and search suspect vessels. In the Caribbean region, where the shiprider policy has been pursued most aggressively, this 'gives the US primary jurisdiction on the high seas and contingent jurisdiction in a country's territorial waters', which has been identified by post-colonial theorists as an exercise in imperialism.[440] This use of law has effectively made the Gulf of Mexico and the Caribbean Sea into an American lake.

So committed was Britain to the public relations aspects of the Caribbean drug war that it deployed Prince William, the future King, in the 'front-line against the Caribbean drug barons'.[441] Two days into his tour of duty as a Royal Navy officer on HMS *Iron Duke*, Sub-lieutenant Wales was involved in a complex transnational maritime policing operation with the UK SOCA, the Maritime Analysis Operation Centre in Lisbon and Shipriders from the USCG.[442] Under the shiprider agreement, HMS *Iron Duke* and its crew were empowered to enforce the US laws in international waters.[443] The operation was reportedly triggered by US intelligence that a 'go-fast' smuggling boat was heading across the Atlantic bound for Europe or North Africa.[444] The Navy spent five days tracking the vessel until it was spotted by a Royal Marine sniper in a Lynx helicopter, several hundred miles northeast of Barbados in poor condition and stationary. The US Coast Guard boarded the boat, arrested five people and seized 45 bales of cocaine weighing 900 kg with an estimated street value of £40 million.[445] The suspects were transported to the USA to face drugs trafficking charges.

Policing piracy

Shiprider is now advocated as the solution to the problems of policing piracy off the coast of East Africa by the United Nations Office on Drug Control and Crime (UNDOC). Its Executive Director, Antonio Maria Costa, said:

> ideally, suspects should be tried in the country where they came from, or in the country that owns the seized ship, but the Somali criminal justice system has collapsed, and countries like Liberia, Panama and the Marshall Islands – where many of the ships are registered – do not want to deal with crimes committed thousands of miles away.

The shiprider agreements being considered were to allow policing agents from, for example, Djibouti, Kenya, Tanzania or Yemen, to join a warship off the Somali coast, arrest 'the pirate' in the name of their country and have them sent to their national court for trial. This fascinating development raises an interesting question. Piracy on the high seas is subject to universal jurisdiction due to its *jus cogens* (the obligation of everyone) and *erga omnes* (a principle which is universal and non derogable) and therefore all nations of the world could potentially be called upon to police it. This raises the question of what, if anything, limits universal jurisdiction in policing piracy? Perhaps those accused of piracy are fair game for any state capable of projecting naval power into the high seas.

The anti-piracy police operations in the Gulf of Aden are kindred to humanitarian missions in broken, failed or failing states. These operations are subject to counter claims, in that some Somalis believed that those labelled 'pirates' were more akin to a national coast guard and customs agency, acting to stop illegal fishing and toxic waste dumping in territorial waters and to exact customs duties. Those claims were projected as doubtful in Western media, but were not baseless. Toxic waste dumping around the coast of Africa – both by illegal Mafia-type organisations and by legal corporate ventures – is well documented (although not widely advertised).[446] The only people who had sought physically to stop this dumping were so-called Somali pirates. The 'taxation practices' may have looked rather like blood and booty, but there was also clear evidence that these same people – former fishermen whose livelihood had been taken away by intensive offshore commercial fishing – had in fact acted to prevent over-fishing and illegal dumping. Indeed, some of the vessels being protected from pirates by the rich world's policing operation in the Gulf of Aden might have been there to fish illegally or dump toxic waste. Little attempt has been made to identify and stop them.[447]

Policing fish

Over-fishing in the North Atlantic exemplifies the failure adequately to police the maritime environment in a global system dominated by notional concerns about sovereign states' interests. Cod fishing in the Atlantic, for example, escalated drastically from an annual average of 250,000 tons (which had been maintained from 1900 to 1960) to 600,000 tons in 1965 and then 800,000 tons by 1970. In this instance, the policing responsibility cannot be adequately undertaken on the basis of the extension of state sovereignty using the 200 mile limit, nor has it been possible to engineer an effective multi-lateral and transnational policing effort for region as a whole. This 'tragedy of the commons' could potentially be overcome by action from global institutions but so far they have not.[448] In 2007 UN Deputy-Secretary General Dr Asha-Rose Migiro said that while progress had been made towards securing the goals of the UNCLOS, implementation of some of its provisions had lagged behind.[449] According to her, '[t]he world's fisheries continue to be depleted [and the] marine environment continues to be degraded by pollution from various sources, including pressure from growing coastal populations and climate change'.[450]

Crimes such as piracy on the high seas makes the headlines and displace common understanding of broader security issues such as the safety of navigation, oil tanker and platform safety, transport of dangerous goods by sea, places of refuge for ships needing assistance and for persons rescued at sea, and the balance between maritime security and the freedom of movement of seafarers. Other maritime security issues, such as the resolution of territorial boundary disputes, rival claims to resources of the seabed, marine environment conservation and maritime military conflict are also crowded out. Sometimes events bring these other issues to light in dramatic fashion.

Policing deepwater oil drilling and exploitation of the seabed

In 2010 the *Deepwater Horizon* disaster made the front covers of *Time*, *Newsweek* and *National Geographic* as the world's worst maritime oil-platform catastrophe since 1988 when the *Piper Alpha* caught fire and exploded killing 167 workers in UK waters of the North Sea.[451] The *Deepwater Horizon* explosion killed 11 people and eventually spilled an estimated five million barrels of oil over an area of approximately 5000 square miles. It quickly came to light that for many years the regulations governing petroleum exploration, production and transportation in the Gulf of Mexico had been progressively loosened by the US government. British Petroleum's deep water drilling operations received a 'categorical exclusion' allowing for 'expedited oil and gas drilling' without an environmental impact study or risk assessment. Lax regulation led to bad drilling practices. The three transnational corporations involved in the venture – BP, which owned the well; Transocean, which owned the rig; and Halliburton, which made the cement casing for the well – ignored test results available in the hours before the explosion that indicated faulty safety equipment.[452] *Deepwater Horizon* was a significant public relations failure for BP but was less so for its American partners in the drilling venture.

Close study of the policing of maritime resource extraction reveals a lack of field-operators with regulatory and enforcement powers with teeth. This is the opposite of the case with policing powers concerned with smuggling, shipping and drug enforcement. Rather than field-operators who are problem solvers and forward thinkers dedicated to preserving a state of prosperity, the high seas and territorial waters of the world are policed by enforcer-technicians dedicated only to limited law enforcement goals. Like fisheries protection, efforts in policing resource extraction are symbolically outweighed by policing piracy and drug smuggling. This pattern echoes the subcultural values of the enforcement operatives best placed to manufacture news about maritime policing.

Policing cyberspace

Cyberspace is intrinsically transnational. The network of computers that comprise it, the creators of its content, its financiers, distributors and consumers may be located anywhere in the world and can interact in their millions simultaneously. These 'new social spaces' challenge our thinking about global policing.[453] Since net-crimes may transgress national boundaries, the implications for territorially based rules, enforcement jurisdiction and regulation were recognised to be problematic early on. The lack of congruence of social mores and criminal offences in different countries posed the problem described by Grabosky and Smith:

> Images, ideas and practices regarded as perfectly acceptable in one place may be regarded as heinous in another. The authorities in one jurisdiction who are untroubled by electronic depictions of nudity, the works of Salman Rushdie, or the virtues of Tibetan independence, are unlikely to expend much time and effort in assisting the authorities in those jurisdictions who are offended by such content.[454]

Nevertheless a catalogue of work for criminal law enforcement was quickly identified: illegal interception of telecommunications; electronic vandalism and terrorism; stealing telecommunications services; telecommunications piracy; pornography and other offensive content; telemarketing fraud; electronic fund transfer crime; electronic money laundering; and the use of telecommunications in the furtherance of criminal conspiracies. The language of 'cybercrime' was symptomatic of a worldwide set of problems common for criminal investigators, prosecutors, and judges. A new vocabulary appeared: botnets, cam-girls, cyberfraud, online gambling, hacktivism, phishing, spyware, trojans, worms, zombie computers and much else. These echoed in the vocabulary of control-speak: technocops or cyber-samurai are engaged in cyberveillance, cryptography, data-mining, logical security, polling, sniffing and sweeping.[455] The public–private partnerships of forensic cyberveillant policing precisely mirror the transnational world of cybercrime and deviance revealing a paradoxical tendency to think in terms of the territorial presuppositions of the transnational-state-system.

The control narrative of the Internet has an intensely individual focus. Policing cyberspace operates through a narrative that shapes actors' awareness and expectation about the ongoing possibility of monitoring and surveillance by diverse audiences for various purposes.[456] By combining fear and control in reflexive virtual communication through, for example, mass media announcements of police success in cyber-operations, the control narrative regulates and controls Internet users. Police operations involving surveillance, deception and entrapment in 'Internet stings' are further examples of such practices.[457] These are not bound by concerns about sovereign state jurisdiction since the 'generative internet' technologically transcends the transnational-state-system (witness the 'Wikileaks effect' and the use of 'new social media' during popular uprisings in Tunisia, Egypt, Lebanon and Libya in 2010–11).[458] Failed attempts to impose territoriality are a recurrent feature of cybercrime policing discourse.

The Great Australian Cyberwall of 2009 is a good example. During a profound moral panic about 'cyberporn', a secret 'black-list' of websites banned by the government and a filtering system capable of preventing access to them from within Australia was exposed in the media. The efficacy and purpose of this censorship was called into question when it emerged that some of the banned sites were innocuous, that there was no mechanism for finding out which sites were on the 'black-list', nor was there a way of requesting removal in the event of an error. Techno-control was so unsophisticated and weak that even high-school students had the computer skills needed to evade them. When neighbouring countries were found to be using similar technology to block local access to news coverage concerning Australian citizens imprisoned in South East Asian jails on drugs offences, the federal government's alliance with web-censorship was likened to 'democracy getting into bed with a loaded gun'.[459] Over-heated rhetoric aside, the Great Australian Cyberwall was by no means a unique attempt to deploy the principle of territoriality as the basis for policing cyberspace.[460]

A significant proportion of cyberspace is outside national control in corporate or other private hands, so the appropriateness and efficacy of policing actions that presuppose, and seem to require, an idea of national sovereignty as conceived in the early modern period are shown in stark relief. In this context, presumptions about the sovereign territorial basis of authority still found in the transnational-state-system seem anachronistic and arguably ought to give way to new policing models more suited to a polycentric global power system. The new boundaries that have been created around ICTs show notions of control and creativity, disciplining and freedom, command and dialogue, state and market in roughly equal measure. The assertion of the logic of territorial-based enforcement is likely to be only partially influential in policing the patterns of ongoing interaction in the new social spaces that have opened up.

Policing mega-events

Mass spectacles are an important manifestation of globalisation. Through mass transport and global communications, the ability for hundreds of thousands of people to converge in one location to pray, protest or party is unprecedented. Whether it is an annual historic religious practice such as *the Haj* pilgrimage to Mecca, periodic sports spectaculars such as the Olympic Games or the football World Cup, or the intermittent and peripatetic carnival of anti-globalisation protest, mega-events provide a fascinating example of how police manipulate territoriality.[461] In each case, the event is transnational in the sense that people from around the world converge in one space within a specified local enforcement jurisdiction. The annual pilgrimage to the Saudi Arabian city of Mecca is a peaceful gathering and yet it presents one of the most challenging public order policing jobs in the world.[462] Mass sports spectaculars offer equally complex policing problems, with the added difficulty of being held in a new city each time.[463] Political protest constitutes a potentially more explosive police–public encounter, and protesters travel internationally to highlight global political issues by asserting the democratic right to protest.[464] The multi-agency policing of these mega-events is always already transnational since knowledge of strategy and tactics in policing public order is common property in the occupational subculture of policing.[465]

The flexible relationship between policing, law and territory is clear in cases of anti-globalisation protests such as the G20/G8 summit in Toronto in June of 2010. At a cost of CAN$1 billion, the security arrangements involved a multi-agency task force drawing police expertise from across North America. Downtown Toronto was contained by a 'small army' of 10,000 uniformed officers and 1000 private security guards. During the summit, more than a thousand arrests were made, the largest mass arrests in Canadian history. Prior to the events it was rumoured that people exercising the right to peaceful protest within 5 meters of the barriers sealing off the summit could be stopped, searched and detained on the basis of a creative interpretation of s. 2.(1) of the Public Works Protection Act. This allowed a number of provincial and municipal officials to appoint 'guards' with special powers to secure 'public works'. Over the days of the summit events, uncounted numbers of persons were stopped and searched and approximately 1000 persons were arrested and detained for up to three days. Few charges were actually pursued. Spokespersons for the Ontario Cabinet office later explained that the memo pertained to courthouses and a few other specific areas inside the perimeter fence and that a '5-meter rule' never existed. The arrests had apparently all been made under normal criminal code violations. Toronto Police Chief Bill Blair admitted that he just wanted to 'get the job done'. A new tool: 'rumour law' was added to the repertoire of the legal ace.[466]

Most reporting of the summit's policing events, and virtually all subsequent coverage of the scandal, disappeared into a vortex of local news reporting. The local police chief, as ranking officer in the enforcement jurisdiction, was a lightning rod for public scrutiny. A small number of anti-globalisation protesters favouring violent direct action provided iconic images of burning police cars and vandalised shops, which were widely disseminated in Europe and North America. After those pictures were released, police violence and mass arrests seemed justifiable. From the police media-relations managers' point of view of this was a successful operation. There was wide transnational dissemination of 'positive messages' of police handling the chaotic potential of the crowd while 'negative messages' about the abuse of police powers and the exceptional undermining of civil liberty was narrowly reported as local news. This shows a masterful ability to think globally and act locally in making choices about police diffusion of information to commercial news media.

Securing mega-events requires flexible policing arrangements. State, corporate and non-governmental actors work together using 'standardised major event templates', 'formal and informal observation programmes', international intelligence sharing and personal exchanges between government and private sector consultancy firms, which creates an epistemic community of experts.[467] It is in these liquid institutional settings that the subculture of transnational policing is evolving. The policing of mega-events generally occurs in exceptional territories that can be created on the basis of the most fluid kinds of law. Mega-events present the creative and adaptive relationship between policing and territory and show that state sovereignty is not simply determinative of policing action; rather, territoriality, legally defined or not, is a tool in police hands. Borders, oceans, cyberspace and mega-events are four examples of the complex territorial objects of the exercise of global policing power. In each case territoriality and law are used opportunistically. Under close analysis these policing practices liquify taken for granted assumptions about 'national sovereignty', the conceptual glue of the transnational-state-system.

Policing transnational flows

The world system has a liquid quality: businesspeople, migrant workers, tourists, goods, services, capital and information are flowing around the globe faster and more extensively than at any point in human history.[468] As Zygmunt Bauman and Katja Franko Aas describe it, we now live in a 'space of flows' rather than a 'space of places'.[469] Every day, millions of people and hundreds of millions of tons of goods move through the seas and skies, across land borders, sometimes under surveillance, searched, inspected or detained. These flows underline one of the contradictions of globalisation. Global neo-liberal capitalism requires free movement of raw materials, component parts, manufactured goods and capital. People must be free to move to work in fields, factories and call centres in order to provide services to capital as it moves from one country to another. And yet, these flows are a source of insecurity – dirty money can pollute the economy, hazardous waste can pollute the environment. Sometimes

undocumented migrants (asylum seekers, migrant workers and criminal depor-
tees) are portrayed as 'pollution' of the national social body. As Bauman puts it,
'the vagabonds are the waste of the world which has dedicated itself to tourist
services'.[470] Policing practices aiming to control and surveille suspect populations are attentive to these flows. The mobility of people across land and sea,
the movement of wealth and financial assets in the global money system, illegal
traffic in weapons and drugs, are phenomena of flows decisively shaped, but not
prevented, by transnational policing. These coursing currents are policed
through a complex division of law enforcement surveillance labour mapped
onto a jurisdictional grid. Paradoxically, policing practices become part of the
structure sustaining the problematic flux.

Policing people: migrants, criminals, terrorists and other suspect populations

The history of the passport illustrates attempts to monopolise the control of
human geographical movement.[471] Policing flows requires technicians to do a
'panoptic sort' using advanced surveillance technologies to create risk or threat
profiles often based on assumptions concerning racial or ethnic identity.[472] Our
everyday life-chances are 'continually checked or enabled and our choices are
channelled using various means of surveillance'.[473] The panoptic sort is a *generalised* practice for the surveillance of suspect populations, its logic separating
the risky from the at-risk, is pervasive and affects everyone.[474] Think about moving through a modern international airport en route to a distant destination,
passport and credit cards in hand. Mobile bodies moving across borders are
objects of policing attention, calculation, prediction and action. Intimate parts
of the body harbour suspicion, and facial expressions have become objects for
close inspection. The face, a mobile surface upon which inner thoughts can be
read (and given meaning by the newest modes of airport security and surveillance), can be justifiable cause for enhanced security screening.[475] The panoptic
sort yields sometimes unexpected results. Recalling the case of Mr Bond from
Chapter 1, Western tourists on wine-tasting holidays normally expect to pass
through the panoptic sorting process with minimal difficulty. Exceptionally,
when identification errors are made, tourists are diverted from the departure
lounge to carceral hardships usually reserved for suitable enemies.

Control speak concerning immigration offenders, illegal aliens, unregistered
workers, terrorists and transnational criminals creates categories of exclusion
and sets in train reverse flows of convicted criminals, suspects, failed emigrants
and asylum seekers, through deportation.[476] At its most extreme, global policing
practice extends to extraordinary rendition in which intelligence agents –
including CIA and MI6 – engage in kidnap, detention and secret flights to

torture camps. 'Othering' is integral to the space of flows because those so labelled are hampered by travel restrictions and other forms of control. The language for describing control in the space of flows works bureaucratically to confine the messy reality of the world. It is used to articulate what control agents think they are doing, but there is more to the casting of suitable enemies and folk devils than the official terms might immediately suggest.[477]

Women drug couriers in the early 1990s offered a disturbing example. Colloquially known as 'drug mules', the smuggling methods included swallowing condoms filled with cocaine or concealing such packages in other bodily orifices. Calling for sentencing reform for these 'prisoners of the drug war', Huling documented how young women, economic losers in the global market place, were exploited in an illicit and deadly shipping industry.[478] It is practically impossible to measure the effect of this kind of interdiction programme on the overall supply of drugs.[479] It certainly led to a massive increase in the imprisonment of women drug couriers in the UK.[480] Between 1992 and 2002, the number of women in British prisons increased by 173 per cent, one in five of whom was a foreign national and nearly one half of whom were Jamaican.[481] Doctors were increasingly faced with requests to perform intimate searches, forensic diagnostic imaging and emergency intervention.[482] These criminalised 'Others' caught in the space of flows are routinely detained, convicted of importation, imprisoned and then deported in a reverse flow. Observing a similar fate for the women victims of human trafficking, Kemala Kempadoo argued that initiatives to prevent trafficking formulated within the framework of a 'war' against transnational organised crime led 'to the criminalisation of migrant women from the global South and the greater control of their mobility, bodies and sexuality'.[483] The research on drug couriers and human trafficking for the purposes of sexual exploitation both indicate that policing creates a form of secondary victimisation for the women involved which tends to find them being deported and grounded indefinitely.

Given the scenes of carnage witnessed in the past decade in New York, London, Bali, Barcelona, Mumbai, Moscow, Iraq and many other places, it is not surprising that the terrorist is the most fearsome folk devil of the new world order. But, in announcing a 'war on terror' shortly after the 9/11 attacks, George W. Bush declared war on an abstract noun,[484] a term selectively applied to specific acts of violence.[485] The language of 'war on terror' fuses the concepts of war and terror.[486] It also implies that terrorism is discinct from ordinary, apolitical violence. The selective use of the language of terrorism provides only arbitrary distinctions between legitimate and illegitimate forms of violence. Terrorism may be directed at civilian targets as a symbolic attack sending messages about governmental authority for the purposes of political change. This implies the premeditated use or threat of symbolic (often chronic and low-level) violence by conspiratorial organisations aiming to communicate a political message that goes beyond the physical damage itself.[487] Defining 'true terrorism' invokes images of the barbarian in an effort to 'symbolically reaffirm and secure civilisation'.[488]

Re-engineering local policing in response to perceptions of heightened terrorist threat de-emphasises routine policing services in communities where 'suspect populations' are thought sparsely distributed, while increasing police intervetion in communities where 'suspect populations' are believed to live, socialise or congregate. This has the effect of transforming 'low policing' everywhere into 'counter-terrorism policing'.[489] Re-engineered around the trope of terrorism, policing becomes increasingly concerned with mobility between zones of risk, so public spaces (especially the spaces of mobility) are redesigned with 'defensive features that are functionally and aesthetically integral'. In many instances, counter-terrorism inaugurates new coercive practices including the use of extensive new legal powers to stop and search (often without requiring suspicion of wrongdoing), integrating intelligence gathering, migration control and street policing.[490]

The problem with terrorism is that although the term is in common usage, there is no commonly agreed definition. Walter Laqueur's major study of political violence is frequently quoted as saying 'the only general characteristic of terrorism generally agreed upon is that terrorism involves violence and the threat of violence'.[491] This definition, as many of the commentators who invoke it are quick to point out, is so amorphous that it can be stretched to include such disparate phenomena as systematic violence against women in the home and state crimes such as genocide as well as denoting a politically motivated suicide bomber. Bruce Hoffman's survey of the extensive literature noted that experts, scholars and governmental programmers produce multiple definitions of the term, not all of which are commensurate.[492] According to Andrew Silke, especially in the period after 9/11, the volume of literature and commentary on terrorism grew to massive proportions but 'the quality of the content leaves much to be desired'.[493] Like 'pornography' and 'organised crime', terms with equally contentious definitional debates, people like to think 'I know it when I see it'. When it comes to policing and counter-terrorist practice there is an attitude that the matter can best be left to professionals.[494] Our viewpoint is a critical one; we agree with Conor Gearty, that matters are not so simple.[495] The identification of terrorism cannot be reduced to ticking off items on a risk based threat assessment since the label is so value-laden.

The traditional ways of drafting legislation which draw on narrative techniques, broadly defined words, tests and expressions make it quite impossible to balance civil and political rights against the constraints on liberty that counter-terrorism law, by its very nature, implies. The meaning of the term is moulded by its usage in government. Popular usage is often filtered through the language of police subculture and projected through mass news and entertainment media. The word resonates with moral opprobrium and emotional appeal and 'as far as the authorities and others are concerned [it is] far too useful an insult to be pinned down and controlled'.[496] Since policing maintains, confirms and asserts the enforceability of law while using law as a tool to make that assertion, terrorism presents legitimation dilemmas.[497] Policing responses to such challenges, invoking violence as a legitimate response to violence, must be carefully crafted for consumption in mass media.[498] In public relations terms, the occupation of policing tries to provide a cultural performance to uphold the authority of 'the police' and affirm a unique prerogative: the claim of legitimacy for violent responses to violence.[499] In the terms of political theory, the terrorism trope has promoted the Hobbesian choice because people have been consumed by national security discourse, which is insufficiently alive to the demands of a broader kind of human security rooted in human flourishing, or to the political liberty necessary for its achievement.[500] The rhetoric of terrorism and counter-terrorism divides the world into 'good guys' and 'bad guys' thereby undermining the possibility of liberal democratic policing which depends on a discourse of common humanity. This is of utility to would-be enforcers and their objects but is antithetical to the general commonwealth.

The theoretical analysis pursued here reveals more than the social construction of the term terrorism. It also shows what remains latent in most other commentary on the subject – namely global policing practice and its effects on populations, territories and flows. In the context of globalisation, international transport hubs such as airports and train stations on the territories of the seigneurial states of the West provide high value symbolic targets because they are nodal points of the circulatory system of what Hardt and Negri call 'Empire' and we call the global social body. Some consider contemporary counter-terrorism policing in the space of flows to be strategic and tactical reactions to the political violence of a 'gobalised civil war'.[501] Thought of as a social body, the real vulnerability of a world system in conflict can be gauged by looking at its system of mobility (the circulatory system) because the security response costs far more in terms of death and unhappiness than the actual costs of the damage done and lives lost through the (largely symbolic) terror-attacks themselves.

Although policing responses must deal with immediate threats and the actors behind them, policing must also respond to the longer-term issues. Sooner or later the paradoxes inherent in the war on terror must give way to the problem solving abilities of police diplomats and field-operators who understand – and are empowered to create – the political, diplomatic and cultural conditions for making peace. Technician-enforcers imposing a world system lock-down cannot ultimately solve the problems of social ordering in that system. However, that is what is being attempted. As the historian Perry Anderson has shown, the seigneurial system of the feudal period similarly 'parcelised' territory with myriad systems of justice and social control such that the great mass of people were bound to the land and had very restricted mobility while the relatively well-off and powerful enjoyed unfettered mobility rights.[502] The transnational-state-system that the transnational practices of police agencies uphold is increasingly a system of mobility control that marks the global exclusive society.[503]

Policing drugs and guns

Policing the global market in narcotic and psychotropic drugs is the 'paradigm example' of transnational policing.[504] The power of drugs as a legitimating device for transnational policing practices stems from the moral resolve that mood-altering drugs need to be destroyed entirely not just because of their presumed capacity to damage the health of the individual user and wider society but because they are thought of as evil.[505] Prohibition rests on the hope that interfering with the flow of drugs – from production and import–export, to distribution and consumption – will make the costs to drug-takers and traffickers so high that it exceeds its perceived use-value and puts an end to drug use.[506] Law, policy and practices inspired by prohibition were developed throughout the 20th century culminating in the 1988 Vienna Convention (discussed above). These international legal instruments required domestic implementing legislation and increasingly coercive policing and punitive criminal justice policies. The high water mark of prohibition was in 1998, when the UN set a 10-year goal to achieve a 'drug free world'.[507] The epic failure to achieve this goal is evident from the 2010 UN estimate that there are 250 million drug users and that the global value of the cocaine market is US$88 billion and the opiate market is worth US$65 billion.[508]

Police strategies have combined analysis of 'criminal networks' and 'hot spots' to develop 'glocal' interventions at the retail level. International research on the policing of street-level markets shows that enforcement strategies have, at best, short-term impacts in specific localities, often accompanied by displacement to other areas.[509] A similar picture emerges from attempts to stifle cultivation, processing and import–export. Police enforcement action tends to take out weaker market actors and leave the more ruthless and well-organised actors untouched. Confiscation and seizure of drugs shipments exceeds only about 10 per cent of drugs in transit, amounting to a modest loss of stock at a cost that can easily be recouped at the retail level. Enforcement action means that participation in the lucrative clandestine market is only open to actors willing and able to mobilise particular kinds of cultural capital with a focus on tough, violent, hard and ruthless masculinity.

Published in 1971, just as the 'total offensive' on drugs was declared, Jock Young's prophetic book *The Drug Takers*, predicted not only that drug prohibition would not work, but that it would have the opposite effect from its manifest intentions.[510] Drawing on labelling theory, Young predicted that instead of reducing drug supply and consumption, criminalisation would 'amplify deviance', foster its popularity and entrench its use. At the time, drug consumption in England was largely confined to relatively small communities of self-defined 'bohemians' and caused little harm measured in terms of addiction, mortality and morbidity. Crucially, drug prohibition created a lucrative clandestine market – it literally *created criminality*. The clandestine market attracts criminal entrepreneurship in an escalating spiral. Illegal markets created and fostered by counter-narcotics enforcement also tend to corrupt local policing agencies. The money generated is so significant that individual police, customs and other officers are often lured into facilitation and drugs money can have the effect of corrupting entire national economies. One of the most important harm-producing qualities of drug prohibition concerns the relationship between illicit markets and violence.[511] Misha Glenny's *McMafia*, showed that illicit markets tend to be more violent than their licit counterparts. The former cannot resolve business disputes through publicly transparent mechanisms, whereas licit market transactions gone wrong can be pursued in open court.[512] Other reseach showed that violence in illicit drugs markets can also be instrumental and targeted, accumulating 'social capital' crucial to survival in marginalised populations.[513]

Economic analyses of the dynamics of wholesale and retail drug markets showed continuing and robust profitability amid long-term falling retail prices.[514] Despite the obvious failure to make marked reductions in the availability and consumption in the worldwide use of drugs over a 10-year period, the UN committed itself again in 2010 to the 'elimination or significant reduction in the global illicit drug supply and demand by 2019'. The extent of production of opiates, cocaine, marijuana and synthetic psychotropics, the scale of trafficking, the profitability, the price and purity of illegal drugs provide few grounds for optimism that the UN's goal of creating a 'drug free world' is ever likely to be attained. As the UN World Drug report itself explained, 'a clear lesson from the history of drug control is that the mere sum of uncoordinated national and sectoral efforts, even successful ones, cannot result in a global success. Another lesson is that countries with limited means cannot resist, and counter the impact of, powerful transnational trafficking flows on their own'.[515] Looking at all the evidence it would be more accurate to say that global drug prohibition has failed on its own terms and has produced collateral harms of corruption, armed violence and community disintegration in many parts of the world.[516]

Understanding the movement of weapons and drugs provides crucial insights into what Manuel Castells has called 'black holes' of global capitalism that exist at every geographic scale from the municipal to the global.[517] Tracing the flow of illegal weapons and drugs is one way of looking at the inter-connections of the global south.[518] A case in point is the 'weaponisation' of the Caribbean.[519] Narco-trafficking is a major problem for police officials but the 'related ills' of the illegal imported guns and ammunition were a greater security threat. According to this analysis:

> ... firearms accompany the drugs like fleas ride on shipboard rats, but firearms stay behind on the islands and the effects spill over onto the streets long after the drugs have been moved on to more lucrative destinations. The resultant weaponisation means that dispute resolution is more explosive.[520]

Examining the links between drugs and guns in the Caribbean region reveals, in microcosm, the global policing of these flows. 'Arming paradise' has happened in three stages. First, Latin American drug traffickers introduced the practice of guarding the transshipment of drugs through force of arms. The Andean region is already highly weaponised due to geopolitical factors, the Caribbean (with the exception of Jamaica) is historically less so. Second, in a transnational environment where formal contracts are impossible and some parties are already armed, the pressure on local criminal networks is to acquire firearms. The increased availability of guns leads to heightened conflict, 'turf wars' between dealers and 'deals gone bad'. The third stage is reached once guns have become commonplace and are used in crimes unrelated to drugs markets, such as robberies, domestic violence and neighbourhood conflict.

Considering that the global drugs prohibition is failing on its own terms, Agozino et al. challenge orthodox thinking with a 'counterfactual thought experiment': imagine that current efforts put into drugs prohibition were instead channelled into a worldwide regime for policing illicit markets in small arms and light weapons.[521] As one West Indian Police Commissioner explained, international policing partners 'are interested in acting on what's affecting them [...] we have a lot of firearms trafficking in the region, for use in the region, yet we don't have the Bureau of Alcohol, Tobacco and Firearms here because the weapons are not going north, it's only drugs that are going north, but [the guns] that's not their concern, that's not their interest'.[522] Asked what would happen if the priorities were reversed and guns and ammunition were the main focus with all of the enforcement resources available in the region, he replied 'we could in very short order reduce homicides in this country, *very* short order'.[523]

The Caribbean provides an example of social exclusion in spatial terms seen by Castells as the 'territorial confinement of systemically worthless populations' from failed states to the inner city ghetto – the 'global south inside the global north'.[524] Epidemiological and public health consequences are symptomatic of the black holes of social exclusion. The link between firearms and illegal drugs markets is not a direct one. Drugs are not simply high-value illegal commodities *requiring* armed guards. Rather, violence is a result of a complex of factors including on firearms availability. Controlling the global flow of illegal handguns and assault rifles seems, to us, obviously more important than controlling the ganja trade. Observing the zeal with which some seigneurial states' policing agencies pursue global drug prohibition and the corresponding reluctance to police the international trade in small arms and light weapons is like listening to an advocate of the death penalty extol the virtues of vegetarianism on the grounds of cruelty to animals.

Policing money

Criminologists and police tend to have a myopic view of policing the global money system because of the systematically distorted language of 'money laundering'.

This concept was born from the practices of some American underworld entrepreneurs of the 1930s – Meyer Lansky among them – who metaphorically cleaned 'dirty money' from the vice rackets, by moving funds through the accounting books of small cash-in-hand businesses such as laundries.[525] The FATF and the construction of a worldwide system of suspicious transactions reporting (STR) by police financial intelligence units (FIUs) discussed in Chapter 3 was built on this metaphor. These FIUs are networked into the financial services system for the purposes of surveillance by legions of 'money laundering reporting officers' or 'compliance officers'. They are civilian employees of banks and insurance companies who help in the policing of money, operating at a distance from and at the behest of, policing agents in the FIUs. In effect, this is a non-voluntary public–private policing partnership. How well does this massive multi-agency surveillance infrastructure police the world money system?

Initially the anti-money laundering regime brought the global money system under partial police surveillance on the basis of going after criminal proceeds associated with the precursor crime of drug trafficking.[526] The aim was to destroy the illicit drugs economy worldwide. However, this has not come to pass.[527] The sheer volume of transactions in the international money system overwhelmed FIUs processing STRs; described by one analyst as being like 'drinking from a fire hose'.[528] It was always going to be very difficult to monitor the trillions of dollars of financial transactions made daily in the global electronic money system.[529] After 9/11 the emphasis shifted to 'terrorist financing', which recognised that 'clean money' could be used for 'dirty' purposes. The fallacy that anti-money laundering could be a purgative for 'dirty money' was finally all washed up.[530] In the mid-1990s criminologists noticed what historians of money already knew – the invention of 'electronic money' and the existence of traditional Hawala or Hundi 'informal' traditional banking systems made total money system surveillance a practical impossibility.[531] In the transnational policing subcultural worldview, the technician-enforcer's response might well have been to welcome the introduction of 'neural networks and knowledge-based systems to develop suspicions electronically'.[532] Stubborn pursuit of the usual suspects continued to produce statistics of law enforcement success with no discernable impact on the global illicit drug supply.[533] In contrast, some of the most successful (and harmful) economic criminals remained free to operate in the higher echelons of the legitimate and formal financial system. Over the two decades since the Bank of Credit and Commerce International (BCCI) scandal broke in 1991 dozens of major white-collar crimes were perpetrated despite the vigilance of financial compliance officers in the banking system and the STR system of the FIUs. How is it that the illicit flows of elite crime seem to escape police money system surveillance?

In February 2011, the *New York Times* reported on Bernard Madoff's first interview for publication since his arrest in 2008. During his interview he alleged that the banks knew about the workings of his US$65 billion Ponzi scheme.

Pointing to the failure to examine discrepancies between his regulatory filings and other information available to them he accused the banks of willful blindness. 'They had to know,' Mr Madoff said, '[b]ut the attitude was sort of, "If you're doing something wrong, we don't want to know."'[534] The blindness might have had a lot to do with the culture of banking. Madoff was doing nothing very out of the ordinary. In two books published two decades apart, Michael Lewis revealed the subculture of Wall Street banking to be every bit as avaricious, gluttonous, ignorant, profane, violent and treacherous (to one another and to their customers) as any street corner Mafiosi ever was.[535] The arcane and mystifying language of CDOs, credit-default swaps, short-selling and derivatives trading, concerning artificial securities largely based on huge numbers of doubtful 'sub-prime' mortgage bonds issued in the USA began to fall to pieces in 2007. It engulfed the world money system in 2008 and was, according to Lewis, the greatest financial fraud in history.[536] Given the size of the other large-scale frauds perpetrated during the period, that is a remarkable thought.[537] What came next in the 'sub-prime' con job is a matter of public record, if only poorly understood. The big financial players – notably then US treasury secretary, Henry 'Hank' Paulson (formerly of the global investment banking and securities firm Goldman Sachs, a primary profiteer in the derivatives trading business) – terrified the US government into handing over billions of dollars to stave off a collapse of the global money system. The general public, and a good many criminologists, have not yet grasped the nature and extent of this confidence trick.

Large-scale fraud and other 'sharp trading practices' were not policed by the global system of FIUs, but these purely financial crimes caused a great deal of human misery.[538] By their very nature, these crimes were more vulnerable than drugs money to the control potential of financial surveillance. The financial law enforcement institutions have evidently not evolved to protect the integrity of the global money system.[539] This is especially noticeable in global flows of money through so-called 'offshore banking havens'. This terminology has an Anglo-American etymology revealing a preoccupation with the finance centres of the Caribbean and Channel Islands. In fact, the major tax havens of Europe – Switzerland, Liechtenstein, Luxemburg and Austria – are all land-locked. In the later 20th century the financial surveillance system had, under the auspices of the war on drugs, infiltrated the global banking system, including the 'offshore system', to an unprecedented degree and this undermined a long held tradition of banking privacy.[540] For a time, transnational policing surveillance of these institutions was confined only to 'criminal assets', most specifically funds associated with illicit drug markets.[541] Interest in the offshore system peaked twice, first after the 9/11 attacks when it came under scrutiny because of concerns about terrorist financing and again in 2009 after the financial derivatives collapse of 2008.

The importance of these treasure islands to the complexities of capitalist finance and the 'men who stole the world' is challenging to convey. One example that puts a human face on the elite social world of global money is the case of multi-millionaire financier Baron Michael Ashcroft of Belize, nominated to the House of Lords in 2000 for his service as Secretary to the UK Conservative Party. Lord Ashcroft was the largest financial contributor to the Party when his considerable offshore financial dealings were inadvertently exposed to public scrutiny following reports from the DEA voicing concerns that Belize was a haven for narco-dollars. The US law enforcement agency's exposure of his offshore financial dealings was a considerable embarrassment.[542] After all, Ashcroft was not only among the world's elite money men, but a key figure within the British government. The ebbs and flows of Ashcroft's wealth through the global money system exemplified the way members of the 'transnational capitalist class' operate.[543] The case revealed interesting facets of the global system. Actors in the mid-range of the transnational-state-system, who are not primarily concerned with international relations, can have unwanted effects in the higher echelons. The story also revealed the mobile and privileged financial world of wealthy, elite, private global actors in the public sector and, in so doing, demonstrated the relative importance of private and 'sub-state' actors. American law enforcement created choppy waters for one transatlantic tycoon, but the architecture of global policing was not built so as to maintain financial surveillance on wealthy elites. Some, like Bernard Madoff, were exposed as elite criminals and punished accordingly. But financial system surveillance, like policing surveillance more generally, is largely focused on 'suitable enemies' at the bottom of the social order.

The story so far has not been altogether bad for Lord Ashcroft, who formally and publically renounced his tax exile status in response to the revelations in 2001 but, nevertheless, continued to do business under the cover of shell companies registered in Belize.[544] In March of 2010 he faced further questions about his non-domiciled status in the UK and allegations of £127 million tax evasion.[545] Political rhetoric about the need to 'crack down' on tax havens gained new ground after the financial crisis of 2008 with new civil society groups, such as the Tax Justice Network (an anti-tax haven group), drawing increasing attention to the issue. The Ashcroft case provides the merest glimpse into the life world of global business elites. There is a formidable force of the entrenched private wealth in the global system. In the policing of flows, the offshore havens for private capital are as integral to the global system as migrant encampments in the frontier border zones.

Policing weak states: where the flows stop

The noblest rhetoric in global policing is the so-called responsibility to protect (R2P) articulated by humanitarian aid agencies, NGOs and the UN.[546] For example, in 2009 the French-based *Médecins sans frontières* (MSF) reported on victims of sexual violence in conflict situations around the world. This report documented an alarming number of individual and gang rapes and the use of sexual violence in civil disorders and armed conflict. In the most disturbing terms, the MSF report focused attention on the practical concerns of providing immediate and long-term care for thousands of victims of sexual violence in various conflict zones around the world. The immediate need was to prevent HIV-infection and to provide treatment for other sexually transmitted diseases, the morning-after pill and, when needed, surgical intervention to repair damaged genitals. Longer-term needs included counselling for psychological trauma and community work to counteract the stigma and rejection of victims. According to the MSF report, 'an optimum package of services should include medical care, psychological support, medical-legal certificates which can be used as evidence in court, and information to help people understand why, how and when to seek care'. [547] It reminded readers that 'the damage done through rape and other forms of sexual violence can be dramatically limited through immediate assistance, but it will never be entirely repaired. Shattered lives can be rebuilt, but the scars will always remain'.[548] The MSF made passing references to the need for police enforcement in these situations. The importance of policing as a social service is certainly true in cases of domestic violence and sexual assault, however there is more to policing and R2P than victim support. Good policing is also about fostering the conditions in which civil social relations can flourish. Sometimes that involves the imposition of order on the disorderly and stopping victimisation before it occurs.

R2P means the employment of coercive means to achieve positive social ends where there is no certain outcome.[549] This is extremely complicated. Alice Hills observed that cultural differences influence perceptions on all sides about the use of force in policing and peacekeeping. She raised questions about how a doctrine of 'minimal force' could be achieved in peacekeeping or peace-building operations in any practical or substantive sense. In conflict situations, multiple cultural frameworks – brought to the situation both by multi-national, police peacekeepers and the conflicting communities they police – are at play. It follows that individual case studies seldom provide clear guidance on what constitutes 'good policing' or the practical meaning of minimal force which is central to liberal policing theory.[550] R2P was, according to some, nothing more than an unwelcome historical echo of Rudyard Kipling's 'white man's burden'. Seen this way, under the global conditions that produced broken, failed or failing states in the first instance, transnational policing could become part of the problem for which it was the intended solution. Observing that humanitarian intervention came to the same kinds of Third World locations as the private security operators working on behalf of the resource extraction industries, peacekeeping was described as the 'military corollary of neo-liberal globalisation [and a] smokescreen for a new politics of containment in peripheralised regions'.[551]

When Port-au-Prince, the Haitian capital city, was levelled by an earthquake on 12 January 2010, there was already a UN mission on the ground. In the aftermath of the earthquake world opinion was focused for some time on the plight of the country. Judging by the financial generosity from the general public in the advanced capitalist economies, the overall sentiment was one of compassion. In only a matter of weeks, however, attention shifted to new panic scenes in different broken, failed or failing states. While the debacle unfolded, the USA military pushed aside the multi-lateral force that was already on the ground in Haiti in the unseemly rush to assert the claim as the major power in the region capable of enforcing hemispheric order. It looked less like humanitarian intervention and more like *Realpolitik*. The domestic political concern in the USA was a potential 'refugee crisis'. US officials made clear that while international law did not prohibit population movement in the wake of natural or man-made disasters, it did permit the creation of 'incentives to stay'. Homeland Security Secretary Janet Napolitano sent a clear message to the Haitian people: 'Please do not have us divert our necessary rescue and relief efforts that are going into Haiti by trying to leave at this point.'[552] US officials used R2P rhetoric and the duty to intervene not to provide security to the people affected by the disaster, but to contain them in ways that served the narrowly defined interests of American national security.

The UN force that had been in the country since 2004 had already left a footprint of its own. This was established when, after an initial request from CARICOM, the UN passed Security Council Resolution 1542 mandating a UN stabilisation mission known by its French name *Mission des Nations Unies pour la stabilisation en Haïti* and French acronym MINUSTAH. This 'assistance' with the restoration and maintenance of the rule of law, public safety and public order in Haiti was the most recent in a long and more or less continuous history of foreign police interventions in Haiti going back to 1915.[553] The stabilisation mission was undertaken because the UN Security Council deemed the situation there to be a 'threat to international peace and security in the region'. Almost from the start of its mandate MINUSTAH, under Brazilian force command, made incursions into Cité Soleil (Sun City) – a notorious shantytown on the western edge of Port-au-Prince – resulting in an uncounted number of casualties. From very early on it was apparent that the operation was falling short of its promise to establish civil order and respect for human rights.

Critics charged that despite one of the strongest human rights mandates in UN peacekeeping history, MINUSTAH did not effectively investigate or report human rights abuses, nor protect human rights advocates. Charged to train and reform the Haitian National Police, MINUSTAH instead provided unquestioning support to police operations resulting in warrantless arrests, detentions, unintended civilian casualties and deliberate extra-judicial killings. Rather than protecting civilians from imminent violence, MINUSTAH instead inflicted stray bullets on them. Disarmament was at the core of MINUSTAH's stabilisation duties, but this never got beyond plans made in conference rooms. When the earthquake struck, Haiti was ruled by guns and terror, not law.[554] The MINUSTAH intervention was not about R2P, but putting 'boots on the ground' to impose order. The armed violence was driven by the desire for political and social change but it blurred into clandestine criminal activities, especially drug trafficking, and the associated disorder led to calls for strong action. However, the transnational policing intervention only seemed to make matters worse. Studies by the MINUSTAH Gender Unit and the United Nations Development Programme (UNDP) in Haiti revealed that the situation was particularly dangerous for women and girls for whom groups of armed men represented a continuous threat of rape, sexual slavery and forced prostitution.[555]

R2P provides the conceptual basis for policing development aid to weak, failing or failed states. Looked at analytically in terms of the policing of suspect populations and controlling territory, these spaces constitute a vortex of social exclusion, poverty, technological under-development, deficiency in social capital and ineffective social institutions. From a neo-liberal perspective, these spaces are fit only for resource extraction and limited labour exploitation of populations thought of as 'the waste of the world'. The pockets of the global south R2P patrols are where the global flows stop. It is into these black holes formed in the social body that drugs and guns are poured.

Conclusion: the consequences of global policing

Global policing involves the control of specific *places* – border zones, the oceans, cyberspace, 'mega-events' and 'weak states' – and the surveillance and control of *flows* of people, money, drugs and guns. These examples illustrate our general theory of policing, but other places such as airports, the skies and space would also be interesting to examine as well as the endangered species, looted antiquities, radioactive materials or toxic waste that pass through them. The liquid quality of late modern life illustrates that global policing comprises both surveillance and control and a descriptive analysis of this reveals its contributions to sustaining the transnational-state-system idea. Policing parcelises territory through myriad systems of control and helps to maintain fuzzy boundaries between public and private global power. The result is that great masses of people are bound to territories and experience tightly and coercively restricted mobility while the rich and powerful enjoy unrestricted global mobility. The transnational-state-system, maintained by new forms of policing, has become a system of mobility control that marks the exclusive society at a global scale.

What are the consequences of global policing for the health of the global social body? The assumption of its functional logic is that border protection, drug enforcement, maritime policing and the 'responsibility to protect' people in weak states combine to make the world a safer place. It is therefore a cruel irony that many policing practices are either useless or iatrogenic. Our examples show that current global policing practice undermines a worldwide state of prosperity. They maintain the territorial confinement of populations defined globally as worthless: from the inner-city ghetto and refugee camp to the failed state. These policing practices shape the flow of illicit commodities, such as guns and drugs, into the 'black holes' of world society as well as the global flow of wealth around them. Policing subculture is tied up with metaphors of territoriality which can be used cunningly in the legitimation games of controlling 'mega-events' or clumsily in the policing of cyberspace. The label 'terrorist' provides a powerful image of a suitable enemy legitimating any and all paramilitary policing efforts. Yet despite the symbolic power of the folk devils used to justify harsh interventions, global policing practice does little to maintain the overall health of the global system.

We are faced with explaining why things turn out the way they do. Stan Cohen has suggested three possibilities: the 'benign transfer model' (that policing policy is for good reasons and will result in good ends); the 'malignant colonialism model' (that both the ends and means of policing policy are malign); and the 'paradoxical-effects model', which suggests that arrangements designed for the best motives can and do have disastrous results.[556] Throughout this book we have illustrated many paradoxes and ironies of policing from a global perspective. These tend to show that, despite the manifest intention of securing peace and prosperity, policing practices often produce more serious harms than they prevent.[557]

In our view, these paradoxes are explained by the meanings produced within the transnational subculture of policing. Despite the variegated institutional architecture of policing and the complexities of the global law enforcement division of labour, despite differences in geographical and socio-cultural locale, our cast of policing characters is organised around a language of suitable enemies and national security. Divesting itself of this subcultural language may help to return to policing the values of maintaining the health of the social body and a general state of prosperity. Noble promises can have paradoxical and unwanted effects. Recognising this, the first step towards global liberal democratic policing is to shift the subcultural language away from a dualistic world view labelling others as 'you' or 'them'. Instead, we need a holistic vision of the world based on a social contract involving 'we' and 'us'.

6

CONCLUSION: THE GLOBAL COPS
HAVE ARRIVED

In the global networked society, police power is no longer constrained by the borders of the nation-state. The idea of the hapless detective standing impotent at the airport cursing in frustration as 'Mr Big' jets off to an untouchable retirement on a distant 'Costa Del Crime' is as anachronistic as the image of Bonny and Clyde driving triumphantly over the state line to escape the local sheriff in depression-era America. Policing today is connected around the world by mobile phone and email, shared databases and personnel exchanges. Thousands of police have global mobility or are stationed permanently overseas.

Policework now extends in a complex global web that enables surveillance of suspect movements and the use of coercive power to disrupt and arrest criminal and terrorist suspects around the world and to render them overseas for trial or detention. With well developed mutual legal assistance treaties, fast-track extradition, regional arrest warrants and a growing number of people working to administer the system, transnational policing is emerging as a new specialism with its own unique subculture. Explaining global policing is made possible through empirical research on how transnational policing works in practice but that research needs to be understood in the context of theories about emerging systems of global governance. Since the power to govern means little, if anything at all, without being able to marshal coercive power, no theory of global governance can be complete without a theory of global policing.

As a mechanism for distributing legitimate coercive force to resolve conflict and secure the ends of safe and peaceful communities, policing is an integral element of all systems of governance.[558] As a set of practices and beliefs, policing is tightly linked to the defining nature of the social system within which it is embedded. Pre-modern policing was tied closely to locality – the village constable and night watchmen are examples of policing in tightly knit communities. Modern policing systems in many parts of the world were constructed within 18th- and 19th-century systems of public administration focused on cities, counties and other sub-national units. In some countries city police chiefs, county chief constables, sheriffs and regional superintendents are supplemented with national police forces, some of which were bequeathed to them by former colonial masters. In the late 20th century, countries without centralised state police forces created new national criminal intelligence services, serious crime agencies or other national policing hubs to link the local and global policing networks.

As we explained in Chapter 2, in the mid-20th century, governance began to evolve from an inter-national to a transnational-state-system, a process that has continued to develop to this day. The institutions of global governance created since the mid-20th century include *political* (e.g. UN, G8), *economic* (e.g. WTO), *legislative* (e.g. UN and ILO), *judicial* (e.g. ICC) and *policing* organisations (e.g. Interpol). What characterises the transnational-state-system is that in addition to relationships between actors operating on behalf of national governments, there are connections and interactions among actors operating 'above', 'below' and 'beyond' the nation-state.[559] As systems of global governance have evolved, police power has begun to fly from its original nesting place within the nation-state-system. Today's 'global cops' could work for a city police force, a private company, a national intelligence hub or a supranational policing agency.

The sociology of policing defines police as being concerned with the maintenance of social order through two distinct means: surveillance and coercion. In Chapter 1 we described the boundaries of the policing field drawing analytical distinctions between 'high' and 'low' forms of police power; 'public' and 'private' security providers and surveillance and control of 'territory' and 'suspect populations'. In Chapter 5 we illustrated these theoretical distinctions by describing new policing practices as emerging in the attempt to secure transnational spaces (e.g. border zones, airports, skies and seas) and to conduct surveillance on flows of people (e.g. migrants and suspect populations) and flows of things (e.g. drugs, money, guns).

These surveillant and coercive practices, while not entirely new, have expanded massively and changed shape dramatically in recent decades. They require continuing close empirical and theoretical scrutiny. Research in the sociology of policing has developed from its initial focus on local beat policing to explore other forms of policework, most recently documenting transnational policing including the practices of customs, immigration, airport security, financial intelligence and private security agencies. By definition, all of these policing agencies have surveillance and coercive powers. All of them are 'knowledge workers' with systems to store and share intelligence collected by technical surveillance, informers and undercover officers. Many also have the power to use physical force to search and seize property, arrest and question suspects, impose travel restrictions and freeze financial assets. A crucial empirical research finding is that police powers now transgress and transcend the boundaries of the nation-state. We have shown that the subculture of transnational policing is no longer anchored by national sovereignty but is writing a new script for policing sovereignty. The evidence suggests that transnational policing constitutes, and is constituted by, the nature of the emerging transnational-state-system.

In Chapter 1, we set out a theory of police legitimacy based on the notion of the social contract.[560] As enlightenment philosopher John Locke put it, because human beings have certain inherent moral rights, any use of coercive power by the state is morally suspect.[561] The power of policing cannot simply be taken for granted: the onus lies with the wielder of coercive power to justify any interference with individual liberty. In terms of classical liberal theory, state power is constrained by reference to democratic relationships within a state that describe a rational and principled separation of governmental power. What distinguishes policing from a mere 'protection racket' is that the people who are policed know, understand and endorse the police mission.[562] That is, the police have legitimate authority. In a democracy, this legitimacy is secured through mechanisms of accountability by which police are answerable to the public whom they both serve and are members of. In Geoffrey Marshall's terms, democratic police should go about their work in ways that are explanatory, co-operative, obedient and subordinate to the will of the people.[563]

It is an axiom of liberal democratic theory that when policing agents abuse their power, they can be called to account by bodies representing the will of the people for the purposes of sanction. These systems of accountability can be legal, political or administrative. A serious problem for any theory of policing beyond the boundaries of the nation-state is in defining who 'the people' are when considered in a global context. In the world system, there is no global *polity* (i.e. an organised world government or representative political organisation) nor a global *demos* (i.e. a common people constituting a democratic state). The problem of global policing then becomes a Gordian knot about the accountability for coercive and surveillant policing power authorised and originating transnationally.

Policing in the world system is not under 'rule-of-law', nor is it 'rule-by-law' but rather 'rule *with* law'. Law is like a tool in the hands of transnational policing actors whose occupational subculture, examined in detail in chapter 4, provides a worldview and rhetoric of justification that largely leaves global policing to be defined in terms of its own script. The resulting insecurity exacerbates a democratic tug-of-war between Rousseauian punitive populism and Hobbsean authoritarianism creating the dangerous possibility of a global social contract torn asunder. In the extreme, transnational paramilitary police power has been used to facilitate assassinations, kidnap, and the illegal rendition by chartered aircraft of 'terrorist suspects' to face torture in other countries.[564] Fortunately such Machiavellian moments are rare. Nonetheless a central problem for the use of global policing power is the absence of a global social contract that could hold global policing to account or provide it with legitimating authority.

This book obliquely confronts calls for a global police force – a supranational investigative body with enforcement powers – an idea which has shown remarkable resilience despite being highly problematic.[565] The 'vision' of a global police force first mooted by UN officials in the 1960s is once again being touted by transnational technocrats. In October 2009, the *New York Times* reported on an Interpol and UNPOL-hosted meeting of justice and foreign ministers from 60 countries (including the USA and China) coming together as a first step in creating a 'global policing doctrine'. It reported that Interpol and the UN were 'poised to become partners in fighting crime by jointly grooming a *global police force* [which] would be deployed as peacekeepers among rogue nations driven by war and organised crime' (emphasis added).[566] Ron Noble, secretary general of Interpol, said that among the most critical tasks were combating illegal arms, drug trafficking and peacekeeping. 'We have a visionary model', he said, 'The police will be trained and equipped differently with resources. When they stop someone, they will be consulting global databases to determine who they are stopping.'[567]

Our analysis of the architecture of global policing sketched out in Chapter 3 shows that UN policing capacity has grown exponentially since the 1960s, a growth that has accelerated during the past decade. At the same time, other global policing agencies – Interpol, the WCO and the FATF – have also grown in capacity, scope and ambition. In our view, a world police force is problematic and is probably destined to remain a law enforcer's dream. It is certainly undesirable in the absence of a global polity based on a principled separation of governmental powers and a demos created out of a widely inclusive system of cultural meaning enshrined with human rights and human security ideals. The essence of the problem for liberal democratic policing theory is the lack of any prospect of a social contract upon which to base the legitimacy claims of such an entity and the absence of an authoritative and representative body that could hold a global police force to account.

While there is no global police force, there is global policing. It seems probable that global policing will continue to play a significant part of the global governance project and seems likely to grow rather than shrink. Every hour of every day, ILOs and a global network of Interpol NCBs, alongside a web of corporate security expertise will probably continue to facilitate policing talk and information exchange, often in the 'transnational space between'. UNPOL will almost certainly carry on with their overseas missions. Regional police bodies will most likely continue to meet, make policy, train and network. Various national intelligence officers will continue to act as agents for the transnational traffic in messages. Overseas liaison officers will go on doing their work stitching together the patchwork quilt of global policing. In a networked society, global policing power can be felt at borders, ports and airports and behind the scenes of national policing bureaucracies. In domestic contexts, local police are increasingly 'globally aware' and seem set to become even more so. The experience of Derek Bond, described in Chapter 1, shows that transnational policing power can extend down to the policing of rural areas as remote as the game parks of KwaZulu-Natal. This is just one illustration of how global policing can affect anyone, in most instances without attracting the attention of the world's media, public scrutiny or democratic accountability mechanisms.

Global policing is an integral component of global governance and one of its defining features. In our view the simple functionalist notion that global policing has arisen because of a need to chase after the global bad guys does not provide a very satisfactory account of the observable transformations. Neither theories of insecurity nor theories of global governance can be complete without a theory of global policing. Any such theory must put the dualistic view of the world divided into good and evil to one side while remaining cognizant that this simplistic functional explanation creates powerful cultural expectations that have real consequences for policing.

In much the same way as domestic policing, transnational policing reflects and reinforces inequality. Priorities, politics and practices are skewed in the interests of the powerful. The policing mission and its patterns of action and justificatory rhetoric are based on the 'usual suspects' being targeted as 'suitable enemies'. And there is no shortage of these: serious organised travelling criminals, suspected terrorists, global protesters, money launderers, fugitives from justice as well as economically marginal migrants more generally. These 'folk devils' legitimate the development of new institutions and the inauguration of new powers. However, not all that is policed causes grave harm (e.g. the production and consumption of marijuana) and some extremely harmful things (e.g. environmental destruction) go un-policed.

Seen in a planetary context, the gulf between the police and the policed is very wide. The existing subculture of transnational policing is dominated by a world view that pits 'enforcers' against 'folk devils'; consequently, it often fails to foster peaceful and safe communities. It is therefore important to challenge the taken for granted assumptions of the transnational-state-system as a container for insecurity. In some places, particularly those where social exclusion and poverty are most entrenched and policing governance weakest, serious violence is endemic and police are often powerless to protect and are themselves sometimes abusive themselves. While some people are confined to insecurity hot-spots where violence and disorder are a fact of everyday life, others inhabit gated enclaves or security bubbles, excluding, or attempting to exclude, global insecurity. This exclusivity, let us not forget, has given rise to what some scholars have called 'social junk' that is, people who have fallen through the cracks – impoverished, economically and ultimately socially excluded.[568]

The construction of these outsiders tends to be couched in racialised terms relegating the black and brown peoples of the global south to the ranks of the permanently excluded. Around the world there are plenty of examples of trans-national policing power having iatrogenic effects that damage human well-being.[569] Such contradictions lead inevitably to a crisis of legitimacy and exacerbate the security–control paradox: the more police are empowered with legal tools, surveillance and coercive technologies in the name of 'providing security', the less secure some people actually become. Trapped in a cycle of insecurity, policing slides into a strategy of colonial war and counter-insurgency in an attempt to enforce peace through superior firepower. The result is 'social dynamite' and the socially excluded become rebellious and violent.[570]

As policing becomes the dominant modality of global social ordering, the destructive association of governance with enforcement power distorts every other aspect of security governance including public health, education and public administration.[571] That is one reason why a theory of global policing is so vital and rather more complex than the usual functionalist thinking assumes. In this book we have concentrated on developing a theoretical language for talking about global policing that not only challenges these functionalist assumptions but also provides a robust analysis based on empirical research findings. In doing so, we show the continuity clearly in the development of transnational police co-operation over the past century and its acceleration at the end of the Cold War. The idea that global policing is a reflexive response to changes in the external security environment – such as the events of 9/11 – is incorrect.

Our theory allows for local subcultural variations in policing practice and is attuned to the fragmentation of the division of policing labour including parts under both private and public auspices. This theory is historically mindful that the roots of the policing idea are part of a conceptual system concerning the nation-state-system. The theory seeks to take into account the complex and often contradictory relations between policing and law as it is played out in a global polycentric power system where a universally recognised source of authority is absent. Finally, this theory explains how a policing field that is practically or organisationally fragmented is held together by the meanings inherent in its occupational subculture and how this system of meaning impinges on the global system by imprinting pre-programmed notions based on the transnational-state-system idea. Global policing arises out of a complex overdetermination arising from multiple factors.

Policing subculture is more important than the letter of the law because it is on the basis of culture that meanings regarding the application of law derive. In other words, legal discourse about policing makes sense of policing in the terms already actually present. We have a particular take on law that describes legal rules as tools and emphasises the discretionary responsibility of social actors in choosing how to rule with law. The symbolic content of law can have effects on cultural meanings and police are not the only social agents who have access to legal tools. However, simply put, the language for talking about transnational crime and insecurity was substantially scripted from within the subculture of transnational policing thus pre-shaping expectations about what policing law is for.

It is striking how the vocabulary of 'crime as business' prevalent in the circuits of UN governance in the early 1970s drew attention to terms like corruption and white-collar criminality by multi-national corporations and to novel types of crime such as environmental destruction. The analytical account of agenda setting presented in this book has shown that the hegemony of 'law enforcement' and 'national security discourse' leaves many lacunae in global policing practice. The shortcomings of global policing have palpable consequences for the overall health of the world system. These patterns are closely related to the continuing influence of high policing often, though not always, at the behest of military or security service agents acting within the circuits of transnational policing. The subcultural discourse of policing is shaped within a complex division of institutional labour and not all the participants have the same degree of influence. The language of insecurity that emerges, and the strategies of containment that come with it, act as a brake on the development of a global social contract or a democratic polity. Currently existing global policing practices call into question liberal democratic policing theory just as a tug-of-war intensifies between advocates of strong authority on the one side and advocates of people power on the other – the inheritors of Hobbes and Rousseau. Consequently, the possibility of a global social contract becomes ever more remote.

An important feature of the emerging transnational-state-system described in Chapter 2, is the 'hollowing out' of the Keynesian 'welfare state' and its gradual replacement with Schumpeterian ideas about a 'workfare state'. This shift in thinking, often referred to as the neo-liberal turn, has had profound consequences for policing. The theory of global policing developed here has stretched to accommodate the hybrid forms of security governance that have emerged between public and private types of policing networks which, we hasten to add, encompass the entire panoply of policing functions including both high and low forms and everything from the militarised policing of border zones to policing drugs, money, guns or fish.

Before all of the global nodes of policing and security governance can be harnessed to the language of human rights and human security, rather than the elimination of enemies, a massive cultural shift in policing would have to take place. The signs are not hopeful, least of all when it comes to observations concerning the privatisation of security functions. Studies of private security companies, private military companies and 'in-house' security in the corporate 'resource extraction industries' show an almost reckless disregard for disempowered communities. Privatised security in urban contexts reflects social class differences patterning the mixed geography of the global south in the global north. Keeping in mind the preponderance of private security and private interest in the production of the global policing apparatus, the predominant preference for private capital accumulation precipitates further insecurity. Private interest provokes public insecurity and then retreats behind walls and security barriers.

The transgressive effects of corporate power in a global system predicated on neo-liberal ideas makes the transnational-state-system fundamentally different from the nation-state-system that preceded it. This transforms the linguistic possibilities for articulating a global social contract and the terms of its legitimacy. Ideas about a global social contract between all individuals are considerably challenged in an age where corporations have become legal persons. The extent and nature of corporate organisation and the ways in which it co-articulates with the global structures of governance in the late modern age are challenges to a just and equitable global social contract.

Our analysis makes this claim on the basis of a social constructionist perspective. It is controversial for many, perhaps most, people to learn that phenomena like 'transnational organised crime' and 'terrorism' are socially constructed. This is no denial on our part of the very real violence associated with illicit markets and political extremism. Of course the violence associated with both phenomena have real consequences. The death and destruction caused by armed violence – irrespective of where in the world it takes place and whether it is carried out by 'criminals', 'gangsters', 'terrorists', 'corporations', 'states' or any other kind of organisation – is a major social and political problem. It is only right that scholars think about solutions to violence whether it is instrumental, expressive or political. The constructivist approach challenges the presumptions that the 'real threats' posed by 'suitable enemies' are enough to justify the construction of a global policing architecture. Still, there can be no doubt that there are people who will kill for an idea or ideological commitment, and who will exploit the economic weakness of others ruthlessly through the means of illicit market transactions. Obviously, we condemn such acts.

It is equally important to acknowledge that appearances can be deceptive and it is not always the case that the social actors claiming to be 'good guys' and pointing fingers at the 'bad guys over there' have anyone's best interests in mind other than their own. Indeed, we would even go so far as to say that it is more important to unmask the taken for granted assumptions, because the rhetoric of 'war on terror' and 'war on crime' have well documented harmful effects. If the solution to the problem of terrorism or drugs trafficking exacerbates the harm associated with the phenomenon at hand, we simply have to reconsider the terms of discourse used to describe the problem. Thinking as police researchers who have spent many years working and researching inside police organisations, we hold an appreciation of policework, especially when it comes to violence.

Sometimes there will be people who can only be prevented by coercive means from doing real harm to others. Police action will therefore feature in any social order; the point is to prevent it from becoming oppressive. Other commentators in this field may eschew normative contemplations in favour of a 'strict examination of empirical developments' along realist assumptions, but we have tried to challenge Manichean thinking while remaining pragmatically engaged with the idea of global policing.[572] There are many authors who provide technocratic analyses prioritising the enforcer's role. In our view it would be better if the diplomats, field-operators and problem solvers moved centre-stage because we firmly believe that one of the most important virtues of good policing is to minimise the use of coercive solutions to social problems.[573] The enforcer role-type will obviously continue as a player in the drama of global policing, but a welcome sign of improvement would be that this role moved from centre-stage to the margins in the theatre of police operations.

In this book we have attempted to describe the forms of transnational policing, their historical genesis and future trajectory so as to raise key theoretical and practical questions about the emerging global system. We have sought to make global policing theoretically visible. In our way of thinking, policing is an essential aspect of any social order but it cannot live up to its normative claims – to maintain the health of the social body and to ensure a generalised state of prosperity – without the legitimacy and accountability that spring from a social contract widely experienced as just. As policing moves into the transnational realm, there will likely evolve a supranational system to regulate its power within and beyond national borders 'from above' and an active globally connected civil society to engage police accountability 'from below'.[574] Developing global policing with the capacity to maintain peace and order and to contribute to good governance means strengthening the democratic ethos or 'constabulary ethic'.[575] Such an ethos would be imbued with notions and principles such as responsiveness to the global commonwealth, adherence to international human rights norms and the values of 'human security'. Accountability would run through its entire blood stream in delivering a service to the public as well in the democratic functioning within policing institutions in order to ensure that global policing reflects the communities that it serves.[576] We hope that making global policing *visible* – empirically and theoretically – will facilitate this process.

In these pages we have engaged with one of the most pressing questions of our time – how peaceful and safe communities be can sustained or created in a world in which the sources of insecurity and the forces of 'law and order' originate beyond the boundaries of the nation-state. This conclusion is therefore a kind of ending, but also a beginning for new thinking about the provision and regulation of good policing in the global system.

ENDNOTES

1 We are both grateful recipients of Economic and Social Research Council (ESRC) grants 'Police co-operation in the English Channel Region' H52427006194, and 'Transatlantic police cooperation' RES000220102. This book draws on the theory and empirical evidence produced through these studies.

2 Malcolm Anderson (1989) *Policing the World*. Oxford: Oxford University Press; Malcolm Anderson, Monica den Boer, Peter Cullen, William Gilmore, Charles Raab and Neil Walker (1995) *Policing the European Union*. Oxford: Oxford University Press; Ethan Nadelmann (1993) *Cops Across Borders: The Internationalization of U.S. Criminal Law Enforcement*. University Park, PA: Pennsylvania State University Press.

3 Anderson et al., *Policing the European Union* see fn 2, p179.

4 Ethan Nadelmann, *Cops Across Borders*, see fn 2, p470.

5 Ibid., see fn 2, p10.

6 Mathieu Deflem (2004) *Policing World Society: Historical Foundations of International Police Cooperation*. Oxford: Oxford University Press; H.-H. Liang (1992) *The Rise of Modern Police and the European State System from Metternich to the Second World War*. Cambridge: Cambridge University Press; M. Mazower (ed.) (1997) *The Policing of Politics in the Twentieth Century: Historical Perspectives*. Oxford: Berghahn Books; James Sheptycki (1995) 'Transnational Policing and the Makings of a Postmodern State'. *British Journal of Criminology*, 35(4): 613–35; James Sheptycki (1998) 'Policing, Postmodernism and Transnationalisation'. *British Journal of Criminology*, 38(3): 485–503.

7 James Sheptycki (ed.) (2000) *Issues in Transnational Policing*. London: Routledge; Andrew Goldsmith and James Sheptycki (eds) (2007) *Crafting Transnational Policing*. Oxford: Hart Publishing; D. Brown (ed.) (2008) *Combating International Crime: The Longer Arm of the Law*. London: Routledge-Cavendish.

8 Bernard Porter (1992) *Plots and Paranoia: A History of Political Espionage in Britain 1790–1988*. London: Routledge, ch. 6.

9 Richard Bach Jensen (2001) 'The United States, International Policing and the War against Anarchist Terrorism 1900–1914'. *Terrorism and Political Violence*, 13(1): 15–46.

10 Mathieu Deflem, *Policing World Society*, see fn 6; Jensen, 'The United States, International Policing', see fn 9.

11 Interpol, *Annual Report* 2007.

12 Ben Bowling (2010) *Policing the Caribbean*. Oxford: Oxford University Press.

13 U. Thant, UN Secretary General (13 June 1963) cited by Beth Greener (2009) *The New International Policing*. London: Palgrave Macmillan, p1.

14 UN Police Adviser Andrew Hughes addressing INTERPOL's 77th General Assembly, 8 October 2008, 'Organized Crime Threatens Peace Efforts, Top UN Police Official Warns Interpol'. UN Police Divison Press Release, 8 October 2008.

15 Ibid., see fn 14; 'Combating terrorism, organised crime among UN police work, says top adviser'. UN Police Division Press Release, 12 February 2009.

16 ICC Assembly of State Parties, *Proposed Programme Budget for 2010 of the International Criminal Court*, Eighth Session, The Hague 18–26 November 2009. ICC-ASP/8/10 advance version, 17 July 2009.

17 Han-Ru Zhou (2005) 'The Enforcement of Arrest Warrants by International Forces: From the ICTY to the ICC'. *Journal of International Criminal Justice*, 4: 202–18.

18 Christopher Mullins, David Kauzlarich and Dawn Rothe (2004) 'The International Criminal Court and the Control of State Crime: Prospects and Problems'. *Critical Criminology*, 285: 304.

19 Sandra Fowler (2008) 'Legal Attachés and Liaison: the FBI', in S. Brown (ed.) *Combating International Crime: The Longer Arm of the Law*, see fn 7, p122.

20 Such as the G7/8/20, the OECD, IMF, UN, ICC, etc.

21 Michael Mann (1997) 'Has Globalization Ended the Rise and Rise of the Nation-state?'. *Review of International Political Economy*, 4(2): 472–96.

22 In Otfried Höffe's vision of a Global Republic, the maintenance of peace, security and the rule of law require 'a permanent global police force'. Otfried Höffe (2007) *Democracy in an Age of Globalisation*. Guildford: Springer.

23 'Wine Tasting Pensioner Finds Himself in Jail and Wanted by the FBI'. *Daily Telegraph* 26 February 2003; 'British Pensioner Hits Out at FBI'. *Guardian* 26 February 2003; Terry Kirby, 'Briton, 72, Arrested on FBI Warrant Is a Victim of Identity Fraud, Family Says'. *Independent* 26 February 2003.

24 David Brown, 'Man Arrested by FBI for Fraud a Briton'. *Independent* 28 February 2003; Terry Kirby, 'Pensioner May Sue US over 17 Days Spent in jail'. *Independent* 27 February 2003.

25 The question of whether US agents are permitted under US Federal law to engage in extraterritorial arrests and the extent to which they may be held accountable for actions overseas has long been controversial. The leading cases stem from the 1990 abduction of Dr Alvarez-Machain from his medical office by Mexican nationals under the direction of the US Drug Enforcement Administration (DEA) and taken from Mexico to the USA to be tried for his alleged role in the murder of a DEA agent in Mexico. After he was acquitted, Alvarez-Machain sought civil claims against the US and a Mexican involved in his abduction. The US Supreme Court ruled in two cases – *Sosa* v. *Alvarez-Machain*, 03–339, and *United States* v. *Alvarez-Machain*, 03–485, on 29 June 2004 – that the Federal Tort Claims Act (FTCA) prohibits claims for injuries that occurred on foreign territory and that the Alien Tort Claims Act (ATCA) does not permit parties to recover claims for arbitrary detention by US officials or their agents acting overseas. In the light of this judgment, it seems unlikely that Derek Bond would have succeeded in his pursuit of damages against the FBI.

26 Katja Franko Aas (2007) *Globalization and Crime*. London: Sage.

27 James Q. Wilson (1975) *Thinking About Crime*, revised edn. New York: Vintage.

28 Mark Galeotti (2005) *Global Crime Today: The Changing Face of Organised Crime*. London: Routledge.

29 Pasquale Pasquino (1991) 'The Foucault Effect: Studies in Governmentality', in Graham Burchell, Colin Gordon and Peter Miller (eds) *Theatricum Politicum: The Genealogy of Capital – Police and the State of Prosperity, with Two Lectures by and an Interview with Michel Foucault*. Chicago, IL: University of Chicago Press, p111.

30 Marcus Dirk Dubber (2005) *The Police Power: Patriarchy and the Foundations of American Government*. New York: Columbia University Press, pxi.

31 Marcus Dirk Dubber and Mariana Valverde (2006) *The New Police Science: The Police Power in Domestic and International Governance*. Stanford, CA: Stanford University Press.

32 Mark Neocleous (1998) 'Policing and Pin-making; Adam Smith, Police and the State of Prosperity'. *Policing and Society*, 8(4): 425–49.

33 Pasquino, 'Theatricum Politicum', see fn 29, p109.

34 Egon Bittner (1980) *The Functions of the Police in Modern Society*. Cambridge: Oelgeschlager; Egon Bittner (1974) 'Florence Nightingale in Pursuit of Willie Sutton: A Theory of Police', in H. Jacob (ed.) *The Potential for Reform of Criminal Justice, Sage Criminal Justice System Annuals*. Beverly Hills, CA: Sage, pp17–44.

35 Jean-Paul Brodeur (2007) 'An Encounter with Egon Bittner'. *Crime, Law and Social Change*, 48: 105–132.

36 Egon Bittner, *The Functions of the Police in Modern Society*, see fn 34, p39.

37 William Muir (1979) *Police: Streetcorner Politicans*. Chicago, IL: University of Chicago Press.

38 David Bayley (1985) *Patterns of Policing: A Comparative International Analysis*. New Brunswick, NJ: Rutgers University Press; P. Chevegny (1997) *Edge of the Knife: Police Violence in the Americas*. New York: Free Press.

39 James Sheptycki (2002) 'Postmodern Power and Transnational Policing: Democracy, the Constabulary Ethic and the Response to Global (In)Security', Geneva Centre for the Democratic Control of Armed Forces, Working Paper Series, No. 19, p20.

40 Hsi-Huey Liang (1992) *The Rise of Modern Police and the European State System from Metternich to the Second World War*. Cambridge: Cambridge University Press; E.H. Monkkonen (1981) *Police in Urban America 1860–1920*. Chicago, IL: University of Chicago Press.

41 Richard Ericson and Kevin Haggerty (1997) *Policing the Risk Society*. Toronto, Canada: Toronto University Press.

42 Stan Cohen (1988a) 'Western Crime Models in the Third World: Benign or Malignant', in Stan Cohen (ed.) *Against Criminology*. New Brunswick, NJ: Transaction Books, original paper presented at the University of Ibadan, Nigeria 1980; Ben Bowling (2011) 'Transnational Criminology and the Globalisation of Harm Production', in Mary Bosworth and Carolyn Hoyle (eds) *What Is Criminology?* Oxford: Oxford University Press.

43 John Kleinig (1996) *The Ethics of Policing*. Cambridge: Cambridge University Press, pp11–22.

44 Cf. Bertrand Russell (1945) *A History of Western Philosophy*. New York: Simon & Schuster.

45 John Kleinig, *The Ethics of Policing*, see fn 43, pp12–14.

46 Bertrand Russell, *A History of Western Philosophy*, see fn 44, p684.

47 Arthur M. Schlesinger, Jr (1973) *The Imperial Presidency*. Boston, MA: Houghton Mifflin Company; William Merren (2005) *Baudrillard and the Media*. Cambridge: Polity Press, p111.

48 David Trend (1997) *Cultural Democracy: Politics, Media and New Technology*. Albany, NY: State University of New York Press.

49 Bertrand Russell, *A History of Western Philosophy*, see fn 44, p616.

50 Charles Tilly (1985) 'War-Making and State-Making as Organized Crime', in P. Evans, E. Reuschemeyer and T. Skocpol (eds) *Bringing the State Back In*. Cambridge: Cambridge University Press, pp169–86.

51 Jean-Paul Brodeur (1983) 'High Policing and Low Policing; Remarks about the Policing of Political Activities', *Social Problems*, 30(5): 507–20.

52 Marc Raeff (1983) *The Well-Ordered Police State: Social and Institutional Change Through Law in the Germanies and Russia, 1600–1800*. New Haven, CT: Yale University Press.

53 Willbur Miller (1977) *Cops and Bobbies: Police Authority in New York and London, 1830–1870*. Chicago, IL: University of Chicago Press.

54 Michael Hardt and Antonio Negri (2000) *Empire*. Cambridge, MA: Harvard University Press, pxii.

55 Ibid., p6.
56 Anne-Marie Slaughter (2004) *A New World Order*. Princeton, NJ: Princeton University Press, pp13–14.
57 George Monbiot (2006) *The Age of Consent: A Manifesto for a New World Order*. New York: New Press.
58 Eg. David Held and Anthony McGrew (2007) *Globalization/Anti-Globalization*, 2nd edn. Cambridge: Polity Press.
59 Roger Cotterell (1992) *The Sociology of Law*, 2nd edn. Oxford: Oxford University Press.
60 Sally Engle Merry (1988) 'Legal Pluralism', *Law and Society Review*, 22(5): 869–96.
61 Roger Cotterell (2003) *The Politics of Jurisprudence: A Critical Introduction to Legal Philosophy*. Oxford: Oxford University Press.
62 Neil Walker (2007) *Policing in a Changing Constitutional Order*. London: Sweet and Maxwell.
63 Robert Reiner (2000) *The Politics of the Police*, 3rd edn. Oxford: Oxford University Press, p116.
64 Tom R. Tyler (1990) *Why People Obey the Law*. New Haven, CT: Yale University Press; Tom R. Tyler (2000) 'Social Justice; Outcome and Procedure', *International Journal of Psychology*, 35: 117–25.
65 Doreen McBarnet (1981) *Conviction: Law, the State and the Construction of Justice*. London: Macmillan; Doreen McBarnet (1982) 'Legal Form and Legal Mystification', *International Journal of the Sociology of Law*, 10: 409–17.
66 Richard Victor Ericson (1983) *The Constitution of Legal Inequality*. The 1983 John Porter Memorial Lecture. Ottawa: Carleton University, Information Services, p32.
67 On socio-legal approaches to law generally see Richard Abel (1995) *The Law and Society Reader*. New York: New York University Press. On police as low visibility decision makers see Joseph Goldstein (1960) 'Police Discretion Not to Invoke the Criminal Process: Low-Visibility Decisions in the Administration of Justice', *Yale Law Journal*, 69(4): 554–62; see also Peter K. Manning (2004) *The Narc's Game: Organizational and Informational Limits on Drug Law Enforcement*. Prospect Heights, IL: Waveland Press; Cyrille Fijnaut and Gary Marx (1995) *Undercover: Police Surveillance in Comparative Perspective*. The Hague: Kluwer.
68 David Kairys (1998) *The Politics of Law: a Progressive Critique*. New York: Basic Books, p435.
69 Sue Ellen Schuerman (1992) 'Establishing a Tort Duty for Police Failure to Respond to Domestic Violence', *Arizona Law Review*, 34: 355–8.
70 Eve Buzawa and Carl Buzawa (2002) *Domestic Violence; The Criminal Justice Response*, 3rd edn. Thousand Oaks, CA: Sage.
71 Egon Bittner (1967) 'The Police on Skid Row', *American Sociological Review*, 32(5): 699–715.
72 Richard Ericson (2007) *Crime in an Insecure World*. Cambridge: Polity. The preceding paragraphs draw extensively on the work of R.V. Ericson, RIP.
73 Christopher Gane and M. Mackarel (1996) 'The Admissibility of Evidence Obtained from Abroad into Criminal Proceedings – The Interpretation of Mutual Legal Assistance Treaties and Use of Evidence Irregularly Obtained'. *European Journal of Crime, Criminal Law and Criminal Justice*, 4: 98–119, esp. p114–115.
74 Roger Grimshaw and Tony Jefferson (1984) *Interpreting Policework*. London: Allen & Unwin; Roger Grimshaw and Tony Jefferson (1984) *Controlling the Constable: Policing Accountability in England and Wales*. London: Allen & Unwin.
75 Mike Brogden (1987) 'The Emergence of the Police – the Colonial Dimension', *British Journal of Criminology*, 27(1): 4–14; D. Anderson and D. Killingray (1991) *Policing the Empire: Government, Authority and Control, 1830–1940*. Manchester: Manchester

University Press; D. Anderson and D. Killingray (1992) *Policing and Decolonisation: Nationalism, Politics and the Police, 1917–1965*. Manchester: University of Manchester Press; S.H. Palmer (1988) *Police and Protest in England and Ireland 1780–1850*. Cambridge: Cambridge University Press; Georgina Sinclair (2006) *At the End of the Line: Colonial Policing and the Imperial Endgame, 1945–80*. Manchester: Manchester University Press; Max Boot (2002) *The Savage Wars of Peace; Small Wars and the Rise of American Power*. New York: Basic Books; Chalmers Ashby Johnson (2004) *Blowback: The Costs and Consequences of American Empire*, 2nd edn. New York: Holt Paperback.

76 Alice Hills (2000) *Policing Africa: Internal Security and the Limits of Liberalization*. Boulder, CO: Lynne Rienner; Biko Agozino (2004) 'Crime, Criminology and Post-Colonial Theory: Criminological Reflections on West Africa', in James Sheptycki and Ali Wardak (eds) *Transnational and Comparative Criminology*. London: Taylor & Francis, pp117–34.

77 Colonial rule in West Central Africa, in what was the Congo Free State (1884–1908) and then later the Belgian Congo 1908–1960 was an extreme exception to this. Crawford Young (1994) *The African Colonial State in Comparative Perspective*. New Haven, CT: Yale University Press.

78 Georgina Sinclair, *At the End of the Line*, see fn 75.

79 John Newsinger (2006) *The Blood Never Dried: A People's History of the British Empire*. London: Pluto.

80 John Brewer (1994) *Black and Blue*. Oxford: Oxford University Press, pp5–10; Georgina Sinclair, *At the End of the Line*, see fn 75.

81 Robert Reiner, *The Politics of the Police*, see fn 63.

82 Mike Brogden (1987) 'The Emergence of the Police – the Colonial Dimension', see fn 75.

83 Trevor Jones and Tim Newburn (1996) *Policing and Disaffected Communities: A Review of the Literature*. A Report to the Standing Advisory Committee on Human Rights. London: Policy Studies Institute, pp3–4.

84 Paul Gilroy (2004) *After Empire: Multiculture or Postcolonial Melancholia*. London: Routledge, p47.

85 On the concept of 'global south', see J. Rigg (2007) *An Everyday Geography of the Global South*. London: Routledge.

86 Institute of Race Relations (1987) *Policing Against Black People*. London: Institute of Race Relations.

87 Graham Ellison and Nathan Pino (2010) *Globalization, Development and Police Reform: Doing it the Western Way?* London: Palgrave Macmillan.

88 Adam Edwards and Pete Gill (2002) 'The Politics Of "Transnational Organized Crime": Discourse, Reflexivity and the Narration of "Threat"', *The British Journal of Politics and International Relations*, 4(2): 245–270.

89 Ulrich Beck (2000) 'What Is Globalization?', in D. Held and A. McGrew (eds) *The Global Transformation Reader: An Introduction to the Globalization Debate*. Cambridge: Polity, pp99–103, quotes from p 101, emphasis in original.

90 James Sheptycki (2002) *In Search of Transnational Policing*. Aldershot: Ashgate.

91 Clifford Shearing and Phillip Stenning (1997) 'From the Panopticon to Disney World: The Development of Discipline', in Ronald V. Clark (ed.) *Situational Crime Prevention: Successful Case Studies*, 2nd edn. Guilderland, NY: Harrow and Heston Publishers; C. Shearing and D. Bayley (1996) 'The Future of Policing', *Law and Society Review*, 30(3): 585–606; Les Johnston (2000) 'Transnational Private Policing: The Impact of Global Commercial Security', in James Sheptycki (ed.) *Issues in Transnational Policing*, see fn 7, pp21–42; Conor O'Reilly (2010) *Policing Global Risks: The Transnational Security Consultancy Industry*. Oxford: Hart Publishing.

92 Richard Ericson and Kevin Haggerty, *Policing the Risk Society*, see fn 41; Kevin Haggerty and Richard Ericson (2000) 'The Surveillant Assemblage', *British Journal of Sociology*, 51(4): 605–622.

93 James Sheptycki, *Issues in Transnational Policing*, see fn 7; Monica den Boer (guest ed.) (2002) *Policing and Society: Special Issue on Police Accountability in Europe*, 12(4).

94 Michael Mann, 'Has Globalization Ended...', see fn 21.

95 Adapted from Ben Bowling (2009) 'Transnational Policing: The Globalisation Thesis; a Typology and Research Agenda', *Policing: A Journal of Policy and Practice*, 3(2): 149–60.

96 Dick Hobbs and Colin Dunnighan (1998) 'Glocal Organised Crime: Context and Pretext', in Vincenzo Ruggeiero, Nigel South and Ian Taylor (eds) *The New European Criminology*. London: Routledge, pp289–303, quotes p289.

97 Maureen Cain (2000) 'Orientalism, Occidentalism and the Sociology of Crime'. *British Journal of Criminology*, 40(2): 239–60.

98 James Sheptycki (1998) 'The Global Cops Cometh: Reflections on Transnationalisation, Knowledge Work and Police Subculture'. *British Journal of Sociology*, 49(1): 57–74.

99 James Sheptycki (2010) 'The Constabulary Ethic Reconsidered', in F. Lemieux (ed.) *International Police Cooperation: Emerging Issues, Theory and Practice*. Cullompton, Devon: Willan Publishing, pp298–319.

100 Robert Reiner (1997) 'Police and Policing', in M. Maguire, R. Morgan and R. Reiner (eds) *The Oxford Handbook of Criminology*, 2nd edn. Oxford: Oxford University Press, pp997–1049, quote p1007.

101 C. Wright Mills (1959) *The Sociological Imagination*. New York: Oxford University Press, p8.

102 Bob Jessop (2004) 'Hollowing Out the 'Nation-state' and Multilevel Governance', in P. Kennett (ed.) *Handbook of Comparative Social Policy*. Cheltenham: A Edward Elgar Publishing, pp11–25, p23; Mann, 'Has Globalization Ended...', see fn 21.

103 David Held (2004) *Global Covenant: The Social Democratic Alternative to the Washington Consensus*. Cambridge: Polity Press.

104 Peter Singer (2002) *One World*. New Haven, CT: Yale University Press.

105 Leslie Sklair (1995) *The Sociology of the Global System*, 2nd edn. Baltimore MD: Johns Hopkins University Press; Leslie Sklair (2009) 'The transnational capitalist class and the politics of capitalist globalisation', in S. Dasgupta and J. NedeNeen (eds). London: Sage. pp82–97.

106 Peter Andreas (2004) 'Illicit International Political Economy: The Clandestine Side of Globalization', *Review of International Political Economy*, 11(3): 642–52; Naomi Klein (2008) *The Shock Doctrine: the Rise of Disaster Capitalism*. Toronto: Vintage Books Canada.

107 Manuell Castells (2007) 'Communication, Power and Counter-Power in the Network Society', *International Journal of Communication*, 1(1): 238–66.

108 Jonathan Zittrain (2008) *The Future of the Internet and How to Stop It*. New Haven CT: Yale University Press.

109 Ben Bowling, 'Transnational Policing', see fn 95.

110 David Harvey (1990) *The Condition of Postmodernity: An Enquiry into the Origins of Cultural Change*. Cambridge, MA: Blackwell.

111 David Held and Anthony McGrew (2000) 'The Great Globalisation Debate: An Introduction', in David Held and Anthony McGrew (eds) *The Globalisation Reader*. Cambridge: Polity.

112 George Monbiot, *The Age of Consent*, see fn 57; Peter Singer (2002) *One World*. fn 104.

113 Steven Spitzer (1975) 'Toward a Marxian Theory of Deviance', *Social Problems*, 22(5): 638–51.

114 Christian Parenti (2008) *Lockdown America: Police and Prisons in the Age of Crisis.* London: Verso.

115 Manuel Castells (1989) *The Informational City: Information Technology, Economic Restructuring and the Urban Regional Process.* Oxford: Blackwell; Manuel Castells (1996) *The Rise of the Network Society, the Information Age: Economy, Society and Culture,* Vol. 1, 2nd edn. Oxford: Blackwell; Manuel Castells (1997) *The Power of Identity, The Information Age: Economy, Society and Culture,* Vol. 2, 2nd edn. Oxford: Blackwell; Manuel Castells (1998) *End of the Millennium, The Information Age: Economy, Society and Culture,* Vol. 3, 2nd edn. Oxford: Blackwell; Manuel Castells, 'Communication, Power and Counter-Power', see fn 107; Lesley Sklair (1995) *Sociology of the Global System.* fn 105; David Held and Anthony McGrew, *Globalization/Anti-Globalization,* see fn 58; I. Wallerstein (2004) *World-Systems Analysis: An Introduction.* Durham, NC: Duke University Press; P. Beyer (2001) *Religion in Process of Globalization.* Würzburg: Ergon Verlag.

116 John Burton (1972) *World Society.* Cambridge: Cambridge University Press, pp28–31.

117 Maurice Punch and T. Naylor (1973) 'The Police: A Social Service', *New Society,* 24(554): 358–61, in Robert Reiner (ed.) (1996) *Policing Vol. 1: Cops, Crime and Control: Analysing the Policing Function.* Aldershot: Ashgate, The International Library of Criminology, Criminal Justice and Penology Series.

118 BBC News Channel, 'UK police end tsunami operation', Tuesday 28 February 2006.

119 Roger Clark (1994) *The United Nations Crime Prevention and Criminal Justice Program: Formulations of Standards and Efforts at Their Implementation.* Washington DC: Procedural Aspects of Law Institute; Adam Edwards and Peter Gill (2004) *Transnational Organised Crime: Perspectives on Global Security.* London: Routledge; Margaret Beare (ed.) (2003) *Critical Reflections on Transnational Organized Crime, Money Laundering, and Corruption.* Toronto, Canada: University of Toronto Press; Petrus Van Duyne and M.D.H. Nelemans (forthcoming) 'Transnational Organised Crime and Plato's Cave', *Handbook of Transnational Organised Crime;* Michael Woodiwiss (2001) *Organized Crime and American Power: A History.* Toronto: University of Toronto Press.

120 UNDOC, United Nations Office on Drugs and Crime (2010) *United Nations Congresses on Crime Prevention and Criminal Justice 1955–2010, 55 Years of Achievement.* Geneva: United Nations Information Service.

121 Roger Clark, *The United Nations Crime Prevention and Criminal Justice Program,* see fn 119, p109.

122 Ezzat Fattah (1997) *Criminology, Past, Present and Future: A Critical Overview.* Basingstoke: MacMillan, p58.

123 The account that follows is mostly derived from James Sheptycki (2004) 'The Accountability of Transnational Policing Institutions: The Strange Case of Interpol', *Canadian Journal of Law and Society,* 19(1): 128–9.

124 Mathieu Deflem and Lindsay C. Maybi (2005) 'Interpol and the Policing of International Terrorism: Developments and Dynamics since September 11', in Lynne L. Snowden and Brad Whitsel (eds) *Terrorism: Research, Readings, & Realities.* Upper Saddle River, NJ: Pearson Prentice Hall, pp175–91.

125 House of Commons Home Affairs Committee (1995) *Organised Crime.* London: HMSO; A. Scherrer (2009) *G8 Against Transnational Organized Crime.* Aldershot: Ashgate; Adam Edwards and Peter Gill (2004) *Transnational Organised Crime: Perspectives on Global Security.* London: Routledge; Margaret Beare (ed.) (2004) *Critical Relections on Transnational Crime, Money Laundering, and Corruption.* Toronto: University of Toronto Press.

126 'After the Twin Towers: The Global Economy Must Be Policed', *Guardian* 29 September 2001, Leader.
127 Peter Andreas and Ethan Nadelmann (2006) *Policing the Globe: Criminalization and Crime Control in International Relations*. Oxford: Oxford University Press, p11.
128 Alan Boyle and Christine Chinkin (2007) *The Making of International Law*. Oxford: Oxford University Press.
129 Jonathan Winer (2004) *Cops Across Borders: The Evolution of Transatlantic Law Enforcement and Judicial Co-operation*. Council on Foreign Relations, URL: http://www.cfr.org/publication/7393/cops_across_borders.html, p2.
130 Mathieu Deflem (2000) 'Bureaucratization and Social Control: Historical Foundations of International Policing', *Law & Society Review*, 34(3): 601–40, p634.
131 Ethan Nadelmann, *Cops Across Borders*, see fn 2.
132 Cyrille Fijnaut and Gary Marx (1995) *Undercover: Police Surveillance in Comparative Perspective*, see fn 67; Gary Marx (1989) *Undercover: Police Surveillance in America*. Los Angeles, CA: University of California Press.
133 James Sheptycki (1997) 'Transnationalism, Crime Control and the European State System: A Review of the Literature'. *International Criminal Justice Review*, 7: 130–40, p136.
134 Maurice Punch (2003) 'Rotten Orchards: "Pestilence", Police Misconduct and System Failure'. *Policing and Society*, 13(2): 171–96; James Sheptycki (1999) 'Political Culture and Structures of Social Control: Police Related Scandal in Low Countries in Comparative Perspective', *Policing and Society*, 9(1): 1–32.
135 Ethan Nadelmann, *Cops Across Borders*, see fn 2.
136 James Sheptycki (2000) 'The "Drug War": Learning from the Paradigm Example of Transnational Policing', in James Sheptycki (ed.) *Issues in Transnational Policing*, see fn 7, pp201–28.
137 Peter Andreas and Ethan Nadelmann, *Policing the Globe*, see fn 127, p41.
138 Edward Jay Epstein (1977) *Agency of Fear; Opiates and Political Power in America*. New York: Putnam and Sons, p105.
139 Peter Andreas and Ethan Nadelmann, *Policing the Globe*, see fn 127, pp49–51.
140 We are thinking here about the policing surveillance scandal that became public in 2011 after it was revealed that a significant team of undercover police operatives had 'infiltrated' groups of ecological activists. See P. Lewis and R. Evans, 'Green Groups Targeted Polluters as Corporate Agents Hid in their Ranks'. *Guardian* 14 February 2011; On environmental criminology more generally see R. White (2008) *Crimes Against Nature: Environmental Criminology and Ecological Justice*. Cullompton, Devon: Willan; P. Bierne and N. South (eds) (2007) *Toward a Green Criminology – Confronting Harms Against Humanity, Animals and Nature*. Cullompton, Devon: Willan.
141 In the UK the Central Authority for Mutual Legal Assistance is part of the Judicial Co-operation Unit and is responsible for processing requests to and from other countries for evidence in criminal investigations and prosecutions. The Extradition Section of the same Unit processes requests to and from other countries for the surrender of persons accused or convicted of extradition crimes.
142 Clive Nicholls, Clare Montgomery and Julian B. Knowles (2007) *The Law of Extradition and Mutual Assistance*, 2nd edn. Oxford: Oxford University Press.
143 Frank Gregory (2000) 'Private Criminality as a Matter of International Concern', in James Sheptycki (ed.) *Issues in Transnational Policing*, see fn 7, pp100–34; Nadelmann, *Cops Across Borders*, see fn 2; Cyrille Fijnaut and Gary Marx, *Undercover: Police Surveillance in Comparative Perspective*, see fn 67.

144 Mathieu Deflem, *Policing World Society*, see fn 6, pp223–4.

145 Richard Abel, *The Law and Society Reader*, see fn 67.

146 Roger Cotterrell (1992) *The Sociology of Law*, see fn 59; Roger Grimshaw and Tony Jefferson (1984) *Interpreting Policework*. fn 74.

147 Named after the famous Trevi fountain in Rome.

148 The *Palma Document* (Madrid, June 1989); the *Declaration of Trevi Group Ministers* (Paris, December 1989); the *Programme of Action* (Dublin, June 1990) and the *Coordinators Report on the Progress on the Palma Document* (Edinburgh, December 1992).

149 Tony Bunyan (1993) *Statewatching the New Europe: A Handbook on the European State*. London: Statewatch.

150 Fenton Bressler (1992) *Interpol*. London: Penguin, p161.

151 Paul Stares (1998) *The New Security Agenda: A Global Survey*, Japan Centre for International Exchange; Barry Buzan, Ole Waever and Jaap de Wilde (1988) *Security: A New Framework for Analysis*. London: Lynne Rienner.

152 Preamble of Council Framework Decision 2002/584/JHA.

153 URL: http://www.fairtrials.net/campaigns/article/justice_in_europe/ (accessed 20 January 2011).

154 Tony Bunyan, *Statewatching the New Europe*, see fn 149, p10–11.

155 William Geller and Norval Morris (1992) 'Relations between Federal and Local Police', in Michael Tonry and Norval Morris (eds) *Modern Policing*. Chicago, IL: University of Chicago Press, pp231–348.

156 Stephen Labaton, 'Administration Drops Plan to Merge Justice Agencies'. *New York Times* 22 October 1993.

157 The institutional cultures owe something to the personalities of the two agencies' founders: Harry J. Anslinger and the legendary J. Edgar Hoover. The launch of the FBI's 10 Most Wanted List by Hoover in early 1950 was a media sensation that is still remembered today. Anslinger's tireless promotion of harsh penalties for illegal drug use is less well remembered. He facilitated the broadcast of scurrilous news stories about cocaine-using Negros, opium-addicted Chinese and lazy Mexican marijuana smokers – stereotypical folk devils said to constitute a danger to the public. Promotion of these views came largely through the chain of newspapers owned by William Randolph Hearst. It is the racist rhetoric that probably prevents the early efforts of the FBN from being remembered with quite the same glory as that of the FBI.

158 As Frank Gregory has documented, this is merely one of a number of cases of 'judicial imperialism'. He cites literature referring to *Verdugo-Urquidez* (1986) and *US v. Noriega* (1990) as other examples of unilateral action by US enforcement agencies that receive favourable treatment in US courts. Frank Gregory (1995) 'Transnational Crime and Law Enforcement: Problems and Processes,' *Transnational Organised Crime*. Vol 4: 105–133.

159 Phillipe Sands (2006) *Lawless World: America and the Making and Breaking of Global Rules*. New York: Penguin; Stephen Grey (2006) *Ghost Plane: The True Story of the CIA Torture Program*. New York: St. Martin's Press; A. C. Thompson, and Trevor Paglen (2006). *Torture Taxi: On the Trail of the CIA's Rendition Flights*. Hoboken, New Jersey: Melville House.

160 Jerry H. Ratcliffe (2002) 'Intelligence-led Policing and the Problems of Turning Rhetoric into Practice', *Policing and Society*, 12(1): 53–66.

161 Report of the Congressional Committees Investigating the Iran-Contra Affair (S. Rep. No. 216, H.R. Rep. No. 433, 100th Cong., 1st Sess.). Washington DC: United States Government Printing Office; Stan Cohen (1996) 'Crime and Politics: Spot the Difference', *British Journal of Sociology*, 47(1): 1–21.

162 Clifford Shearing (1992) 'The Relations Between Public and Private Policing', in Michael Tonry and Norval Morris (eds) *Modern Policing*, see fn 155, pp399–434.

163 Peter Andreas and Ethan Nadelmann, *Policing the Globe*, see fn 127, p115.

164 Rita Abrahamsen and Michael Williams (2011) *Security Beyond the State: Private Security in International Politics*. Cambridge: Cambridge University Press; Graham Ellison and Conor O'Reilly (2006) 'Eye Spy Private High: Reconceptualising High Policing Theory'. *British Journal of Criminology*, 46(4): 641–60; Conor O'Reilly (2010) *Policing Global Risks*, see fn 91.

165 Wilbur Miller, *Cops and Bobbies*, see fn 53.

166 Nils Christie (1986) 'Suitable enemy', in Herman Bianchi and Rene von Swaaningen (eds) *Abolitionism: Toward a Non-repressive Approach to Crime*. Amsterdam: Free University Press.

167 Alice Sampson, Paul Stubbs, David Smith, Geoffrey Pearson and Harry Blagg (1988) 'Crime Localities and the Multi-Agency Approach', *British Journal of Criminology*, 24(4): 478–93; William Saulsbury and Ben Bowling (1991) *The Multi-Agency Approach in Practice: The North Plaistow Racial Harassment Project*. London: Home Office; A. Karabinas, B. Monaghan and J. Sheptycki (1996) 'An Evaluation of the Craigmillar Youth Challenge', *The Howard Journal*, 35(2): 113–30, doi: 10.1111/j.1468–2311.1996. tb00864.x.

168 Clive Harfield (2006) 'SOCA; a Paradigm Shift in British Policing', *British Journal of Criminology*, 46(4): 743–61.

169 Peter Kraska (2001) *Miltarizing the American Criminal Justice System: The Changing Roles of the Armed Forces and the Police*. Boston, MA: Northeastern University Press; Peter Kraska (2007) 'Militarization and Policing – Its Relevance to 21st Century Policing'. *Policing: A Journal of Police and Practice*, 1(4): 501–13.

170 Donatella Della Porta and Abby Peterson (2005) 'Special Issue: Policing Political Protest After Seattle', *Policing and Society*, 15(3); Luis A. Fernandez (2008) *Policing Dissent: Social Control and the Anti-globalization Movement*. Chapel Hill, NC: Rutgers University Press.

171 Kevin Haggerty and Richard Ericson (2001) 'The Military Technostructures of Policing', in Peter Kraska (ed.) *Miltarizing the American Criminal Justice System: The Changing Roles of the Armed Forces and the Police*, see fn 169, pp43–44.

172 Pete Gill and Mark Phythian (2006) *Intelligence in and Insecurity World: Surveillance, Spys and Snouts*. Cambridge: Polity Press; Peter Gill, Stephen Marrin and Mark Phythian (2008) *Intelligence Theory: Key Questions and Debates*. London: Routledge.

173 Jerry Ratcliffe (2008) *Intelligence-led Policing*. Cullompton, Devon: Willan; Jerry Ratcliffe (ed.) (2004) *Strategic Thinking in Criminal Intelligence*. Annadale, NSW: Federation Press; Marc Alain (2001) 'The Trapeze Artists and the Ground Crew – Police Co-operation and Intelligence Exchange Mechanisms in Europe and North America: A Comparative Empirical Study', *Policing and Society*, 11(1): 1–28.

174 Gregory F. Treverton (2008) *Reorganising US Domestic Intelligence: Assessing the Options*. Santa Monica, CA: RAND Corp. Homeland Security Program and the Intelligence Policy Centre, prepared for the Department of Homeland Security.

175 Angus Smith (1997) *Intelligence Led Policing: International Perspectives on Policing in the 21st Century*. Lawrenceville, NJ: International Association of Law Enforcement Intelligence Analysts.

176 Loch Johnson (ed.) (2007) *Strategic Intelligence*. Westport, CT: Praeger Security International, p8–9.

177 Ibid., p8–9.

178 Tim Newburn (2007) 'Governing Security: The Rise of the Privatized Military', in David Downes, Paul Rock, Christine Chinkin and Conor Gearty (eds) *Crime, Social Control and Human Rights. From Moral Panics to States of Denial: Essays in Honour of Stanley Cohen*. Cullompton, Devon: Willan, pp195–210; Conor O'Reilly, *Policing Global Risks*, see fn 91; Peter Singer (2003) *Corporate Warriors: the Rise of the Privatized Military Industry*. Ithaca, NY: Cornell University Press.

179 Jeremy Scahill (2007) *Blackwater: The Rise and Fall of the World's Most Powerful Mercenary Army*. New York: Nation Books.

180 Scott Burris, Peter Drahos and Clifford Shearing (2005) 'Nodal Governance'. *Australian Journal of Legal Philosophy*, 30: 30–58; Clifford Shearing and Jennifer Wood (2003) 'Nodal Governance, Democracy and the New "Denizens"'. *Journal of Law and Society*, 30(3): 400–19; Jennifer Wood and Enrique Font (2007) 'Crafting the Governance of Security in Argentina: Engaging with Global Trends', in Andrew Goldsmith and James Sheptycki (eds) *Crafting Transnational Policing*, see fn 7; Jennifer Wood and Michael Kempa (2005) 'Understanding Global Trends in Policing: Explanatory and Normative Dimensions', in J. Sheptycki and A. Wardak (eds) *Transnational and Comparative Criminology*. London: Taylor & Francis, pp287–316.

181 Ben Goold and Liora Lazarus (eds.) *Security and Human Rights*. Portland, OR: Oxford University Press; Goldsmith and Sheptycki, *Crafting Transnational Policing*, see fn 7; Nathan Pino and Michael Wiatrowski (eds) (2006) *Democratic Policing in Transitional and Developing Countries*. Ashgate: Aldershot.

182 Biko Agozino (2004) 'Crime, Criminology and Post-Colonial Theory: Criminological Reflections on West Africa', in J. Sheptycki and A. Wardak (eds) *Transnational and Comparative Criminology*. London: Routledge/Glasshouse, pp117–134; Suzana Sawyer and Edmund Terence Gomez (2008) *Transnational Governmentality and Resource Extraction: Indigenous Peoples, Multinational Corporations, Multilateral Institutions and the State*. United Nations Research Institute for Social Development, Conflict and Cohesion Paper No. 13; David Szablowski (2007) *Transnational Law and Local Struggles: Mining Communities and the World Bank*. Oxford: Hart Publishing; Human Rights Watch, Nigeria (May 1999) *Crackdown in the Niger Delta*, 11(2a); Human Rights Watch (February 2005) *Rivers and Blood; Guns, Oil and Power in Nigeria's River State*, a Human Rights Briefing Paper.

183 Richard Sennett (1998) *The Corrosion of Character: The Personal Consequences of Capitalism*. New York: W.W. Norton and Co.; Jock Young (2007) *The Vertigo of Late Modernity*. London: Sage.

184 Robert Reiner (2007) *Law and Order: An Honest Citizen's Guide to Crime Control*. Cambridge: Polity Press.

185 Ibid., see fn 100, quote p1007.

186 Fenton Bressler, *Interpol*, see fn 150, p161.

187 Malcolm Anderson (1989) *Policing the World: Interpol and the Politics of International Police Co-operation*. Oxford, UK: Clarendon; M. Barnett and L. Coleman (2005) 'Designing Police: Interpol and the Study of Change in International Organisations'. *International Studies Quarterly*, 49: 593–619; Fenton Bressler, *Interpol*, see fn 150; Mathieu Deflem (2002) *Policing World Society*, see fn 6; Michael Fooner (1989) *Interpol: Issues in World Crime and International Criminal Justice*. New York: Plenum Press.

188 James Sheptycki, 'The Accountability of Transnational Policing Institutions', see fn 123.

189 Ibid., see fn 123, pp119–21.

190 Idib., see fn 123, pp119–21.

191 Interpol General Assembly Resolution (2006) Subject: Statement to Reaffirm the Independence and political neutrality of Interpol, AG_2006–RES–04, p1.

192 Rutsel Silvestre J. Martha (2010) *The Legal Foundations of Interpol*. Oxford: Oxford University Press.

193 James Sheptycki, 'The Accountability of Transnational Policing Institutions', see fn 123, p115.

194 Fenton Bressler, *Interpol*, see fn 150.

195 US Department of Justice (2009) *Audit Report 09–35, The United States National Central Bureau of Interpol*. US Department of Justice, Washington, DC: Office of the Inspector General.

196 Cheah Wui Ling (2010) 'Mapping Interpol's Evolution: Functional Expansion and the Move to Legalization', *Policing: A Journal of Policy and Practice*, 4(1): 28–37.

197 Ethan Nadelmann, *Cops Across Borders*, see fn 2.

198 Interpol General Assembly Resolution (2006) *Subject: Resolution Statement to Reaffirm the Independence and Political Neutrality of Interpol*. AG_2006-RES-04, p2.

199 Robert Lloyd, Jeffrey Oatham and Michael Hammer (2007) *2007 Global Accountability Report*. London: One World Trust.

200 Ben Bowling, *Policing the Caribbean*, see fn 12, p290–1.

201 Pravin Gordan (2007) 'Customs in the 21st Century', *World Customs Journal*, 1(1): 49–54.

202 International Convention on the Simplification and Harmonization of Customs Procedures (Kyoto, 18 May 1973) entered into force: 25 September 1974, URL: http://www.unece.org/trade/kyoto/.

203 Pravin Gordan, 'Customs in the 21st Century', see fn 201.

204 Ibid., see fn 201.

205 Gareth Lewis (2009) 'The Impact of ICT on Customs'. *World Customs Journal*, 3(1): 3–12, p5; Stephen Holloway (2009) 'The Transition From eCustoms to eBorder Management'. *World Customs Journal*, 3(1): 13–26, p16.

206 Memorandum of Understanding between the World Customs Organisation and the International Criminal Police Organisation, signed in Lyon, 9 November 1998.

207 Steve Charnovitz (2001) 'International Law Weekend Proceedings: Economic and Social Actors in the World Trade Organisation'. *ILSA Journal of International and Comparative Law*, 259, International and Comparative Law Association.

208 Peter Gonzales (2002) 'CARICOM, the European Union and International Linkages in External Trade Negotiations'. Paper presented at The Symposium on The European Union: A Polity in Transformation and a Model of Transition in the Americas Miami European Union Center and the Jean Monnet Chair, University of Miami.

209 Camillo Gonsalves (5 November 2009) *Statement to the United Nations General Assembly, 64th Session, 38th Plenary Meeting on International Drug Control*. New York.

210 William Gilmore (1999) *Dirty Money: The Evolution of Money Laundering Countermeasures*. Strasburg: Council of Europe Publishing.

211 Thirty-four jurisdictions and two regional organisations were members: Argentina, Australia, Austria, Belgium, Brazil, Canada, China, Denmark, European Commission, Finland, France, Germany, Greece, Gulf-Cooperation Council, Hong-Kong (China); Iceland, India, Ireland, Italy, Japan, Kingdom of the Netherlands, Luxembourg; Mexico; New Zealand, Norway, Portugal, Republic of Korea, Russian Federation, Singapore, South Africa, Spain, Sweden, Switzerland, Turkey, the United Kingdom and the United States.

212 Valsamis Mitsilegas (2003) *Money Laundering Counter-Measures in the European Union: A New Security Paradigm Versus Fundamental Legal Principles*. The Hague: Kluwer Law

International; David Garland (2001) *The Culture of Control: Crime and Social Order in Contemporary Society*. Chicago, IL: University of Chicago Press, p452; Phil Williams and Ernesto Savona (1996) *The United Nations and Transnational Organized Crime*. London: Frank Cass, p44; James Sheptycki (2000) 'Policing the Virtual Launderette: Money Laundering, New Technology and Global Governance', in James Sheptycki (ed.) see fn 7, pp134–76; Peter Grabosky and Russell G. Smith (1998) *Crime in the Digital Age: Controlling Telecommunications and Cyberspace Illegalities*. Canberra, NSW: Federation Press.

213 URL: http://www.fas.org/irp/agency/ustreas/fincen/ops.htm (accessed 24 January 2011).

214 Mike Levi (2002) 'Money Laundering and Its Regulation'. *The Annals of the American Academy of Political and Social Science*, 582(1): 181–94, doi: 10.1177/000271620258200113.

215 Mike Levi and Peter Reuter (2006) 'Money Laundering', in Michael Tonry (ed.) *Crime and Justice: A Review of Research*, 34: 289–375.

216 The UN has had a 'high policing' capacity more or less since its inception. The Security and Safety Section of the UN set up in 1946 tasked with protecting UN buildings and the security of UN staff overseas, comprised mainly of US military personnel. This body also had a role in the early days of the civilian police operations, though it is quite separate from the UN Police Division. A suicide truck-bomb attack on the UN Headquarters at the Canal Hotel in Baghdad on 19 August 2003 killing 22 UN staff and visitors and injuring more than 150 persons, exposed the vulnerability of UN missions in the 'new security' environment. In a 2004 General Assembly Resolution, the UN merged into a single security framework the security management component of the Office of the United Nations Security Coordinator, the Security and Safety Services (SSS) that secures headquarters and other offices, and the civilian security component of the Department of Peacekeeping Operations headed by an Under-Secretary-General. The only source we have found on this is Cecil T.J Redman (2004) *From the Caribbean to the United Nations: International Security Is My Business*. Shawville, Quebec: Life Profiles.

217 Beth Greener, *The New International Policing*, see fn 13; Alice Hills (2009) 'The Possibility of Transnational Policing', *Policing and Society*, 19(3): 300–17.

218 U. Thant, UN Secretary General (13 June 1963) 'The Forgotten Agenda: Human Rights and Protection in Cold War Peacekeeping', cited by Katarina Månsson (2005) 'The Forgotten Agenda: Human Rights Protection and Promotion in Cold War Peacekeeping'. *Journal of Conflict & Security Law*, 10(3): 379–403; Beth Greener, *The New International Policing*, see fn 13, p1.

219 Duncan Chappell and John Evans (1997) *The Role, Preparation and Performance of Civilian Police in United Nations Peacekeeping Operations*. Vancouver: International Centre for Criminal Law Reform and Criminal Justice Policy.

220 UN Police website (accessed 9 February 2011).

221 UN Police Adviser Andrew Hughes (8 October 2008) 'Organized Crime Threatens Peace Efforts, Top UN Police Official Warns Interpol', in addressing INTERPOL's 77th General Assembly; 'Combating Terrorism, Organized Crime Among UN Police Work, Says Top Adviser', UN Police Division Press Release (12 February 2009).

222 Erwin Schmidl (ed.) (2000) *Peace Operations Between War and Peace*. London: Frank Cass; Ririn Mobekk (2005) *Identifying Lessons in United Nations International Policing Missions*. Geneva: DCAF.

223 Frank Gregory (1996) 'The United Nations Provision of Policing Series (CIVPOL) within the Framework of "Peacekeeping" Operations: An Analysis of the Issues'. *Policing and Society*, 6(44): 145–61.

224 Elizabeth Wilmshurst (1999) 'Jurisdiction of the Court', in R.S. Lee (ed.) *The International Criminal Court: The Making of the Rome Statute*. The Hague: Kluwer Law International, p136.

225 ICC Assembly of State Parties (17 July 2009) *Proposed Programme Budget for 2010 of the International Criminal Court*, Eighth Session, 18–26 November 2009. The Hague: ICC-ASP/8/10.

226 Cherif Bassiouni and Christopher Blakesley (1992) 'The Need for an International Criminal Court in the New World International Order', *Vanderbilt Journal of Transnational Law*, 151.

227 Han-Ru Zhou, 'The Enforcement of Arrest', see fn 17.

228 Ibid., see fn 17.

229 Sherene Razack (2004) *Dark Threats and White Knights: The Somalia Affair, Peacekeeping and the New Imperialism*. Toronto: University Of Toronto Press, p42.

230 Other regional entities are set out in Table 1.2.

231 Malcolm Anderson et al., *Policing the European Union*, see fn 2.

232 Ibid., see fn 2, p12–13.

233 Eugene McLaughlin (1992) 'The Democratic Deficit: European Union and the Accountability of the British Police'. *British Journal of Criminology*, 32(4): 473–87; Ian Loader (2002) 'Governing European Policing: Some Problems, and Prospects'. *Policing and Society*, 12(4): 291–305.

234 Monica den Boer and Willy Bruggeman (2007) 'Shifting Gear: Europol in the Contemporary Policing Era'. *Politique européenne*, 3(23): 77–91; Monica den Boer (2002) 'Towards an Accountability Regime for an Emerging European Policing Governance'. *Policing and Society*, 12(4): 275–90; James Sheptycki, *In Search of Transnational Policing*, see fn 90.

235 Björn Müller-Wille (2006) 'Improving the Democratic Accountability of EU Intelligence'. *Intelligence and National Security*, 21(1): 100–28.

236 James Sheptycki (2001) 'Patrolling the New European (In)Security Field: Organisational Dilemmas and Operational Solutions for Policing the Internal Borders of Europe'. *European Journal of Crime, Criminal Law and Criminal Justice*, 9(2): 144–60.

237 Thomas Mathieson (2000) 'On the Globalisation of Social Control: Towards an Integrated Surveillance System in Europe', in P. Green and A. Rutherford (eds) *Criminal Policy in Transition*. Oxford: Oxford University Press, p175.

238 Malcolm Anderson et al., *Policing the European Union*, see fn 2, p175 and 179; Pete Gill (1994) *Policing Politics: Security Intelligence and the Liberal Democratic State*. London: Frank Cass.

239 James Sheptycki, 'Patrolling the New European (In)Security Field', see fn 236, quote p156–7.

240 M.C. Ricklefs, Bruce Lockhart, Alberrt Lau, Portia Reyes and Maitrii Aung-Thwin (2010) *A New History of South East Asia*. London: Palgrave Macmillan.

241 Peter Katzenstein (2005) *A World of Regions, Asia Europe in the American Imperium*. Ithaca, NY: Cornell University Press.

242 M.C. Ricklefs et al., *A New History of South East Asia*, see fn 240.

243 James Findlay (2008) 'Global Terror and Organised Crime: Symbiotic or Synonymous?'. *Asian Journal of Criminology*, 3(1): 75–89.

244 Nicholas Dorn and Michael Levi (2008) 'East Meets West in Anti-Money Laundering and Anti-Terrorist Finance: Policy Dialogue and Differentiation on Security, the Timber Trade and "Alternative" Banking'. *Asian Journal of Criminology*, 3(1): 91–110.

245 Ko-Lin Chin (2009) *The Golden Triangle: Inside Southeast Asia's Drug Trade*. Ithaca, NY: Cornell University Press.

246 Chin's ethnographic work is verified by the research of others. See for example C. Grundy-Warr, R. King and G. Risser (1996) *Cross-Border Migration, Trafficking and the Sex Industry: Thailand and Its Neighbours*. Durham: International Boundaries Research Unit IBRU Research Bulletin. More than a decade prior to Chin's field work they observed that trans-border illicit markets represented a growing problem in a part of the world when formerly ideological and alienating borders suddenly became critical crossing-points for businesses and communities.

247 Roderic Broadhurst (2009) 'Book Review: Ko-Lin Chin *The Golden Triangle: Inside Southeast Asia's Drug Trade*'. *Australian & New Zealand Journal of Criminology*, 42(3): 423–7.

248 David Garland (2001) *The Culture of Control: Crime and Social Order in Contemporary Society*. Chicago, IL: University of Chicago Press.

249 James Sheptycki (2009) 'Transnationalisation, Orientalism and Crime'. *Asian Journal of Criminology*, 3(1): 13–35; Jonathon Simon (2009) *Governing through Crime: How the War on Crime Transformed American Democracy and Created a Culture of Fear*. Oxford: Oxford University Press.

250 Ko-Lin Chin (2003) *Heijin: Organized Crime, Business, and Politics in Taiwan*. Armonk, NY: M.E. Sharpe; James Finckenaeur and Ko-Lin Chin (2007) *Asian Transnational Organized Crime*. New York: Nova Science Publishers.

251 Monica de Boer and Patrick Doelle (2002) 'Converge or Not to Converge... That's the Question: A Comparative Analysis of Europeanisation Trends in Criminal Justice Organisations', in M. den Boer (ed.) *Organised Crime: A Catalyst in the Europeanisation of National Police Agencies?* Maastricht: European Institute of Public Administration, pp1–71.

252 Ben Bowling and James Ross (2006) 'The Serious Organised Crime Agency: Should We Be Afraid?'. *Criminal Law Review*, DEC: 1019–1034, quote taken from p1031.

253 Gregory Treverton, *Reorganising US Domestic Intelligence*, see fn 174, quotes from pp25–7.

254 Ibid., see fn 174, quotes from pp25–7.

255 Ibid., see fn 174, pp25–7.

256 Kevin Haggerty and Richard Ericson, 'The Surveillant Assemblage', see fn 92.

257 US Department of Justice, *Audit Report 09–35*, see fn 195.

258 James Sheptycki (2004) 'Organisational Pathologies in Police Intelligence Systems: Some Contributions to the Lexicon of Intellience-led Policing'. *European Journal of Criminology*, 1(3): 307–32.

259 Robert Reiner, *The Politics of the Police*, see fn 63.

260 Alice Hills (2009) *Policing Post-Conflict Cities*. London: Zed Books; M. Hinton (2008) *Policing Developing Democracies*. London: Routledge; D. Bayley (2006) *Changing the Guard: Developing Democratic Police Abroad*. Oxford: Oxford University Press; Philip Stenning (2007) 'Review of *The State on the Streets*, by Mercedes Hinton and *Changing the Guard*, by David Bayley'. *British Journal of Criminology*, 47(2): 346–50.

261 Personal communication to authors.

262 Rita Abrahamsen and Michael Williams, *Security Beyond the State*, see fn 164; Graham Ellison and Conor O'Reilly, 'Eye Spy Private High: Reconceptualising High Policing Theory', see fn 164; Les Johnston and Clifford Shearing (2003) *Governing Security: Exploration in Policing and Justice*. London: Routledge; Les Johnston (2000) 'Transnational Private Policing: The Impact of Global Commercial Security', in James Sheptycki (ed.) see fn 7, p21–42; Conor O'Reilly, *Policing Global Risks*, see fn 91; Clifford Shearing (1992) 'The Relations Between Public and Private Policing', in Michael Tonry and Norval Morris (eds) *Modern Policing*, see fn 155, pp399–434;

Shearing and Stenning, 'From the Panopticon to Disney World', see fn 91; Clifford Shearing and David Bayley (1996) 'The Future of Policing'. *Law and Society Review,* 30(3): 585–606; Jennifer Wood and Benoît Dupont (eds) (2006) *Democracy, Society and the Governance of Security.* Cambridge: Cambridge University Press.

263 Rita Abrahamsen and Michael Williams, *Security Beyond the State,* see fn 164, p19–20.
264 Peter Kraska (2004) *Theorizing Criminal Justice.* Long Grove, IL: Waveland Press, pp14–15.
265 Rita Abrahamsen and Michael Williams, *Security Beyond the State,* see fn 164, pp82–4; see also Les Johnston and Clifford Shearing, *Governing Security,* see fn 262; Jennifer Wood and Benoît Dupont (eds), *Democracy, Society and the Governance of Security,* see fn 262.
266 Graham Ellison and Conor O'Reilly, 'Eye Spy Private High: Reconceptualising High Policing Theory', see fn 164.
267 Ian Bannon and Paul Collier (2003) *Natural Resources and Violent Conflict: Options and Actions.* Washington DC: International Bank for Reconstruction/The Word Bank, pp166–7; C. Kinsey (2006) *Corporate Soldiers and International Security: The Rise of Private Military Companies.* London: Routledge, pp125–7; S. Sawyer and E.T. Gomez (2008) *Transnational Governmentality and Resource Extraction: Indigenous Peoples, Multinational Corporations, Multilateral Institutions and the State.* United Nations Research Institute for Social Development, Conflict and Cohesion Paper No. 13; David Szablowski (2007) *Transnational Law and Local Struggles: Mining Communities and the World Bank.* Oxford: Hart Publishing; Human Rights Watch, *Crackdown in the Niger Delta,* see fn 182; Human Rights Watch, *Rivers and Blood,* see fn 182.
268 B. Whitaker (1964) *The Police.* London: Penguin Books. This author advocated a progression towards regional police forces, suggesting there be nine, as a means of improving police effectiveness and efficiency in an era of increasingly mobile problems of crime and disorder.
269 Tim John and Mike Maguire (2004) *The National Intelligence Model: Key Lessons from Early Research.* Home Office Online Report 30/04; James Sheptycki (2002) *Review of the Influence of Strategic Intelligence on Organized Crime Policy and Practice.* Home Office Special Interest Paper No. 14. London: Home Office.
270 R. Evans and P. Lewis, 'Met Counter-terrorism Chief to Take Over Protest Spy Unit'. *Guardian* 25 January 2011.
271 James Sheptycki (2007) 'Police Ethnography in the House of Serious Organized Crime', in A. Henry and D.J. Smith (eds) *Transformations of Policing.* Aldershot: Ashgate, pp51–78, esp. pp51–3.
272 James Sheptycki (2003) 'The Governance of Organised Crime in Canada', *The Canadian Journal of Sociology,* 28(3): 489–517, quote p510.
273 Ben Bowling, *Policing the Caribbean,* see fn 12, pp106–11.
274 Janet Chan (2001) 'The Technological Game: How Information Technology Is Transforming Police Practice'. *Criminal Justice,* 1(2): 139–59; Janet Chan (2003) 'Police and New Technologies', in Tim Newburn (ed.) *The Handbook of Policing.* Cullompton: Willan, pp655–79.
275 Clive Harfield (2008) 'The Organization of "Organized Crime Policing" and its International Context'. *Criminology and Criminal Justice,* 8(4): 483–507, esp. p500.
276 Katharyne Mitchell and Katherine Beckett (2008) 'Securing the Global City: Crime, Consulting, Risk, and Ratings in the Production of Urban Space'. *Indiana Journal of Global Legal Studies,* 15(1): 75–100.
277 Richard V. Ericson and Clifford Shearing (1986) 'The Scientification of Police Work', in G. Böhme and N. Stehr (eds) *The Knowledge Society.* Dordrecht: D. Reidel Publishing Co.

278 Ben Bowling (1999) 'The Rise and Fall of New York Murder: Zero Tolerance or Crack's Decline'. *British Journal of Criminology*, 39(4): 531–54; Andrew Karmen (2000) *New York Murder Mystery*. New York: NYU Press; Andrew Golub, Bruce Johnson and Eloise Dunlap (2007) 'The Race/Ethnicity Disparity in Misdemeanour Marijuana Arrests in New York City'. *Criminology and Public Policy*, 6(1): 131–64; Bernard E. Harcourt and Jens Ludwig (2007) 'Reefer Madness: Broken Windows Policing and Misdemeanour Marijuana Arrests in New York City, 1989–2000'. *Criminology and Public Policy*, 6(1): 165–82. Maurice Punch (2007) *Zero Tolerance Policing*. Bristol: Policy Press.

279 Vincent E. Henry (2002) 'The Need for a Coordinated and Strategic Local Police Approach to Terrorism: A Practitioner's Perspective'. *Police Practice and Research*, 3(4): 31–336.

280 Vincent E. Henry (2003) *The Compstat Paradigm: Management Accountability in Policing, Business and the Public Sector*. New York: Looseleaf Law Publications, esp. ch. 8 'Beyond Policing: Applying Compstat in Security Management'.

281 He subsequently left the NYPD to become Chief of the Los Angeles Police Department (LAPD) where he remained until 2009. At that time he publicly announced that he would be joining a private security firm based in New York City.

282 Diane E. Davis (2008) 'The Giuliani Factor: Crime, Zero Tolerance Policing and the Transformation of the Public Sphere in Downtown Mexico City', in Gareth A. Jones (ed.) *Public Sphere and Public Space in Mexico*. London: Palgrave Macmillan.

283 Letta Tayler, 'Giuliani's Crime Plan for Mexico City a Work in Progress'. *The Seattle Times* 11 August 2004.

284 Chris Hawley, 'Crime Fuels Demand for Security in Mexico'. *USA Today* 5 August 2007, World Section.

285 F. Mena and Dick Hobbs (2010) 'Narcophobia: Drugs Prohibition and the Generation of Human Rights Abuses'. *Trends in Organised Crime*, 13: 60–74; Julia Buxton (2006) *The Political Economy of Narcotics: Production, Consumption and Global Markets*. London: Zed Books.

286 Kees Koonings and Dirk Kruijt (2007) *Fractured Cities: Social Exclusion, Urban Violence in Latin America*. London: Zed Books; Alice Hills *Policing Post-Conflict Cities*, see fn 260; Teresa Caldeira (2000) *City of Walls: Crime, Segregation and Citizenship in São Paulo*. Berkeley, CA: University of California Press; M. Davis (1992) *City of Quartz*. London: Vintage.

287 Didier Bigo (2000) 'Liaison Officers in Europe: New Officers in the European Security Field', in James Sheptycki (ed.) *Issues in Transnational Policing*, see fn 7, p67 and 77.

288 James Sheptycki (1998) 'Police Co-operation in the English Channel Region 1968–1996'. *European Journal of Crime, Criminal Law and Criminal Justice*, 6(3): 216–36; James Sheptycki, 'Patrolling the New European (In)Security Field', see fn 236; Detlef Nogala (2001) 'Policing Across a Dimorphous Border: Challenge and Innovation at the French–German Border', *European Journal of Crime, Criminal Law and Criminal Justice*, 9(2): 130–43.

289 Didier Bigo, 'Liaison Officers in Europe', see fn 287, p67.

290 Ibid., see fn 287, p75.

291 Ibid., see fn 287, p75.

292 Ben Bowling, *Policing the Caribbean*, see fn 12, ch8. NB: the acronym FCO stands for Foreign and Commonwealth Office.

293 BBC; Profile Mark Shields; Omar Anderson, 'Not Guilty: Adams, Cops Walk Free'. *Jamaica Gleaner* 21 December 2005.

294 Marc Alain, 'The Trapeze Artists...', see fn 173.

295 Robert Reiner, 'Police and Policing', see fn 100.

296 David Downes and Paul Rock (2003) *Understanding Deviance*, 4th edn. Oxford: Oxford University Press; David Downes (1966) *The Delinquent Solution*. New York: The Free Press; S. Hall, C. Critcher, T. Jefferson, J.N. Clarke and B. Roberts (1978) *Policing the Crisis: Mugging, the State and Law and Order*. London: Palgrave MacMillan; J. Ferrell, K. Hayward and Jock Young (2008) *Cultural Criminology: An Invitation*. London: Sage.

297 James Sheptycki (2007) 'High Policing and the Security Control Society'. *Policing*, 1(1): 70–9.

298 Peter Andreas and Ethan Nadelmann, *Policing the Globe*, see fn 127, p232.

299 Robert Reiner, *The Politics of the Police*, see fn 63, pp118–21.

300 Ethan Nadelmann, *Cops Across Borders*, see fn 2, p110.

301 Robert Reiner, *The Politics of the Police*, see fn 63, pp115–38.

302 W.I. Thomas and D.S. Thomas (1928) *The Child in America: Behavior Problems and Programs*. New York: Knopf, pp571–72, cited by Jock Young (1971) *The Drug Takers: The Social Meaning of Drug Use*. London: McGibbon and Kee.

303 David Downes (1966) *The Delinquent Solution: A Study in Subcultural Theory*. London: Collier-Macmillan: Free Press, pp1–10.

304 This general point has been made by many police researchers including James Q. Wilson (1968) *Varieties of Police Behavior*. Robert Reiner (2010) provides a detailed overview (see fn 63) as does John Kleinig, *The Ethics of Policing*, see fn 43, pp77–80. See also Monique Marks (2000) 'Transforming Police Organizations from Within'. *British Journal of Criminology*, 40(4): 557–73; E. Paes-Machado and C.L. De Albuquerque (2002) 'Jungle ID: Educational Reform Inside the Brazilian Paramilitary Police'. *Policing and Society*, 13(1): 59–78; N. Conti (2010) 'A Visigoth System: Shame, Honor and Police Socialization'. *Journal of Contemporary Ethnography*, 39: 187–214.

305 Robert Reiner (2010) *The Politics of the Police* see fn 63, pp119–20; John Kleinig, *The Ethics of Policing*, see fn 43, pp77–80.

306 A useful distinction has been drawn between 'on the job trouble' – referring to police organisational difficulties – and 'in the job trouble', which refers to the fallout from contentious operations. See P. Waddington (2003) 'Policing Public Order and Political Contention', in Tim Newburn (ed.) *Handbook of Policing*. Cullompton: Willan.

307 Jerome Skolnick (1966) *Justice Without Trial: Law Enforcement in Democratic Society*. London: Palgrave Macmillan.

308 Maurice Punch (2009) *Police Corruption: Deviance, Accountability and Reform in Policing*. London: Willan.

309 Egon Bittner (1967) 'Police Discretion in Emergency Apprehension of Mentally Ill Persons'. *Social Problems*, 14: 279–92; Egon Bittner (1974) 'Florence Nightingale in Pursuit of Willie Sutton: A Theory of Police', see fn 34.

310 Egon Bittner (1970) *The Functions of Police in Modern Society*. Oelgeschlager: Gunn & Hain, p56

311 One interesting take on this literature is P.A.J. Waddington (1999) 'Police (Canteen) Sub-Culture: An Appreciation'. *British Journal of Criminology*, 39(2): 287–309; see also Janet Chan (1996) 'Changing Police Culture'. *The British Journal of Criminology*, 36(1): 109–34.

312 William Muir (1979) *Police; Streetcorner Politicians*, see fn 37, p48.

313 Elizabeth Reuss-Ianni (1983) *Two Cultures of Policing: Street Cops and Management Cops*. New Brunswick, NJ: Transaction Books.

314 George Rigakos (2002) *The New Parapolice: Risk Markets and the Commodification of Social Control*. Toronto: University of Toronto Press.

315 Monique Marks (2005) *Transforming the Robocops: Changing Police in South Africa*. Durban: University of Kwazulu-Natal Press; Laura Huey (2007) *Negotiating Demands:*

The Politics of Skid Row Policing in Edinburgh, San Francisco and Vancouver. Toronto: University of Toronto Press.

316 Philip Stenning, Christopher Birkbeck, Otto Adang, David Baker, Thomas Feltes, Luis Gerardo Gabaldón, Maki Haberfeld, Eduardo Paes Machado and P. A. J. Waddington (2009) 'Researching the Use of Force: The Background to the International Project'. *Crime, Law and Social Change*, 52(2): 95–110; J. Skolnick and J. Fyfe (1993) *Above the Law: Police and Excessive Use of Force*. New York: The Free Press.

317 Janet Chan, D. Brereton, M. Legosz and S. Soran (2001) *E-Policing: The Impact of Information Technology on Police Practices*. Brisbane: Queensland Criminal Justice.

318 Manuel Castells, *The Rise of the Network Society*, see fn 115, pp164–6.

319 Peter Manning (2008) *The Technology of Policing: Crime Mapping, Information Technology and the Rationality of Crime Control*. New York: New York University Press.

320 Bridgette Wessels (2007) *Inside the Digital Revolution: Policing and Changing Communication with the Police*. Aldershot: Ashgate. Chapters 6 and 7 tell the story of a European Union funded project with the London Metropolitan Police Service for the adoption of advanced telematics communications between police and public 'in the delivery of services, the dissemination of information, and the interactive provision of advice and support' (p15). This account provides insights into the way ICT is configured within the police occupational culture.

321 Jerry H. Ratcliffe, 'Intelligence-led Policing...', see fn 160, pp53–66.

322 Nina Cope (2004) 'Intelligence-led Policing or Policing-led Intelligence: Integrating Volume Crime Analysis into Policing'. *British Journal of Criminology*, 44: 188–203.

323 James Sheptycki (2004) 'Organizational Pathologies in Police Intelligence Systems: Some Contributions to the Lexicon of Intelligence-led Policing'. *The European Journal of Criminology*, 1(3): 307–32.

324 S. Herbert (2006) 'Police Subculture Reconsidered'. *Criminology*, 36(2): 343–70; Narayanan Ganapathy (2005) 'Theorizing Police Response to Domestic Violence in the Singaporean Context: Police Subculture Revisited'. *Journal of Criminal Justice*, 33(5): 429–39.

325 E.A. Paoline (2003) 'Taking Stock: Toward a Richer Understanding of Police Culture'. *Journal of Criminal Justice*, 31(3): 199–214.

326 Martin Innes and James Sheptycki (2004) 'From Detection to Disruption: Intelligence and the Changing Logic of Police Crime Control in the United Kingdom'. *International Criminal Justice Review*, 14: 1–24.

327 Richard Ericson and Kevin Haggerty, *Policing the Risk Society*, see fn 41.

328 Roger Grimshaw and Tony Jefferson (1984) *Interpreting Policework*. London: Allen & Unwin.

329 M. Marks (2004) 'Researching Police Transformation the Ethnographic Imperative'. *British Journal of Criminology*, 44(6): 866–88.

330 Richard V. Ericson (1994) 'The Royal Commission on Criminal Justice System Surveillance', in M. McConville and L. Bridges (eds) *Criminal Justice in Crisis*. Aldershot: Edward Elgar; Richard V. Ericson (1994) 'The Division of Expert Knowledge in Policing and Security'. *British Journal of Sociology*, 5(2): 149–76.

331 Peter K. Manning and John van Maanen (1978) *Policing: A View from the Street*. New York: Random House; Peter K. Manning, *The Narc's Game*, see fn 67; Ethan Nadelmann (1987) 'The DEA in Latin America: Dealing with Institutionalized Corruption'. *Journal of Interamerican Studies and World Affairs*, 29(4): 1–39.

332 Police researchers have also used the dramaturgical metaphor to categorise variations in cop culture. For example, Rober Reiner's (*The Politics of the Police*, see fn 63,

pp132–4) categories include (i) the bobby, (ii) the new centurion, (iii) the uniform carrier, and (iv) the professional. Kleinig's (1996, see fn. 43) categories of role types are (a) the crimefighter, (b) the emergency operator, (c) the social enforcer, and (d) the social peacekeeper.

333 S. Leman-Langlois (2008) *Technocrime*. Cullompton: Willan.

334 M. Peterson (2005) *Intelligence-Led Policing: The New Intelligence Architecture*. US Department of Justice: International Associations of Chiefs of Police.

335 Haggety and Ericson, 'The Surveillant Assemblage', see fn 92.

336 C. Norris and G. Armstrong (1999) *The Maximum Surveillance Society; The Rise of CCTV*. Oxford: Berg Publishers.

337 G. Armstrong, C. Norris and J. Moran (eds) (1999) *Surveillance, CCTV and Social Control*. Aldershot: Ashgate.

338 Mike Maguire and Tim John (2006) 'Intelligence Led Policing, Managerialism and Community Engagement: Competing Priorities and the Role of the National Intelligence Model in the UK'. *Policing and Society*, 16(1): 67–85.

339 Martin Innes (2003) *Investigative Murder; Detective Work and the Police Response to Criminal Homicide*. Oxford: Oxford University Press.

340 A. Henry and D.J. Smith (2007) *Transformations of Policing*, see fn 271.

341 James Sheptycki (2004) 'Organizational Pathologies in Police Intelligence Systems: Some Contributions to the Lexicon of Intelligence-led Policing'. *The European Journal of Criminology*, 1(3): 307–32.

342 Ben Bowling, Amber Marks and Cian Murphy (2009) 'Crime Control Technologies', in R. Brownsword and K. Yeung (eds) *Regulating Technologies*. Oxford: Hart.

343 But see B. McRae and D. Hubert (2001) *Human Security and the New Diplomacy: Protecting People, Promoting Peace*. Montreal and Kingston: McGill-Queen's University Press, which looks at policing in weak, failing or failed states from a critical security studies perspective.

344 James Sheptycki, 'The Global Cops Cometh', see fn 98, p68.

345 James Sheptycki (1997) 'Upholding the Boundaries of Order; The Mounties, Serial Sex Crime and the Transnational Pursuit of Serial Killers'. *The British Journal of Canadian Studies*, 12(2): 257–72.

346 See P.A.J. Waddington (1999) 'Police (Canteen) Sub-Culture: An Appreciation'. *British Journal of Criminology*, 39(2): 287–309, esp. p302, and the distinction between 'in the job' and 'on the job' trouble.

347 Ben Bowling, *Policing the Caribbean*, see fn 12.

348 Peter K. Manning and John van Maanen, *Policing: A View from the Street*, see fn 331; Peter K. Manning, *The Narc's Game*, see fn 67.

349 Bernd Belina and Gesa Helms (2003) 'Zero Tolerance for the Industrial Past and Other Threats: Policing and Urban Entrepreneurialism in Britain and Germany'. *Urban Studies*, 40(9): 1845–67.

350 Ari Agut (2004) 'Scandal as Norm Entrepreneurship Strategy: Corruption and the French Investigating Magistrates'. *Theory and Society*, 33(5): 529–78.

351 David Musto (1999) *The American Disease: Origins of Narcotic Control*, 3rd edn. Oxford: Oxford University Press, pp210–14.

352 R. Smith (2009) 'Entrepreneurship, Police Leadership and the Investigation of Crime in Changing Times'. *Journal of Investigative Psychology and Offender Profiling*, 5(3): 209–25.

353 Dick Hobbs (1991) 'A Piece of Business: The Moral Economy of Detective Work in the East-End of London'. *The British Journal of Sociology*, 42(4): 597–608, quote p597.

354 Aaron Doyle (2003) *Arresting Images: Crime and Policing in Front of the Television Camera*. Toronto, Canada: University of Toronto Press.

355 Willem De Lint (2002) 'Autonomy, Regulation and the Police Beat', *Social and Legal Studies: An International Journal*, 11: 475–502.

356 V. Packard (1957/2007) *The Hidden Persuaders*. Brooklyn, NY: IG Publishing.

357 Peter Manning (1992) *Organizational Communication*. New York: Aldine de Gruyter, p149.

358 Willem De Lint, Sirpa Virta and John Edward Deukmedjian (2007) 'The Simulation of Crime Control: A Shift in Policing?'. *American Behaviour Scientist*, 50(12): 1631–47, esp. p1636.

359 Kent Roach (1999) *Due Process and Victim's Rights: The New Law and Politics of Criminal Justice*. Toronto: University of Toronto Press; M. Beare (2008) *Honouring Social Justice*. Toronto: University of Toronto Press.

360 J. Ransley, J. Anderson and T. Prenzler (2007) 'Civil Litigation Against Police in Australia: Exploring its Extent, Nature, and Implications for Accountability'. *Australia and New Zealand Journal of Criminology*, 40(2): 143–60.

361 A. Leong (2007) *The Disruption of International Organised Crime: An Analysis of Legal and Non-legal Strategies*. Aldershot: Ashgate.

362 Anne O'Rourke, Vivek Chaudhri and Chris Nylan (2005) 'Torture, Slippery Slopes, Intellectual Apologists and Ticking Bombs'. *University of San Francisco Law Review*, 40(85): 85–105.

363 Doreen McBarnet (1981) *Conviction*. Atlantic Highlands, NJ: Humanities Press; Conor Gearty (2007) 'Rethinking Civil Liberties in a Counter-Terrorism World'. *European Human Rights Law Review*, 2: 111–19.

364 Cyrille Fijnaut and Gary Marx, *Undercover: Police Surveillance in Comparative Perspective*, see fn 67.

365 Gary Marx (forthcoming) 'Review: Snitching, Criminal Informants and the Erosion of American Justice'. *Theoretical Criminology*; Home Office (2002/2007) *Covert Human Intelligence Sources; Code of Practice: Pursuant to Section 71 of the Regulations of Investigatory Powers Act 2000*. London: The Stationery Office.

366 Roger Billingsley (2009) *Covert Human Intelligence: The 'Unlovely' Face of Policework*. Hampshire, UK: Waterside Press.

367 Tony Bunyan (1977) *The History and Practice of the Policing Police in Britain*. London: Quartet Books; M. Mazower, *The Policing of Politics...*, see fn 6.

368 Nick Fyfe and J. Sheptycki (2006) 'International Trends in the Facilitation of Witness Co-operation in Organized Crime Cases'. *The European Journal of Criminology*, 3(3): 319–55.

369 James Sheptycki (2010) 'Book Review: Covert Human Intelligence: A View from the Police, Roger Billingsley (ed.) *Covert Human Intelligence Sources: The 'Unlovely Face of Police Work'*, Hampshire, UK: Waterside Press, 2009'. *Crime Law and Social Change*, 53: 205–6.

370 J.A. Barnes (1994) *A Pack of Lies: Towards a Sociology of Lying*. Cambridge: Cambridge University Press.

371 J.-P. Brodeur (1984) 'Policing Beyond 1984'. *The Canadian Journal and Sociology*, 9(2): 195–207; Richard V. Ericson (1981) 'Rules for Police Deviance', in Clifford D. Shearing (ed.) *Organizational Police Deviance: Its Structure and Control*. Toronto: Butterworths, pp83–110; Richard V. Ericson (2007) *Crime in an Insecure World*. Cambridge: Polity.

372 J.-P. Brodeur (2007) 'High and Low Policing in Post-9/11 Times'. *Policing: A Journal of Policy and Practice*, 1(1): 25–37.

373 Egon Bittner, 'The Police on Skid Row', see fn 71; David Weisburd, Stephen D. Mastrofski, James J. Willis and Rosann Greenspan (2006) 'Changing Everything So

That Everything Can Remain the Same: Compstat and American Policing', in David Weisburd and Anthony Braga (eds) *Prospects and Problems in an Era of Police Innovation: Contrasting Perspectives*. Cambridge: Cambridge University Press, pp284–301.

374 William Muir, *Police: Streetcorner Politicians*, see fn 37.

375 H. Goldstein (1979) 'Improving Policing: A Problem-Oriented Approach'. *Crime and Delinquency*, 25: 236–58; H. Goldstein (1990) *Problem-Oriented Policing*. New York: McGraw-Hill.

376 Ben Bowling (1998) *Policing Violent Racism*. Oxford: Oxford University Press, esp. p121.

377 R.J. Chaskin (2001) 'Building Community Capacity: A Definitional Framework and Case Studies from a Comprehensive Community Initiative. *Urban Affairs Review*, 36(3): 291–323.

378 G. Berkeley (1969) *The Democratic Policeman*. Boston, MA: Beacon Press.

379 William Muir, *Police: Streetcorner Politicians*, see fn 37. This role-type is sometimes referred to as the 'crime fighter' or 'new centurion'; Robert Reiner, *The Politics of the Police*, see fn 63.

380 Quoted in James Sheptycki, 'The Global Cops Cometh', see fn 98, p69.

381 James Sheptycki, 'Book Review: Covert Human Intelligence', see fn 369, pp298–319.

382 John Kleinig, *The Ethics of Policing*, see fn 43, pp24–5.

383 Jerome Skolnick and James Fyfe (1993) *Above the Law: Police and the Excessive Use of Force*. New York: Free Press.

384 John-Paul Brodeur (1998) *How to Recognize Good Policing: Problems and Issues*. Washington, DC: Police Executive Research Forum.

385 K. Dowler, T. Fleming and S.L. Muzzatti (2007) 'Constructing Crime: Media, Crime and Popular Culture'. *Canadian Journal of Criminology and Criminal Justice*, 48(6): 837–50.

386 J. Flyghed (2002) 'Normalizing the Exceptional: The Case of Political Violence'. *Policing and Society*, 13(1): 23–41; J. Moran (2007) 'Generating More Heat than Light? Debates on Civil Liberties in the UK'. *Policing: A Journal of Policy and Practice*, 1(1): 80–93.

387 Janet Chan (1997) *Changing Police Culture: Policing in a Multicultural Society*. Cambridge: Cambridge University Press; P.A.J. Waddington, 'Police (Canteen) Sub-culture', see fn 346.

388 Robert Reiner, *The Politics of the Police*, see fn 63, p89; Frances Heidensohn (1992) *Women in Control? The Role of Women in Law Enforcement*. Oxford: Oxford University Press.

389 Howard Becker (1963) *Outsiders: Studies in the Sociology of Deviance*. New York: Free Press; S. Cohen (2002) *Folk Devils and Moral Panics: 30th Anniversary Edition*. London: Routledge; Stan Cohen and Jock Young (1973) *The Manufacture of News: Social Problems, Deviance and the Mass Media*. London: Constable; D. Hebdige (1979) *Subculture: The Meaning of Style*. London: Routledge; Hall et al., *Policing the Crisis*, see fn 296; Nils Christie, 'Suitable enemy', see fn 166; L. Wacquant (1999) '"Suitable Enemies": Foreigners and Immigrants in the Prisons of Europe'. *Punishment and Society*, 1(2): 215–22; J. Ferrell, K. Hayward and J. Young (2008) *Cultural Criminology: An Introduction*. London: Sage, p4.

390 Stan Cohen, *Folk Devils and Moral Panics*, see fn 389; Cohen and Young, *The Manufacture of News*, see fn 389.

391 Stuart Hall et al., *Policing the Crisis*, see fn 296.

392 James Q. Wilson (1968) *Varieties of Police Behavior*. Cambridge, MA: Harvard University Press; Doreen McBarnet (1982) 'Legal Form and Legal Mystification'. *International Journal of the Sociology of Law*, 10: 409–17.

393 Robert Reiner, *The Politics of the Police*, see fn 63, p117, S.D. Mastrofski (2004) 'Controlling Street-Level Discretion'. *The Annals*, 593: 100–18.

394 M. Beare and T. Murray (2007) *Police and Government Relations: Who's Calling the Shots*. Toronto: University of Toronto Press.

395 Ibid., see fn 394, p18 and pp183–256.

396 Ibid., see fn 394, p18.

397 David Dixon (1997) *Law in Policing: Legal Regulation and Police Practices*. Oxford: Oxford University Press; Tony Jefferson and Roger Grimshaw (1984) *Controlling the Constable*. London: Allen & Unwin; Roger Grimshaw and Tony Jefferson (1984) *Interpreting Policework*. London: Allen & Unwin.

398 Kent Roach (1999) *Due Process and Victim's Rights: The New Law and Politics of Criminal Justice*. Toronto: University of Toronto Press.

399 Ibid., p17.

400 Geoffrey Marshall (1978) 'Police Accountability Revisited', in D. Butler and A.H. Halsey (eds) *Policy and Politics*. London: Macmillan. Reprinted in Tim Newburn (ed.) (2004) *Policing: Key Readings*. Collumpton: Willan.

401 Clifford Shearing (2002) 'A Nodal Conception of Governance: Thoughts on a Policing Commission'. *Policing and Society*, 11(3–4): 259–72; Mike Brogden (2002) 'The Patten Report: A Unitary Solution to a Multi-dimensional Problem?' *Policing and Society*, 11(3–4): 273–95; M. Beirne (2002) 'Progress or Placebo? The Patten Report and the Future of Policing in Northern Ireland'. *Policing and Society*, 11(3–4): 297–319.

402 Ian Loader (2000) 'Plural Policing and Democratic Governance'. *Social Legal Studies*, 9(3): 323–45; David Bayley and Clifford Shearing (2001) *The New Structure of Policing: Description, Conceptualization and Research Agenda, a Research Report*. Washington, DC: US Department of Justice; Jennifer Wood and Benoît Dupont (eds) *Democracy, Society and the Governance of Security*, see fn 262; Phillip Stenning (2009) 'Governance and Accountability in a Plural Policing Environment – the Story So far'. *Policing: A Journal of Policy and Practice*, 3(1): 22–33.

403 Clifford Shearing and Les Johnston (2010) 'Nodal Wars and Network Fallacies: A Genealogical Analysis of Global Insecurities'. *Theoretical Criminology*, 14(4): 495–514.

404 Sam Walker (2005) *The New World of Police Accountability*. Thousand Oaks, CA: Sage; A. Goldsmith and C. Lewis (2000) *Civilian Oversight of Policing: Governance, Democracy and Human Rights*. Oxford: Hart.

405 Thomas Mathiesen (1997) 'The Viewer Society: Foucault's Panopticon Revisited'. *Theoretical Criminology*, 1(2): 215–34.

406 Sam Walker, *The New World of Police Accountability*, see fn 404, p42.

407 Didier Bigo, 'Liaison Officers in Europe', see fn 287, p85.

408 Malcolm Anderson, *Policing the European Union*, see fn 2. p. 52.

409 Ibid., p. 66.

410 Marshall, *Police Accountability Revisited*, see fn 400.

411 Robert Reiner, *The Politics of the Police*, see fn 63, pp116–18.

412 Suzanne Krasmann argues that an 'enemy penology' has developed within theories of criminal law more generally based on a narrative about crime that sees its subject not as criminals but enemies who, rather than being brought to justice, must be 'combated [and] excluded, if not extinguished': S. Krasmann (2007) 'The Enemy on the Border: Critique of a Programme in Favour of a Preventive State'. *Punishment and Society*, 9(3): 301–18.

413 Katja Franko Aas (2007) 'Analysing a World in Motion. Global Flows Meet "Criminology of the other"'. *Theoretical Criminology*, 11(2): 283–303, p292; N. Wonders (2006) 'Global Flows, Semi-Permeable Borders and New Channels of

Inequality', in Sharon Pickering and Leanne Weber (eds) *Borders, Mobility and Technologies of Control*. Amsterdam: Springer, pp63–86.

414 Leanne Weber and Ben Bowling (2008) 'Valiant Beggars and Global Vagabonds: Select, Eject, Immobilize'. *Theoretical Criminology*, 12(3): 355–75.

415 Karine Côté-Boucher (2008) 'The Diffuse Border: Intelligence-Sharing, Control and Confinement along Canada's Smart Border'. *Surveillance and Society*, 5(2): 142–65.

416 Source for Figure 5.1: Leanne Weber and Ben Bowling (2004) 'Policing Migration: A Framework for Investigating the Regulation of Global Mobility'. *Policing & Society*, 14(3): 195–212.

417 V. Carty (2004) 'Transnational Labor Mobilizing in Two Mexican Maquiladoras: The Struggle for Democratic Globalization'. *Mobilization: An International Quarterly*, 9(3): 295–310; Diana Washington Valdez (2006) *The Killing Fields: Harvest of Women*. Burbank, California: Peace at the Border; Mark Bowden (2010) *Murder City: Ciudad Juarez and the Global Economy's New Killing Fields*. New York: Nation Books.

418 Julie Erfani and A. Murphy (2007) 'Whose Security? Dilemmas of US Border Security in the Arizona-Sonora Borderlands', in Emmanuel Brunet-Janilly (ed.) *Comparing Border Security in North America and Europe*. Ottawa: University of Ottawa Press, pp41–74.

419 Matthew Sparke, James D. Sidaway, Tim Bunnell and Carl Grundy-Warr (2004) 'Triangulating the Borderless World: Globalisation, Regionalisation and the Geographies of Power in the Indonesia–Malaysia–Singapore Growth Triangle'. *Transactions of the Institute of British Geographers*, 29(4): 485–98; Tim Bunnell, James D. Sidaway and Carl Grundy-Warr (2006) 'Introduction: Re-Mapping the Growth Triangle: Singapore's Cross-Border Hinterland'. *Asia Pacific Viewpoint*, 47(2): 235–40.

420 E.F. Isin and K. Rygiel (2007) 'Of Other Global Cities: Frontiers, Zones, Camps', in H. Wimmen (ed.) *Cities and Globalization: Challenges for Citizenship*. London: Saqi Books, p170–209.

421 D. O'Rourke and J. Sheptycki (2011) 'Existential Predicaments and Constabulary Ethics', in R. Lippens and J. Hardie-Bick (eds) *Crime, Governance and Existential Predicaments*. London: Routledge.

422 Peter Andreas (2009) *Border Games: Policing the US–Mexico Divide*. Ithaca, NY: Cornell University Press, pxi.

423 I.C.B. Dear and Peter Kemp (2005) *Oxford Companion to Ships and the Sea*. Oxford: Oxford University Press.

424 Peter Singer (2002) *One World*. New Haven, CT: Yale University Press; A. Boyle (1991) 'Saving the World? Implementation and Enforcement of International Environmental Law Through International Institutions'. *Journal of Environmental Law*, 3(2): 229–45.

425 Martin Murphy (2009) *Small Boats, Weak States, Dirty Money: Piracy and Maritime Terrorism in the Modern World*. London: Hirst & Co.; John S. Barnett (2002) *Dangerous Waters: Modern Piracy and Terror on the High Seas*. London: Plume/Penguin; William Langewiesche (2007) *The Outlaw Sea: Chaos and Crime on the World's Oceans*. London: Granta; Jon Vagg (1995) 'Rough Seas? Contemporary Piracy in South East Asia (Riau Archipelago, Indonesia)'. *British Journal of Criminology*, 35(1): 63–80; Jon Vagg (1997) 'Piracy, Corruption and the Rule of Law', *Trends in Organised Crime*, 3(4): 72–6.

426 Peter Andreas and Ethan Nadelmann, *Policing the Globe*, see fn 127, pp26–8.

427 United Nations General Assembly (29 August 2003) *Oceans and the Law of the Sea*. United Nations General Assembly, Report of the Secretary General, Addendum, Fifty-eighth session, A/58/65/Add.1, paragraph 1.

428 The Convention also created the Exclusive Economic Zone (EEZ), providing jurisdictional rights for nation states to exploit all the resources in the water and on and beneath the seabed for 200 miles from its shore.

429 Article 6(1) of the High Seas Convention requires that ships shall sail 'under the flag of one State only' and, apart from exceptional cases, 'shall be subject to its exclusive jurisdiction on the high seas'.

430 Michael Byers (2004) 'Policing the High Seas: The Proliferation Security Initiative'. *American Journal of International Law*, 98(3): 526–45.

431 Ibid., see fn 430.

432 Ibid., see fn 430.

433 Convention between the UK and the US respecting the Regulation of the Liquor Traffic, concluded in Washington on 23 January 1924, cited by John Siddle (1982) 'Anglo American Co Operation in the Suppression of Drug Smuggling'. *International and Comparative Law Quarterly*, 31: 726–47; see also, Joseph Kramek (2000) 'Bilateral Maritime Counter-Drug and Immigrant Interdiction Agreements: Is This the World of the Future'. *The University of Miami Inter-American Law Review*, 31: 121.

434 24. 19 USC 1401 (i) cited by Siddle, 'Anglo American Co Operation', see fn 433.

435 26. 19 USC 1401 (j) cited by Siddle, 'Anglo American Co Operation', see fn 433.

436 The Government of the United Kingdom and the Government of the United States Exchange of Notes concerning co-operation in the suppression of the unlawful importation of narcotic drugs into the United States, 13 November 1981, see Appendix I; John Siddle, 'Anglo American Co Operation', see fn 433.

437 John Siddle, 'Anglo American Co Operation', see fn 433.

438 Reuters, 'Castro Assails the U.S. for Attack on Vessel'. *New York Times* 2 February 1990.

439 David Stout, 'Coast Guard Using Sharpshooters to Stop Boats'. *New York Times* 14 September 1999.

440 Hilborne Watson (2003) '"The Shiprider Solution" and Post-Cold War Imperialism: Beyond Ontologies of State Sovereignty in the Caribbean', in Cynthia Barrow-Giles and Don Marshall (eds) *Living at the Borderlines: Issues in Caribbean Sovereignty and Development*. Kingston: Ian Randal Publishing, p232; Ivelaw Griffith (1997) *Drugs and Security in the Caribbean: Sovereignty Under Seign*. University Park, PA: University of Pennsylvania Press.

441 *The Sun*, 3 July 2008; see also Ben Bowling (2008) 'The Prince, the Iron Duke and the Drugs Barons: Tactical Success and Strategic Failure in the Caribbean Drugs Wars'. Presentation to the World Criminology Congress, Barcelona, July 2008. (Unpublished manuscript.)

442 Hilborne Watson, 'The Shiprider Solution', see fn 440.

443 Article 4(3) states that the shiprider 'has the power to enforce the laws of the United States in U.S. waters, or seaward therefrom, in the exercise of the right of hot pursuit or otherwise in accordance with international Law' [i.e. on high seas with the permission of the flag state, in the case of piracy or slave trafficking or if the vessel is carrying no flag]; and 'authorise UK law enforcement vessels on which they are embarked to assist in the enforcement of U.S. law'.

444 'Prince William Takes Part in £40m bust'. *Times* 2 July 2008.

445 'Iron Duke Strikes a Blow to Cocaine Smugglers'. Royal Navy Press Release, 2 July 2008.

446 R. Scott Frey (1998) 'Hazardous Waste Stream in the World-System', in P.S. Ciccantell and S.G. Bunker (eds) *Space and Transport in the World-System*. Westport, CT: Greenwood, p84–106; R. White (2008) 'Toxic Cities: Globalizing the Problem of

Toxic Waste. *Social Justice*, 35(3): 107–13; Jennifer Clapp (2001) *Toxic Exports: The Transfer of Hazardous Wastes from Rich Countries to Poor Countries*. Ithaca, NY: Cornell University Press; N. Dorn, Stijn Van Daele and Tom vander Beken (2007) 'Reducing Vulnerabilities to Crime of the European Waste Management Industry: The Research Base and the Prospects for Policy'. *European Journal of Crime, Criminal Law and Criminal Justice*, 15(1): 23–36.

447 Colum Lynch, 'UN Authorizes Land, Air Attacks of Somali Pirates: International Effort to Secure Sea Route May Stumble Amid Political Disarray in East African Nation'. *Washington Post* 17 December 2008; Xan Rice, 'US Launches Anti-piracy Navel Force to Combat Hijacking Off Somalia'. *Guardian* 9 January 2009; George Monbiot, 'From Toxic Waste to Toxic Assets, the Same People Always Get Dumped On'. *Guardian* 21 September 2009.

448 Alan Boyle (1991) 'Saving the World? Implementation and Enforcement of International Environmental Law Through International Institutions'. *Journal of Environmental Law*, 3(2): 229–45.

449 At which time 157 states had ratified the Convention, but not the US. While the US government promised to respect the treaty's provisions it was never put before the Senate, mainly because it was regarded as compromising US sovereignty. To date the US has yet to ratify the UNCLOS.

450 Quoted in *A Global Agenda; Issues Before the United Nations* 2009–2010. New York: United Nations Association of the United States of America, 2002, p143.

451 W.G. Carson (1982) *The Other Price of Britain's Oil: Safety and Control in the North Sea*. Oxford: Martin Robertson; Charles Woolfson and M. Beck (2000) 'The British Offshore Oil Industry After Piper Alfa'. *Journal of Environmental and Occupational Health Policy*, 10(1–2): 11–65.

452 Jeffrey Collins, 'Interior Secretary Ken Salazar Says Effort to Stop Gulf Oil Leak Hits Snag, but Work Continues'. *Los Angeles Times* 15 May 2010; Susan Goldenberg, 'Gulf Oil Spill: Firms Ignored Signs Before Blast, Inquiry Hears; Documents Suggest BP, Transocean and Halliburton Ignored Tests Indicating Faulty Safety Equipment, Says Committee'. *Guardian* 13 May 2010.

453 Peter Manning (2000) 'Policing New Social Spaces', in James Sheptycki (ed.) *Issues in Transnational Policing*, see fn 7, pp177–200.

454 Peter N. Grabosky and Russell G. Smith (1998) *Crime in the Digital Age*. Canberra: The Australian Institute of Criminology, p10.

455 S. Leman-Langlois (ed.) (2008) *Technocrime: Technology, Crime and Social Control*. Cullumpton: Willan; D. Wall (2007) *Cybercrime: The Transformation of Crime in the Information Age*. Cambridge: Polity Press.

456 David L. Altheid (2004) 'The Control Narrative of the Internet'. *Symbolic Interaction*, 27(2): 223–45.

457 James Sheptycki (forthcoming) 'Technocrime, Criminology and Marshall McLuhan,' in *Technocrime: Policing and Surveillance*. Stephen Leman-Langlois (ed.) London: Routledge.

458 J. Zitrain (2008) *The Future of the Internet – and How to Stop It*. New Haven, CT: Yale University Press.

459 Asher Moses, 'Leaked Australian Blacklist Reveal Banned Sites'. *The Sydney Morning Herald* 29 March 2009; Asher Moses, 'Fatal Flaws in Website Censorship Plan, Says Report'. *The Sydney Morning Herald* 23 December 2008; Australian Associated Press, 'Teenager Crack's Governments $84 Million Porn Filter'. *The Sydney Morning Herald* 25 August 2007; Australian Associated Press, 'Internet Porn a Sign of the Blues: Study'. *Sydney Morning Herald* 8 December 2008.

460 Paul Schiff Berman (2002) 'The Globalization of Jurisdiction'. *University of Pennsylvania Law Review*, 151(2): 311–545, esp. pp529–30; S.J. Kobrin (2004) 'Safe Harbours are Hard to Find: The Trans-Atlantic Data Privacy Dispute, Territorial Jurisdiction and Global Governance'. *Review of International Studies*, 30: 111–31.

461 James Sheptycki (2005) 'Policing Political Protest When Politics Go Global'. *Policing and Society*, 15(3): 327–52.

462 R.R. Bianchi (2004) *Guests of God: Pilgrimage and Politics in the Islamic World*. Oxford: Oxford University Press.

463 Phil Boyle and Kevin D. Haggerty (2009) 'Spectacular Security: Mega-Events and the Security Complex'. *International Political Sociology*, 3(3): 257–74.

464 Donatella Della Porta, Abby Peterson and Herbert Reiter (eds) (2006) *The Policing of Transnational Protest*. Aldershot: Ashgate; L. Wood (2009) 'Taking to the Streets Against Neoliberalism: Global Days of Action and Other Strategies', in Bruce Podobnik and Thomas Reifer (eds) *Transforming Globalization: Challenges and Opportunities in the Post 9/11 Era*. Leiden, NL: Brill Academic Press.

465 J.D. McCarthy, C. McPhail and J. Crist (1999) 'The Diffusion and Adoption of Public Order Management Systems', in Donatella Della Porta, Hanspeter Kriesi and Dieter Rucht (eds) *Social Movements in a Globalising World*. London: Macmillan, pp71–94.

466 'G20 Probe Is More Smoke and Mirrors from the Liberals'. *The Globe and Mail* 22 September 2010; 'Province to Prove "Secret Law", G20 Police Powers'. *The Globe and Mail* 22 September 2010; 'Ontario Ombudsman Wrapping Up Probe into G20 "Secret Law"'. *The Globe and Mail* 1 December 2010.

467 Phil Boyle (forthcoming) 'Mobilizing Knowledge: The Olympics and Security Knowledge Networks', in Colin Bennett and Kevin Haggerty (eds) *Security Games: Surveillance and Control at Mega-Events*. London: Routledge.

468 Katja Franko Aas, 'Analysing a World in Motion', see fn 413.

469 Zygmunt Bauman (2000) *Liquid Modernity*. Cambridge: Polity Press; Manuel Castells (1996) *The Rise of the Network Society*. Malden, MA: Blackwell Publishers.

470 Zygmunt Bauman (1998) *Globalization: The Human Consequences*. Cambridge: Polity Press, p92.

471 J. Torpey (2000) *The Invention of the Passport: Surveillance, Citizenship and the State*. Cambridge: Cambridge University Press, p58; Weber and Bowling, 'Valiant Beggars and Global Vagabonds', see fn 414; Weber and Bowling, 'Policing Migration', see fn 416.

472 Dean Wilson and Leanne Weber (2008) 'Surveillance, Risk and Preemption on the Australian Border'. *Surveillance and Society*, 5(2): 124–41.

473 David Lyon (2003) *Surveillance as Social Sorting: Privacy, Risk and Digital Discrimination*. London: Taylor & Francis, p2.

474 James Sheptycki (1997) 'Insecurity, Risk Suppression and Segregation: Some Reflections on Policing in the Transnational Age'. *Theoretical Criminology*, 1(3): 303–16.

475 P. Adey (2009) 'Facing Airport Security: Affect, Biopolitics, and the Preemptive Securitization of the Mobile Body'. *Environment and Planning D: Society and Space*, 27(2): 274–95.

476 Liz Fekete (2005) 'The Deportation Machine: Europe, Asylum, and Human Rights'. *Race and Class*, 47(1): 64–91; J.A. Warner (2005) 'The Social Construction of the Criminal Alien in Immigration Law, Enforcement Practice and Statistical Enumeration: Consequences for Immigrant Stereo-typing'. *Journal of Social and Ecological Boundaries*, 1(2): 6–80; W. Chan (2005) 'Crime, Deportation and the Regulation of Immigrants in Canada'. *Crime, Law and Social Change*, 44(2): 153–80; G. Nicholls (2007) *Deported: A History of Forced Departures from Australia*. Sydney: New South Wales University Press.

477 Stan Cohen (1984) *Visions of Social Control*. Cambridge: Polity.

478 T. Huling (1995) 'Drug Couriers: Sentencing Reform for Prisoners of War'. *Criminal Justice*, 15: 15–27.

479 E. Bramley-Harker (2001) *Sizing the UK Market for Illicit Drugs*. Research, Development and Statistics Directorate, Ocassional Paper No. 74. London: Home Office.

480 R.L. Harper, G.C. Harper and J.E. Stockdale (2002) 'The Role and Sentencing of Women in Drug Trafficking Crime'. *Legal and Criminal Psychology*, 7(1): 101–14.

481 Julia Sudbury (2005) 'Mules, Yardies and Other Folk Devils: Mapping Cross-border Imprisonment in Britain', in Julia Sudbury (ed.) *Global Lockdown: Race, Gender and the Prison-Industrial Complex*. London: Routledge, p167.

482 R.J. Booker, J.E. Smith and M.P. Rodger (2009) 'Packers, Pushers and Stuffers – Managing Patients with Concealed Drugs in UK Emergency Departments: A Clinical and Medico-legal Review'. *Emergency Medical Journal*, 26: 316–20, p316.

483 K. Kempadoo (2005) 'Victims and Agents of Crime: The New Crusade Against Trafficking', in Julia Sudbury (ed.) *Global Lockdown: Race, Gender and the Prison-Industrial Complex*, see fn 481, p35.

484 Rodney Allan (2002) 'Terrorism and Truth'. *Alternative Law Review*, 27: 57.

485 P. Sproat (1997) 'Can the State Commit Acts of Terrorism? An Opinion and Some Qualitative Replies to a Questionnaire'. *Terrorism and Political Violence*, 9(4): 117–50; J. Moran and M. Pythian (2008) *Intelligence, Security and Policing Post-9/11: The UK's Response to the 'War on Terror'*. Basingstoke: Palgrave MacMillan.

486 N. Rogers (2008) 'The Play(fullness) of Law'. Unpublished PhD dissertation. Lismore, NSW: Southern Cross University, pp39–40.

487 M. Crenshaw (1981) 'The Causes of Terrorism'. *Comparative Politics*, 13(4): 379–99.

488 L. Godden (2006) 'Terrorism: Reinvoking the Barbarian to Secure the Space of Civilisation'. *Australian Feminist Law Journal*, 24: 69–94.

489 Alpa Parmar (2011) 'Counter Terrorist or Counterproductive'. *Policing and Society*, Special Issue on Stop and Search; D. Weisburd, B. Hasisi, T. Jonathan and G. Aviv (2010) 'Terrorist Threats and Police Performance: A Study of Israeli Communities'. *British Journal of Criminology*, 50(4): 725–47.

490 H. Petroski (2004) 'Technology and Architecture in an Age of Terrorism'. *Technology and Society*, 26(2–3): 161–7.

491 See, for example, Meredith Leigh (undated) 'Problems in Drafting Anti-terrorism Laws in Australia, a Legal Opinion by M. Leigh, First Assistant Parliamentary Counsel, Australian Office of Parliamentary Counsel'.

492 A. Silke (2004) *Research on Terrorism: Trends, Achievements and Failures*. London: Frank Cass, p2.

493 Ibid., see fn 492, p2.

494 M. Deflem (2010) *The Policing of Terrorism: Organizational and Global Perspectives*. London: Routledge.

495 Conor Gearty (2010) *Escaping Hobbes: Liberty and Security for Our Democratic (Not Anti-Terrorist) Age*. LSE Legal Studies Working Working Paper No 3/2010.

496 Quoted in A. Silke, *Research on Terrorism*, see fn 492, p7.

497 D. Bigo and A. Tsoukala (2008) *Terror, Insecurity and Liberty: Illiberal Practices of Liberal Regimes after 9/11*. London: Routledge; C. Walker (2006) 'Clamping Down on Terrorism in the United Kingdom'. *Journal of International Criminal Justice*, 4(5): 1137–51.

498 G. Mythen and S. Walklate (2006) 'Communicating the Terrorist Risk: Harnessing a Culture of Fear?'. *Crime, Media and Culture*, 2(2): 123–42.

499 N. Rogers, 'The Play(fullness) of Law', see fn 486, p43.

500 Conor Gearty, *Escaping Hobbes: Liberty and Security for Our Democratic (Not Anti-Terrorist) Age*, see fn 495.

501 M. Crenshaw (2001) 'Why America? The Globalization of Civil War'. *Current History*, DEC: 425–32.

502 Perry Anderson (1974/1996/2000) *Passages from Antiquity to Feudalism*. London: Verso.

503 Jock Young (1994) *The Exclusive Society: Social Exclusion, Crime and Difference in Late Modernity*. London: Sage; J. Young (2007) *The Vertigo of Late Modernity*. London: Sage.

504 James Sheptycki, 'The Drug War', see fn 7; Ivelaw Griffith, *Drugs and Security in the Caribbean Basin: Sovereignty Under Siege*, see fn 440.

505 David Musto, *The American Disease: Origins of Narcotic Control*, see fn 351; Peter Andreas and Ethan Nadelmann, *Policing the Globe*, see fn 127, p247.

506 Ethan Nadelmann (1988) 'US Drug Policy: A Bad Export'. *Foreign Policy*, 70: 83–108; Ethan Nadelmann (2007) 'Think Again: Drugs'. *Foreign Policy*, 162: 24–30.

507 In 1998, the UN General Assembly Special Session on drugs committed to 'eliminating or significantly reducing the illicit cultivation of the coca bush, the cannabis plant and the opium poppy by the year 2008' and to 'achieving significant and measurable results in the field of demand reduction'.

508 United Nations (2010) *World Drug Report*. United Nations Office of Drugs and Crime. URL: http://www.unodc.org.

509 C. Aitken, D. Moore, P. Higgs, J. Kelsall and M. Kerger (2002) 'The Impact of a Police Crackdown on a Street Drug Scene: Evidence from the Street'. *International Journal of Drug Policy*, 13(3): 193–202; D. Dixon and L. Maher (2002) 'Anh Hai: Policing, Culture and Social Exclusion in a Street Heroin Market'. *Policing and Society*, 12(2): 93–118; D. Dixon and L. Maher (2005) 'Policing, Crime and Public Health'. *Criminal Justice*, 5(2): 115–43; T. May, A. Harocopos, P.J. Turnbull and M. Hough (2000) *Serving Up: The Impact of Low-level Police Enforcement on Drug Markets*. Police Research Paper 133. London: Home Office.

510 Jock Young, *The Drug Takers*, see fn 302.

511 P. Andreas and J. Wallman (2009) 'Illicit Markets and Violence: What Is the Relationship?'. *Crime, Law and Social Change*, 52(3): 225–9.

512 M. Glenny (2008) *McMafia: A Journey Through the Global Criminal Underworld*. New York: Alfred Knopff.

513 S. Sandberg (2011) 'Street Capital: Ethnicity and Violence on the Streets of Oslo'. *Theoretical Criminology*, 12(2): 153–71; S. Hallsworth and D. Silverstone (2009) '"That's Life Innit": A British Perspective on Guns, Crime and Social Order'. *Criminology and Criminal Justice*, 9(2): 359–77; S. Hallsworth and T. Young (2008) 'Gang Talk and Gang Talkers: A Critique'. *Crime, Media and Culture*, 4(2): 175–95.

514 G. Newman (ed.) (1999) *Global Report on Crime and Justice*. Published for the United Nations Office for Drug Control and Crime Prevention and the Centre for International Crime Prevention. New York: Oxford University Press; Geoff Pearson and Dick Hobbs (2001) *Middle Market Drug Distribution*. Home Office Research Development Statistics Directorate; S.D. Levitt and S.A. Venkatesh (2000) 'An Economic Analysis of a Drug-Selling Gang's Finances'. *The Quarterly Journal of Economics*, 115: 755–89.

515 United Nations, *World Drug Report*, see fn 508.

516 Ben Bowling, 'Transnational Criminology...', see fn 42; Jerry Rattcliff and James Sheptycki (2004) 'Setting the Strategic Agenda', in Rattcliff (ed.) *Strategic Thinking in Criminal Intelligence*. Annadale, NSW: The Federation Press, pp194–210; James Sheptycki (2007) 'Transnational Crime and Transnational Policing'. *Sociology Compass*, 1: 1; Jock Young, *The Drug Takers*, see fn 302; Peter Reuter (1997) 'Why Can't We Make Prohibition Work Better?'

Some Consequences of Ignoring the Unattractive'. *Proceedings of the American Philosophical Society*, 141(3): 262–75; Susan S. Everingham and C. Peter Rydell (1994) *Modeling the Demand for Cocaine*. Santa Monica, CA: RAND Drug Policy Research Centre; Eric L. Jensen, Jurg Gerber and Clayton Mosher (2004) 'Social Consequences of the War on Drugs: The Legacy of Failed Policy'. *Criminal Justice Review*, 15(1): 100–21; Carey Goldberg, 'Wealthy Ally for Dissidents in the Drug War'. *New York Times* 11 September 1996.

517 Manuel Castells, *End of the Millennium...*, see fn 115.

518 D. Corva (2008) 'Neoliberal Globalization and the War on Drugs: Transnationalizing Illiberal Governance in the Americas'. *Political Geography*, 27(2): 176–93; E. Sheppard and R. Hagar (2004) 'From East–West to North–South'. *Antipode: A Radical Journal of Geography*, 36(4): 557–63.

519 Ben Bowling, *Policing the Caribbean*, see fn 12; B. Agozino, B. Bowling, E. Ward and G. St. Bernard (2009) 'Guns, Crime and Social Order in the West Indies'. *Criminology and Criminal Justice*, 9(3): 287–305.

520 Ibid., see fn 519, p294. Agozino et al. see fn 519.

521 See also Ethan Nadelmann (1988) 'US Drug Policy: A Bad Export'. *Foreign Policy*, 70: 83–108; R. MacCoun and P. Reuter (2001) *Drug War Heresies*. Cambridge: Cambridge University Press. On the challenges of pursuing transnational control of illegal guns see P. Cook, W. Cukier and K. Krause (2009) 'The Illicit Firearms Trade in North America'. *Criminology and Criminal Justice*, 9(3): 265–86; K. Krause (2002) 'Review Essay: Multilateral Diplomacy, Norm Building, and UN Conferences: The Case of Small Arms and Light Weapons'. *Global Governance*. 8: 247–63.

522 Agozino et al., 'Guns, Crime and Social Order...', see fn 519, p299.

523 Ben Bowling, *Policing the Caribbean*, see fn 12, p82.

524 Manuel Castells, *End of the Millennium...*, see fn 115, p169; J. Rigg (2007) *An Everyday Geography of the Global South*. London: Routledge.

525 James Sheptycki, 'Policing the Virtual Launderette...', see fn 212, pp135–76.

526 William Gilmore, *Dirty Money: The Evolution of Money Laundering Countermeasures*, see fn 210.

527 M.-F. Cuellar (2003) 'Criminal Law: The Tenuous Relationship between the Fight Against Money Laundering and the Disruption of Criminal Finance'. *Journal of Criminal Law and Criminology*, 93(2–3): 311–466.

528 James Sheptycki (2004) *Review of the Influence of Strategic Intelligence on Organised Crime Policy and Practice*. Research, Development and Statistics Directorate Special Interest Paper No. 14. London: Home Office, p17.

529 Jack Weatherford (1997) *The History of Money*. New York: Crown Publishers.

530 M. Levi and W.C. Gilmore (2002) 'Terrorist Finance and the Rise and Rise of Mutual Evaluation: A New Paradigm Got Crime Control?', in M. Peith (ed.) *Financing Terrorism*. The Hague: Kluwer Academic; R.T. Naylor (2006) *Satanic Purses: Money, Myth and Misinformation in the War on Terror*. Montreal: McGill-Queen's University Press; P. Sproat (2007) 'An Evaluation of the UK's Anti-money Laundering and Asset Recovery Regime'. *Crime Law and Social Change*, 47(3): 169–84; P. Sproat (2007) 'The New Policing of Assets and the New Assets Of Policing: A Tentative Financial Cost–Benefit Analysis of the UK's Anti-money Laundering and Asset Recovery Regime'. *Journal of Money Laundering Control*, 10(3): 277–99.

531 M. Levi (1996) 'Money Laundering: Risks and Countermeasures', in Adam Graycar and Peter Grabosky (eds) *Money Laundering in the 21st Century: Risks and Countermeasures*. Canberra: Australian Institute of Criminology, p1–11.

532 Ibid., see fn 531, quote from p11.

533 M. Levi (1997) '"Evaluating the New Policing": Attacking the Money Trail of Organized Crime'. *Australian and New Zealand Journal of Criminology*, 30(1): 1–25.

534 'From Prison, Madoff Says Banks "Had to Know" of Fraud', *New York Times* 15 February 2011.

535 M. Lewis (2010) *The Big Short: Inside the Doomsday Machine*. New York: W.W. Norton and Co.; M. Lewis (1989) *Liar's Poker; Rising Through the Wreckage on Wall Street*. New York: W.W. Norton and Co.

536 An earlier shake-down of this type is the downfall of long-term capital management in 1998. See R. Lowenstein (2000) *When Genius Failed: The Rise and Fall of Long-Term Capital Management*. New York: Random House.

537 N. Passas (1996) 'The Genesis of the BCCI Scandal'. *Journal of Law and Society*, 23(1): 57–72; D. Friedrichs (2004) 'Eron ET Al: Paradigmatic White Collar Crime Cases for the New Century'. *Critical Criminology*, 12(2): 113–32; R.T. Naylor (2003) 'Towards a General Theory of Profit-driven Crimes'. *British Journal of Criminology*, 43(1): 81–101.

538 See United Nations (2009) *The World Financial and Economic Crisis and its Impact on Development*. General debate on the world financial and economic crisis and its impact on development, Report of the Secretary-General, 1–3 June, New York.

539 Mike Levi and David Nelken (eds) (1996) *The Corruption of Politics and the Politics of Corruption*. Oxford: Blackwell; Mike Levi (2008) *The Phantom Capitalists*, 2nd edn. Andover: Ashgate.

540 R.T. Naylor (2002) *Wages of Crime; Black Markets, Illegal Finance and the Underworld Economy*. Montreal: McGill-Queens University Press.

541 V. Mitsilegas (2003) *Money Laundering Counter-Measures in the European Union: A New Paradigm of Security Governance Versus Fundamental Legal Principles*. The Hague: Kluwer Law International.

542 'Ashcroft to sell off Belize Bank: Outgoing Tory Treasurer to Dispose of Offshore Finance Operation that Sparked Feud with Government'. *Guardian* 20 August 2001.

543 Lesley Sklair (2001) *The Transnational Capitalist Class*. Oxford: Blackwell.

544 'Ashcroft's Millions: from Belize Tax Havens to Tories via Southampton'. *Guardian* 5 March 2010.

545 'Lord Ashcroft: New Demands for a Full Tax Inquiry'. *Guardian* 3 March 2010.

546 Andrew Goldsmith (2009) 'It Wasn't Like Normal Policing: Voices of Australian Peacekeepers in Operation Serene, Timor-Leste 2006'. *Policing and Society*, 19(2): 119–33; Andrew Goldsmith and James Sheptycki (2007) *Crafting Transnational Policing*, see fn 7.

547 *Médecins Sans Frontières* (2009) *Shattered Lives: Immediate Medical Care for Sexual Violence Victims*. Brussels: Médecins Sans Frontières Operational Centre. *Médecins Sans Frontières* is an international humanitarian organisation that brings emergency medical care to populations in over 60 countries. Quotes p14 and p8, respectively.

548 Ibid., see fn 547, quotes p8.

549 James Sheptycki, 'The Constabulary Ethic Reconsidered, see fn 99; James Sheptycki (2010) 'The Raft of the Medusa: Further Contributions Towards a Constabulary Ethic'. *Cahiers Politiestudies* Special Issue, Policing in Europe. No. 16 pp39–56.

550 Alice Hills, *Policing Post-Conflict Cities*, see fn 260.

551 Sherene Razack, *Dark Threats and White Knights*, see fn 229, p47. These criticisms are compounded after observing how countries like Australia, Canada and the USA have historically and contemporarily dealt with their own indigenous populations.

552 Spencer S. Hsu, 'Officials Prevent Haitian Earthquake Refugees From Coming to US'. *The Washington Post* 9 January 2010.

553 Max Boot reports in his book *The Savage Wars of Peace* (2002, New York: Basic Books) that the first foreign intervention in Haiti came in 1915 with a landing force of US

marines. According to him 'the more unstable a country, the more likely the U.S. was to intervene. And no country was more unstable than Haiti. Of the 22 rulers between [independence in] 1843 and 1915 only one served out his term of office. During those years there were 102 civil wars, coups d'etat, revolts and other political disorders' (pp156–7). In Boot's estimation, in the history of Haiti 'the only thing more unsavoury than US intervention was US non-intervention', p181.

554 Harvard Law Student Advocates for Human Rights (2005) *Keeping the Peace in Haiti? An Assessment of the United Nations Stabilization Mission in Haiti Using Compliance with Its Prescribed Mandate as a Barometer for Success.* Cambridge, MA: Havard Law Student Advocates for Human Rights and Centro de Justiça Global Rio de Janeiro and São Paulo Brazil, p48.

555 Benedetta Faedi (2008) 'The Double Weakness of Girls: Discrimination and Sexual Violence In Haiti'. *Stanford Journal of International Law* 44: 147–99; Sandra Jordan, 'Haiti's Children Die in UN Crossfire'. *Observer* 1 April 2007.

556 Stan Cohen, 'Western Crime Models in the Third World...', see fn 42.

557 Ben Bowling, 'Transnational Criminology...', see fn 42.

558 Robert Reiner, *The Politics of the Police*, see fn 63.

559 Ian Loader (2002) 'Governing European Policing: Some Problems, and Prospects', see fn 233.

560 John Kleinig, *The Ethics of Policing*, see fn 43.

561 Ibid., see fn 43.

562 Charles Tilley (1985) 'War-Making and State-Making as Organized Crime', see fn 50, pp169–86.

563 Geoffrey Marshall, 'Police Accountability Revisited', see fn 400.

564 Philippe Sands, *Lawless World: America and the Making and Breaking of Global Rules*, see fn 159; A. Goldfarb and M. Litvinenko (2007) *The Poisoning of Alexander Litvinenko and the Return of the KGB*. New York: Simon & Schuster.

565 S.D. Brown (2008) *Combating International Crime: The Longer Arm of the Law,* see fn 7, p5.

566 'Interpol and UN back "Global Policing Doctrine"'. *New York Times* 11 October 2009.

567 Ibid.

568 Steven Spitzer, 'Toward a Marxian Theory of Deviance', see fn 113.

569 Stan Cohen , 'Western Crime Models in the Third World...', see fn 42. Ben Bowling, 'Transnational Criminology...', see fn 42.

570 Spitzer, see fn 113.

571 Paul Gilroy, *After Empire*, see fn 84, p47.

572 M. Deflem, *The Policing of Terrorism*, see fn 494, p29.

573 Ben Bowling (2008) 'Fair and Effective Police Methods: Towards 'Good Enough' Policing'. *Scandinavian Studies in Criminology and Crime Prevention*, 8(1): 17–23.

574 Ben Bowling, *Policing the Caribbean*, see fn 12, pp311–5.

575 James Sheptycki, 'The Raft of the Medusa', see fn 549.

576 Ben Bowling, Coretta Phillips, Alexandra Campbell and Maria Docking (2004) *Human Rights and Policing: Eliminating Racism, Discrimination and Xenophobia from Policework*. United Nations Institute for Social Research and Development.

NAME INDEX

References beginning with 'n' relate to endnotes on pages 137 to 168

SUBJECT INDEX

abduction, 48; *see also* kidnapping;
  rendition
accountability for policing, 1, 7–10, 19,
  44–50, 54–6, 65, 70–1, 94–100, 130,
  132, 136
Afghanistan, 1, 4, 62
Africa, 5, 9–10, 20, 27, 55, 60, 63, 79, 81,
  84, 105–8
agents provocateurs, 39
air travel, 9, 31
airport security, 6, 25, 84, 114, 129
Al Bashir, Omar Hassan Ahmad, 63
Alvarez-Machain case, 47–8
amalgamation of police services, 74
anarchism, 3
anti-globalisation protests, 112–13; *see also*
  mega-events, policing of
armed forces, 72, 105; *see also* defence
  forces; military forces; soldiers
arrest, 4–5, 8–10, 44–5, 54–7, 63, 69, 71,
  74–5, 79, 95, 107–8, 112–13, 121,
  125, 128–9
arrest warrants, 5, 9–10, 44, 55, 63,
  75, 128
Association of Chief Police Officers
  (ACPO), 74
Association of South East Asian Nations
  (ASEAN), 66–8
  Police Chiefs (ASEANPOL), 5, 64–8
Australia, 111
  Federal Police (AFP), 6, 25
authoritarianism, 130
autonomy of police institutions, 38–9, 42

banking, 60, 68, 121–2
Basel Convention on Hazardous
  Waste, 58–9
Belgium, 19, 69
Belize, 123
Blackwater (company), 26, 51
border protection, 58, 103, 126
border zones, 34, 42–3
  with diffuse borders, 102–3
borders, national, 6–7, 10, 26, 44–7, 57,
  101–4, 113–14, 128, 132, 136
Brazil, 6, 75, 80, 125
Britain, 3, 22, 61, 69, 104, 107

British Empire, 21
British Petroleum (BP), 109

Canada, 3, 60, 64, 74
capacity building, 93
capital, 15–16, 22, 30–1, 52, 73, 113,
  118–19, 123–6, 135; *see also* money;
  money laundering; neo-liberalism
Caribbean region, 3, 5, 25, 56, 59, 79–81,
  106–7, 119–22
Central America, 48
China, 6, 63, 67–8, 75, 107, 131
Chinoy case, 39
CIA *see* United States: Central
  Intelligence Agency
civil law, 19, 95
Civilian Policing Programme, 61–2
coastguard services, 84, 105–7
cocaine, 25, 107, 115, 118–19
coercive force, use of, 83, 128–30, 136;
  see also power, coercive
Cold War, 42–4, 66, 133
collaboration between police officers,
  3–5, 42
colonial regimes, 20–2, 27, 32, 39, 79–81,
  107, 128–9, 133; *see also* post-colonial
  regimes
'command and control' style of policing, 93
Commonwealth countries, 41
communication, interception of, 19, 110
communication technology, 4, 23, 26, 50,
  98, 102; *see also* information and
  communication technology
Compstat model, 75–6
Congo, 4, 61–3
constabularies *see* police, policing
'constabulary ethic', 21, 84, 136
'controlled delivery' of drugs, 39
Convention on International Trade in
  Endangered Species (CITES), 40–1, 58–9
cooperation
  bilateral agreements, 3, 6, 29, 38, 41–2,
    48, 79, 104–7
  informal, 43, 79
  international, 2–5, 25–6, 29–30, 37–8,
    43–4, 47, 49–50, 57–9, 66–9, 133
  with metropolitan countries, 68